D1526986

DISCARDED

THE ECONOMICS OF HIGH INFLATION

The Economics of High Inflation

Paul Beckerman

MACMILLAN

First published 1992 by
MACMILLAN ACADEMIC AND PROFESSIONAL LTD
Houndmills, Basingstoke, Hampshire RG21 2XS
and London
Companies and representatives
throughout the world

ISBN 0–333–56380–8

A catalogue record for this book is available
from the British Library.

Copy-edited and typeset by Povey/Edmondson
Okehampton and Rochdale, England

Printed in Great Britain by
Billing and Sons Ltd, Worcester

Contents

Acknowledgements and Disclaimer

The writer gratefully acknowledges comments on earlier versions of different chapters by Werner Baer, Azucena Beckerman, Melissa Birch, Neal Epstein, Thomas Hutcheson, Marcia Koth de Paredes, and Nancy Worth. The writer also gratefully acknowledges comments on Chapter 9 by participants in the conference on "The Economic Crisis of Latin America in the 1980s and the Opportunities of the 1990s," at the University of Illinois, Urbana-Champaign, September 6–8, 1990. Many other friends and colleagues have contributed to the set of ideas this book presents. Special thanks are due to Azucena Beckerman for her help and forbearance while this book was being written. This work was begun when the writer was teaching and carrying out research in Lima, Peru, under a Fulbright grant in 1980 and 1981.

The views and conclusions presented here are the writer's alone. They do not necessarily represent the views of any institutions with which the writer is now or has recently been associated. In particular, they should not be taken to represent the views of the World Bank, its Board of Executive Directors, or the countries they represent. The writer alone is responsible for any errors of fact and judgement.

1 The Inflation Enigma —puzzle or mystery

During the 1970s and 1980s a number of national economies slipped into chronic inflation at double- and triple-digit annual rates. Such Latin American nations as Argentina, Brazil, and Peru have had particularly persistent problems, but many nations—Israel and Yugoslavia, for example—have also endured severe inflation over extended periods. At this writing, inflation is likely to remain a problem in many nations for some years to come. This book aims to elucidate the economic processes that sustain chronic high inflation, and to explain why it has proven so stubbornly resistant to both "orthodox" and "heterodox" stabilization approaches.

The analysis presented here draws on various schools of thought, although it remains within the "neo-classical" paradigm. It focuses on the self-perpetuating character of inflation: once set off by some "shock," each price-level increase generates pressure for further price-level increases, through a tangle of inter-related effects on people's anticipations, money and credit creation, the public sector's participation in the economy, competition among economic entities for shares of purchasing power, productivity, contract formulation, the threat of bankruptcy, and price setting. Several generations of Latin American analysts have discussed the self-perpetuating character of chronic inflation, describing it variously as "inflation feedback" and "inflation inertia."[1] Indeed, the familiar expression "inflation spiral" conveys essentially the same idea.

The idea that inflation can be self-perpetuating runs against the neo-classical tenet that market forces drive economic systems into "equilibrium." In an inflationary process, paradoxically, the price level rises toward but always remains short of equilibrium. The present argument is that, while price-level rises may in some ways be self-equilibrating, they also activate various disequilibrating forces. Chronic inflation results where the disequilibrating forces persistently overwhelm the equilibrating forces. Orthodox neo-classical analysts characteristically take the view that the disequilibrating forces could only be "non-market forces"—principally, money issue to finance public-sector expenditure. This book argues that the matter is more subtle and more intricate. The distinction between "market" and "non-market" forces is not always helpful: in real economies with

1

active public sectors and banking systems market and non-market forces operate and interact mutually in the inflation-feedback process. Thus, for example, suppose the banking authorities agree to support banks that are providing credit to a large firm threatened with bankruptcy by surging costs; clearly, in this instance, market and non-market forces are interacting to produce what would likely be an inflationary impulse.

An inflation is a sustained depreciation of the purchasing power of an economy's monetary unit. Several aspects of this seemingly uncontroversial definition bear emphasis. First, as something that happens to an economy's monetary unit, any inflation is unfailingly a "monetary phenomenon." Second, however, since a monetary unit's purchasing power is the rate at which goods and services exchange for money, any inflation is a "goods-and-services phenomenon" as well as, and no less than, a monetary phenomenon. These are semantic and tautological points, to be sure; while therefore difficult to dispute, neither says anything fundamental about the causes of inflation.

Debate about inflation often explicitly or implicitly concerns whether the value of money falls or the value of goods and services rises. For example, the stated objective of the Bullion Committee—the British parliamentary commission convened in 1810 to investigate the inflation of the time, in testimony before which David Ricardo first achieved renown—was to determine whether the value of goods (in particular, gold bullion) was rising or the value of money was falling.[2] The correct answer is plainly "both": saying that the money value of goods and services rises is the same as saying that the value in goods and services of money falls.

This book takes the following proposition as a starting premise—not, it should be emphasized, as a conclusion: the purchasing power of money is determined by its scarcity relative to goods and services. This is neo-classical value theory applied to money. Neo-classical value theory holds that the relative values of things are determined by their relative scarcities—i.e., by their relative states of supply and demand.[3] Thus, the premise is that the purchasing power of money diminishes whenever money becomes abundant relative to goods, i.e., whenever more money exists than economic entities all together wish to hold. The public bids down the monetary unit's purchasing power by demanding goods in exchange for money, or—equivalently—by offering money for goods.

The truism that money's relative scarcity determines its value is not in itself a theory of *inflation*. The definition of inflation given above

has another significant aspect: an inflation is a *sustained* fall in the
purchasing power of money. For any general price rise to qualify as
inflation, it must continue over an extended time—month after month,
quarter after quarter. A "once-and-for-all" decline in a monetary
unit's purchasing power—say, a once-and-for-all doubling of all
prices from one day or one month to the next—fails to satisfy the
definition. A theory of inflation must explain what sustains an
inflationary price rise—why, having fallen, the monetary unit's
purchasing power continues to fall.

Since any nation's money supply is regulated—in principle, set—by
the "monetary authority," it would seem to follow that sustained
monetary abundance is possible only where the monetary authority
allows the money stock persistently to exceed public willingness to
hold it. The usual reason for excessive money-supply growth, orthodox
analysts maintain, is public-sector budget deficits: unwilling or unable
to borrow in private financial markets, governments borrow from their
central banks, which create the money they lend. If the authorities
could be persuaded to control public-sector deficits, or to finance them
in domestic or external financial markets, inflationary pressure would
presumably diminish.

Latin American experience in the 1980s suggests that this orthodox
analysis oversimplifies the nature of the problem. First, many nations
found that sharp public-sector budget-cutting and monetary control
failed to stifle inflation permanently, even though they often generated
agonizing recessions. Proponents of orthodoxy often argue, with some
circularity, that if inflation persisted the budget-cutting and monetary
stringency must have been insufficient. Some people came to suspect
that orthodox remedies could work only at lethal dosages, meaning
that in a practical sense they could not work. Second, in a high-
inflation context, the fiscal and monetary authorities may lose the
scope of control that theory ascribes to them. For example (as
discussed in Chapters 3 and 4), the fiscal authorities may be unable
easily to increase tax revenues, or to reduce expenditures without
violating contractual obligations. Or (as discussed in Chapters 3 and
6), the monetary authorities may be unable to limit money-supply
growth without forcing interest rates so high that they generate
widespread bankruptcy—perhaps even widening the public-sector
deficit if the public sector is itself heavily indebted.

The objective of monetary stringency is to reduce aggregate demand
for goods and services to the quantity the economy is able to provide
and to reduce the money supply to what the economy is willing to

hold. Since a nation's money supply is also its credit supply, monetary restriction amounts simultaneously to credit restriction. Credit restriction disrupts productive activity, reducing the quantity of goods and services the economy provides. This is a troubling point: if an economy's purpose is to provide goods and services, stabilization that works by disrupting economic activity would seem inherently problematic. The usual response is that uncontrolled inflation is likely to disrupt an economic system even more, and so policy-makers must apply monetary restriction for as long as it takes to work the inflation out of the economy. In any case, the disruption caused by stabilization is presumably temporary. Some analysts appear to believe "stabilizing recessions" make economies "leaner" and more efficient. This is by no means certain; they might even make economies weaker and less efficient.

True, in recent years, in economies where orthodox programs had failed, heterodox programs tended also to fail, Israel's 1985 program excepted. (Mexico's more recent program, not discussed in this book, appears at this writing also to have been relatively successful.) Two important points need to be stressed, however. First, the fact that orthodox approaches have exacted a high price, but even so have often failed, suggests that economic analysts should continue seeking better, less painful alternatives. Second, economists and policy-makers do not fully understand the self-sustaining processes of inflation. Assuming the basic insight is correct, they remain some way from knowing how to manage policy where inflation has self-perpetuating characteristics.

Inflation is one of many means by which economies determine the purchasing-power allocation—the way in which wealth (the existing purchasing-power stock) and income (the flow of newly-created purchasing power) are shared among economic entities or groups. High inflation is a manifestation that a society broadly disagrees about how its purchasing power should be shared. It is sustained as long as the disagreement remains unresolved and as long as economic entities have the means to remain in the inflationary competition. Economic entities engage in inflationary competition not only through increases in money prices, but also by securing the use of newly-created credit and money. The purchasing-power allocation at issue in an inflationary competition need not be—indeed, is unlikely to be—the "size distribution"; that is, inflationary competition does not necessarily pit poorer against wealthier people. It is more likely to be a multi-dimensional competition among the groups that make up complex modern industrial societies, including different kinds of worker, industrialist, importer, exporter, primary producer, the public sector, the public sector's contributors and beneficiaries, and so on.

Indeed, "competition" might not be quite the right word. In game-theory terms, inflationary competition is not always "zero-sum." In an inflationary context, there is too much purchasing power around compared to what is available to purchase. Individual economic entities, however, may find it in some degree beneficial that other economic entities have excessive purchasing power. True, demand for everything is higher—a bad thing for each economic entity demanding goods and services; but at the same time demand for each entity's product is higher—a good thing for each economic entity supplying goods and services. Moreover, all other things being equal, the larger the total purchasing power outstanding, the larger the proportion of contractual obligations that can be honored. This benefits everyone because modern complex industrial economies hang together on layered, mutually interdependent obligations. Suppose economic entity A is aware that if agent C fails to honor his debt to B, B might fail to honor his debt to A; A will then consider it a good thing that C has adequate purchasing power.

That is, inflationary competition may actually be a positive-sum, rather than a negative- or zero-sum game, at least in its initial phases. The positive-sum character might even keep the authorities from acting too vigorously against it at first. Indeed, some inflation episodes may have a "game cycle": at the outset, positive-sum aspects may dominate a society's thinking, and so inflation is permitted to continue; over time, as inflationary competition intensifies, zero- and negative-sum aspects intensify. Once they predominate, the society becomes more inclined to accept stabilization, but by then stabilization may become more difficult.

The mixed theory of inflation that emerges when inertial processes and competition for purchasing power are taken into account with more conventional economic theory has characteristics that some economists may find analytically disquieting. One is that the mixed theory may lose the characteristic of reversibility. In the "hydraulics" of conventional macroeconomic theory, if a policy change is infla-tionary, its quantitative opposite should be stabilizing. For example, in conventional theory, all other things being equal, money-supply growth is inflationary while monetary tightening is stabilizing. The mixed theory introduces other possibilities. Under money-supply expansion, one set of economic entities might respond in inflationary ways; under money-supply tightening, another set of economic entities might respond in ways that are even more immediately inflationary— e.g., wholesale producers might raise prices, at least in the short term, in response to rising credit costs.

The argument of this book—that any chronic inflation is sustained by powerful self-propagating mechanisms, including a "struggle for shares" among the various entities that constitute an economic society—has implications for policy formulation. Where inflation has persisted for many years and has developed powerful feedback mechanisms, rapid solutions may (i) prove impermanent or (ii) come at devastating cost—possibly requiring a sharp decline in economic growth. Inflationary economies have all attempted policy packages incorporating price freezes, special taxes, emergency expenditure cuts, credit restrictions, and the like. All too often, even where these measures reduce inflation temporarily, they ultimately prove unsustainable; sooner or later they must be relaxed, and then inflation quickly revives. Each policy failure dangerously reduces people's confidence in public policy. Indeed, certain kinds of short-term policy measure—for example, tight monetary policy that raises interest rates on public-sector obligations—are likely to prove inflationary rather than stabilizing.

The struggle against long-standing inflation is, accordingly, best perceived as a patient, medium- to long-term policy effort. In a society with chronic inflation, the public sector, the financial system, and the system of foreign economic relations characteristically become foci of the struggle over purchasing-power claims. Any economy's public sector employs people at higher or lower wages, purchases and sells goods and services at higher or lower prices, provides subsidies and collects taxes, and borrows money and pays interest on accumulated debt. Any economy's financial system creates money and credit and channels interest from producers to savers, often opening or closing off the way to economic progress for particular entities. For any national economy, world economic developments often operate like a wheel of fortune, making different groups of people in the society suddenly richer or poorer. What makes an inflationary economy different is that, taken together, the public and private sectors, the banking system, and the external economy together tend to provide and exercise far more purchasing-power claims than the economy's productive structure can simultaneously satisfy: inflation is then the means of sorting out the discrepancy. Those dissatisfied by the outcome of the inflation then press new claims and demands on the public sector and on the banking system; to the extent they succeed, inflation continues.

Latin America's present inflationary processes generally date back to the 1970s. With few exceptions, the military regimes then permitted their governments to run inefficiently, and they substituted their dictates for genuine social accord. They and their private sectors then found it easy to borrow in world capital markets, which were highly liquid on account of oil exporters' accumulating surpluses. In the early 1980s, however, when interest rates on floating-rate debt surged sharply and world financial markets closed off, these nations found their interest bills surging without means of financing them. Their inability to cope partly explains why the military turned their societies back to constitutional regimes. These regimes not only had to deal with the external crisis and with the atrophied administrative systems, but also with years of accumulated demands on the part of people who had had no voice in their government while the external debt accumulated, but who were now called upon to pay the economic price. It should hardly seem surprising that inflation worsened sharply.

To overcome chronic inflation, societies must make their public and private sectors and their financial systems more effective and disciplined, more subject to socially agreed rules and hence more capable of resisting claims and demands. Restructuring, reform, reconstitution are inevitably necessary to foster rules of purchasing-power allocation that everyone in society can accept. To relieve inflation over the longer term—to remove the standing threat of inflation more or less permanently—societies need effective, respected systems to reconcile different groups' claims on purchasing-power. This will be difficult to accomplish in societies with lengthy inflation experience, and is likely to require time.

2 Why Inflation is "A Bad Thing"

1 INTRODUCTION: WHY INFLATION IS AN ECONOMIC PROBLEM

Inflation causes trouble for economic systems in four interrelated ways.[1] First, inflation erodes the money unit's purchasing power—the so-called "inflation tax." Anticipation of further erosion reduces people's desire to hold money and other assets denominated in the money unit. This may have certain favorable short-term consequences, but on balance the longer-term consequences are assuredly negative. Second, the inflation rate over any time interval frequently surprises people, so that individuals and enterprises end up with different amounts of purchasing power than they originally planned. The surprise may be agreeable or disagreeable: for example, if prices rise more than originally expected, "economic entities" (i.e., households and firms) that owe money are agreeably surprised, while those owed money are disagreeably surprised.

Third, at any moment the inflation rate over any future time interval is uncertain. Such "price-level uncertainty" makes economic planning more contingent and speculative than it would otherwise be. This affects economic behavior, mostly for the worse. Fourth, inflation occurs unevenly over an economy's price array. The measured inflation rate over any time interval is a weighted average of money price rises; particular prices may rise at quite different rates. In a market economy prices are likely in any case to move at different rates, but inflation apparently magnifies the variations among price movements. Such higher "relative-price dispersion" implies that relative prices may shift sharply, an unsystematic ways, over the course of an inflation. There are two broad implications. First, the price system may inadequately reflect relative scarcities of goods and services, and so provide misleading, inappropriate signals to sellers and purchasers. The second is that future prices become harder to predict—again, making economic planning more contingent and speculative than it otherwise would be.

2 EXPECTED INFLATION AND THE DISPOSITION TO HOLD MONEY

Once an inflation is under way, people come to expect it to continue. Accordingly, they anticipate purchasing-power losses on any assets denominated in the money unit—not only on money itself, but on such assets as interest-bearing bank deposits and contracted receivable accounts. Any anticipated loss on a money-denominated financial asset can be compensated to the extent the asset's yield can rise. This possibility is discussed below. The initial discussion treats the effect of expected inflation on the economy's desire to hold "narrowly-defined" money, whose yield is assumed to be fixed at zero.

Defined practically, money is "very liquid" wealth, wealth that its owners can exchange rapidly for anything available for sale. In modern economies the most liquid kind of wealth is the currency issued by the central bank, followed closely by checking accounts at commercial banks. These forms of wealth together constitute an economy's "narrowly-defined" money—what economists call "M1." The kind of wealth whose liquidity is presumably closest to narrowly-defined money is interest-bearing commercial-bank deposits—savings accounts, "time deposits," and the like—since withdrawals from such accounts can usually be made easily and rapidly. Economists therefore incorporate these with "narrowly-defined" money in their definition of "broadly-defined" money, "M2." Higher-numbered Ms incorporate progressively less liquid kinds of asset.

Narrowly-defined money ordinarily pays no yield, although this has begun to change in some nations. Some forms of broadly-defined money pay interest, but typically at low rates compared to those available on less liquid assets. Accordingly, the higher a person's expectation of inflation over some future time interval, the larger the expected purchasing-power loss on money holdings, whether defined narrowly or broadly. In general, the lower the prospective yield on a financial asset—whether a corporate stock, a bond, a piece of antique furniture, or a *peso* bill—the less inclined people will be to hold that asset. Accordingly, a (higher) prospect of inflation discourages people (all the more) from holding money. Empirical evidence from recent Latin American experience seems broadly consistent with this argument. Inflation rates were sharply higher in the 1980s than in the late 1970s in Argentina, Bolivia, Brazil, Ecuador, Mexico, and Peru, and lower only in Colombia, Chile, and Venezuela. For the first group of nations, there was a sharp decline over these years in the ratio of narrowly- and broadly-defined money to gross domestic product (GDP).[2]

A decline in an economy's desire to hold money has favorable and unfavorable economic consequences. On the favorable side, when people move their wealth out of money, they move it into something else. When an individual buys a new equity issue in a productive enterprise, or an interest-bearing financial asset, resources are made available to finance productive activity and capital formation. Interest rates tend to fall as more financial resources are available; stock prices tend to rise. In this way the prospect of inflation discourages what John Maynard Keynes's *General Theory* described as "speculative" money holdings[3]—wealth held in the relatively unproductive form of "idle" money balances rather than in more productive, socially useful forms, by people presumably speculating that they stand to lose less on cash balances than on riskier applications.

On the unfavorable side, people and firms induced by expected inflation to hold less money than they otherwise would tend to operate somewhat less efficiently. Money held for what Keynes described as the "transactions motive" enables people and firms to make payments more efficiently. Money held for what he described as the "precautionary motive" enables them to meet sudden emergencies and opportunities. That is, holding smaller cash balances makes it harder for individuals and firms to carry out transactions, and leaves them less prepared for contingencies. In a real sense, this imposes higher costs on an economy's functioning.

Furthermore, some of the forms of wealth into which people might move from money place it further from productive applications. Currency apart, most money holdings are held in bank checking accounts, where they are available to be passed on in the form of short-term credit. If wealth is held as gold, antique furniture, or foreign exchange, it is effectively removed from the economy's financial circulation, and made unavailable to would-be borrowers. Short-term credit may be crucial to finance working capital for production and commerce (as discussed in Chapter 4), so that a decline in money holdings may have real consequences for production.

Recent macroeconomic analysis has emphasized the importance of inflation expectations. Broadly speaking, two things result from a generalized increase in an economy's inflation expectations *per se*. The first is that people become less disposed to hold money and money-denominated assets, except to the extent that their yields rise in compensation. The second, to be discussed in the following section, is a subtler matter: some people who arranged their financial affairs *on the expectation that expectations would be lower* may be surprised by some of the consequences of the higher expectations. Both these consequences may have "good" points: some of the wealth that "flees" from money may be made available to other parts of the financial system; and for some people the surprise may be agreeable, depending on the particular configuration of their balance sheets.

Imagine an economy at a moment when (impossibly) there exist no old, outstanding contracts, financial arrangements, or fixed incomes, and at which every economic arrangement in the present and future is under negotiation. In such an economy, because no old arrangements remain in force, changes in inflation expectations should not matter to anyone. Suppose that while the negotiations proceed, all participants uniformly change their conviction about the future inflation rate: originally they had expected zero inflation; now they confidently expect the price level to rise 25 per cent over the coming month and another 25 per cent over the subsequent month. Assume that people are interested not in the quantity of money they expect to pay or receive, but rather in the quantity of purchasing power they expect to receive. That is, people have no "money illusion": they calculate rationally in terms of what they can buy, not in terms of how much money they have.

Accordingly, so long as everyone agrees on the expected inflation rate over the coming two months, changed inflation expectations should make no *real* difference for the agreements everyone will reach. Suppose that before expectations changed two people were prepared to sign a contract under which one would have paid the other 100 *pesos* at the end of each month. They should be equally willing to sign the same contract after the change in expectations, only for 125 *pesos* at the end of the first month and for (125 times 1.25 =) 156.25 *pesos* at the end of the second month. The purchasing power of 125 *pesos* after a month of 25 per cent inflation is the same as the purchasing power of 100 *pesos* after a month of zero inflation. On this argument a change in inflationary expectations should not affect any economy's *real* behavior.

One thing that makes this seemingly common-sense argument not quite correct is that, as noted above, higher inflation expectations reduce the desire to hold money. People would move their wealth out of money into other forms of holding wealth. This would probably increase the valuations of and reduce the "real" interest rates on those other assets, and might in turn affect people's disposition to negotiate particular contractual arrangements. (Money outstanding is an "old" contract in this context.)

In effect, where the price level varies, the "exchange rate" of money for goods varies over time. In planning for the future, people must use the different exchange rates for different moments. Once a society acquires significant inflation experience, the arithmetic becomes second nature, particularly for business people. For example, over any period in which prices generally rise 25 per cent, the money unit loses 20 (note, *not* 25) per cent of its purchasing power. The reasoning is that if it now takes 125 *pesos* to buy what 100 *pesos* used to buy, then each *peso* buys only 80 per cent as much as before (1/125 is 80 per cent of 1/100). If people confidently expect the money unit that they use in transactions a month from now to have 20 per cent less purchasing power, they can easily take account of this fact in making contracts: when the period ends, 125 money units will have the same purchasing power as 100 now.

Similar arithmetic applies to payments of interest and principal on loans. Suppose a borrower and lender had been prepared to agree on a 100-*peso*, one-month loan at 1 per cent interest when they expected zero inflation: the lender was prepared to purchase an asset of 100 pesos yielding 1 per cent, i.e., promising a 101-*peso* payment of principal and interest at the month's end. Now the money unit is expected to have 20 per cent less purchasing power at the month's end. In order to provide the same purchasing power, the payment at the month's end should be (101 times 1.25 =) 126.25 *pesos*. This quantity has the same purchasing power after 25 per cent inflation (or 20 per cent monetary depreciation) as 101 *pesos* following zero inflation. Thus, in principle, if the interest rate were to rise from 1 to 26.25 per cent, borrowers and lenders should be just as willing to make the same transaction. In "real," or purchasing-power, units, both interest rates are 1 per cent.

It seems reasonable to assume that people do their calculations and negotiations in terms of purchasing power. When calculating what they should do—lend, borrow, or abstain from financial transactions—on the basis of some "money" interest rate n, they presumably use a real interest rate r that they estimate from n and from their inflation expectation x. Alternatively—assuming they agree on an expectation x—parties negotiating a loan may be presumed to agree on r, and then to set n to be consistent with r. The familiar "Fisher" formula relates the "real," or purchasing-power, interest rate r to the "nominal" interest rate n and the expected inflation rate x (all taken to be decimals):[4]

$$r = (n\text{-}x)/(1 + x)$$

Some analysts believe, on various grounds, that many people have "money illusion"—that is, that they calculate according to the amount of money, not purchasing power, they expect to receive or spend, and so take no account of expected inflation. The notion that people have "money illusion" is, at a minimum, suspect as an explanation of anything, since it suggests a measure of irrationality. The assumption that, in general, people act rationally and self-interestedly on the basis of calculations regarding their present and future access to real goods and services is not only fundamental in neo-classical analysis, but consistent with most people's experience. In the absence of strong evidence to the contrary, it is safest to suppose that people who experience inflation learn how it affects their ability to acquire real goods and services, and take anticipated inflation into account when making decisions. This book therefore assumes that, while their inflation expectations may turn out incorrect or be subject to uncertainty, people simply do not have "money illusion."

Inflation may affect the rate at which real interest earnings are taxed, and this may have some consequences for the real economy. All other things being equal,—i.e., given the tax rate on nominal interest and the prevailing real interest rate – the higher the inflation rate, the higher the tax will effectively be on the *real* interest rate.[5] Changes in anticipated inflation and tax rates should cause movements in real as well as nominal interest rates, as borrowers and lenders determine who, in effect, bears the "tax incidence."

The essential distinction between narrowly-defined money and other financial assets denominated in money units is that, in general, the latter can increase their money yield to compensate their holders for any increase in the expected decline in the money unit's purchasing power. For contracts and assets other than money, expected future inflation should present no obstacle to negotiating their yields or values. In general, however, money itself does not pay interest to compensate for expected purchasing-power losses. (Chapter 5 explains why payment of interest on money to compensate for anticipated inflation is likely to prove futile.)

The economic behavior induced by the prospect of a loss on money holdings is one "real" consequence of inflation. Inflation may usefully be described as a tax on money holdings. The "tax rate" per *peso* paid over any period is the negative of the real rate of return on money, calculated from the formula above with n equal to zero and x as the inflation rate (again, all in decimal terms):

$$-x/(1+x)$$

The tax "revenue" goes to whomever issued the money liability, in the form of a diminished liability in purchasing power. From some viewpoints—most obviously, from the viewpoint of the revenue recipient—the inflation tax has positive aspects. Considered as a tax it is relatively easy to collect. People try to avoid it, however, by reducing their money holdings. Indeed, an ironic consequence is that, as people reduce their money holdings in response to higher inflation, the inflation-tax base, and so the purchasing-power flow of inflation-tax revenue yield from a given inflation rate, diminishes. Or, alternatively, a higher inflation rate becomes necessary to produce any required flow of inflation-tax revenue.

3   INFLATION SURPRISES

People presumably use expectations of future inflation in formulating decisions about consumption, saving, asset holdings, liability positions, and contract agreements. Over the course of any inflation episode, the inflation rate varies, sometimes considerably. Inevitably, people's expectations often turn out incorrect. Had they foreseen the inflation rate correctly, they might have acted differently—although if everyone had acted differently, the inflation rate would probably have turned out differently.

The surprise can be agreeable or disagreeable, depending on each person's circumstances. Incorrectly anticipated inflation affects the economy's purchasing-power allocation. When inflation turns out higher than had generally been anticipated, lenders effectively transfer purchasing power to borrowers: the *ex post* real rate of return turns out higher than the *ex ante* real rate of return—x turns out higher in the Fisher formula than originally anticipated. Similarly, those who sell under contract (including those who sell their labor under contract) transfer purchasing power to those who purchase under contract. An inflation rate higher than originally anticipated is a happy surprise to debtors (and to purchasers under contract generally), an unhappy surprise to lenders (and to sellers under contract generally); *vice versa* for an inflation rate that turns out lower than anticipated.

This is one reason why an inflation rate that turns out higher than people had generally anticipated tends to stimulate economic activity. Since higher-than-anticipated inflation provides people who owe money a surprise "windfall" gain, they end up with more purchasing power at their disposal. Fewer are likely to go bankrupt. Productive firms tend to be debtors, since they generally hire labor and finance, and purchase supplies under contract at prices based partly on managers', workers', financiers', and suppliers' inflation anticipations. If inflation turns out higher than anticipated, and output prices rise higher than originally expected, firms tend to earn higher profits than anticipated.

For some people, however, higher-than-anticipated inflation is a disagreeable surprise. Firms' workers, financiers, and suppliers receive less purchasing power than they had expected—although at least the financiers and suppliers have the consolation of paying less purchasing power than they had expected to *their* workers, financiers, and suppliers. Having been unpleasantly surprised, workers, financiers, and suppliers will be on guard in coming periods. As soon as possible, they will try to revise their contracts, not only to compensate for inflation that has occurred, but also to compensate for the inflation the unpleasant surprise induces them to anticipate. The happily surprised parties may be willing—or in some instances may be forced by competition—to meet these demands from the additional resources they are surprised to have.

An increase in everyone's inflation *expectations* can also work out to be an unpleasant surprise for individual economic agents. People respond to higher inflation expectations by negotiating higher contracted prices and interest rates. This applies only to "new" assets and contracts. Anyone who has an "old" asset, or has a commitment under an "old" contract, may take a loss as a consequence of the increased inflation expectation, at least until the asset matures or the contract is revised. Market values of old, "marketable" financial assets decline if higher money interest rates are offered on new assets. For example, if new notes yielding 25 per cent appear, old notes yielding 20 per cent decline in market value: since promises of 125 *pesos* one month from now are available today for 100, a promise of 120 pesos at the same moment can only be worth 96 today:

$$125/100 = 120/96$$

The fall in value from 100 to 96 *pesos* is a true loss, reflecting a firm's or an individual's loss of purchasing power as a consequence of increased inflation expectations: newer bonds would provide a higher rate of return. (Of course, declining inflation expectations would raise the value of any bond whose yield had been premised on higher inflation expectations.)

4   PRICE-LEVEL UNCERTAINTY

In an "ideal"—but purely theoretical—inflation, everyone would correctly anticipate the inflation rate; all goods and services prices would rise synchronously at the same rate, apart from occasional adjustments presumably reflecting real supply and demand changes. The inflation rate would cause no surprises and be subject to no uncertainty. By assumption, relative prices would always be in the relative alignment appropriate to supply and demand conditions. The economic cost of such an inflation would be the tax on money balances and its consequences, balanced by whatever gains result from people's reduced disposition to hold money.

Alternatively, one might imagine a—no less theoretical—"semi-ideal" inflation, with inflation surprises but no price-level uncertainty. Although sometimes surprised by the inflation rate, people would somehow (implausibly) go on assuming the validity of their present inflation expectations. Again, prices would still always be in the relative alignment appropriate to supply and demand conditions. The economic cost of such an inflation would be the costs arising from the "tax" on money balances and from the disagreeable surprises, offset by whatever benefits result from the disposition to hold less money and the agreeable surprises.

In reality, however, having been surprised, people are unlikely to maintain faith in their ability to predict future inflation. Their expectations will come to be characterized by uncertainty. Accordingly, consider a "neutral" inflation—a still theoretical kind of inflation in which people regard future price levels as uncertain, but in which relative prices are always at their appropriate values. "Price-level uncertainty" in itself affects economic behavior, imposing costs on economic functioning with few redeeming benefits.[6]

Obviously, no one can ever be perfectly certain about any future price level. People may thus be presumed to attach greater or lesser uncertainty to their inflation expectations. The "degree" of uncertainty may be characterized by individuals' responses to the following question: "Within what range of percentage points above and below your expectation do you suppose the inflation rate will lie, with a probability of—say—95 per cent?" The wider this "confidence interval," the greater is each individual's uncertainty.

For any expected inflation rate, the associated uncertainty may be larger or smaller. People may be presumed generally to be "risk-averse"—that is, all other things being equal, they prefer to have assets and liabilities whose yields are more certain. By definition, risk-averse people are prepared to sacrifice some expectation of gain in exchange for greater certainty of gain. This implies that, for any given expected inflation rate, different degrees of price-level uncertainty induce people to behave differently.

As an example, imagine a "Dutch" auction of a given supply of one-year government bonds whose coupon interest rate is 25 per cent.[7] Their purchasing-power yield is uncertain to the extent inflation is uncertain. For any given expected inflation rate, the bonds should sell at a lower price (or higher discount), the wider is the confidence interval of the public's inflationary expectation. Consider two situations: in both, the expected inflation rate is 20 per cent, but in the first the public believes the probability is 95 per cent that the inflation rate will turn out between 19 and 21 per cent, whereas in the second the 95 per cent confidence interval is 15 to 25 per cent. In the first case, the public believes the probability is 95 per cent that the bonds will yield between 3.31 and 5.04 per cent in real terms; in the second, between zero and 8.70 per cent (using the "Fisher" formula given above). The public's risk aversion implies that the auction price would turn out lower in the second case than in the first: risk-averse people will offer less for riskier bonds. The bonds will pay a higher effective yield in the second case, and so cause the government a higher financing burden in purchasing power.[8]

Intuition and experience suggest that, for any given time horizon, the higher the inflation expectation, the higher the uncertainty attaching to it. That is, less uncertainty attaches to an expected annual 5 per cent inflation rate than to an expected annual 100 per cent inflation rate. Excepting quite special circumstances, expected inflation rates are generally on the order of magnitude of the current inflation rate. It is therefore broadly fair to say that future inflation rates are more uncertain, the higher is the current inflation rate. Furthermore, at any given moment, future inflation rates are more uncertain, the longer the future time period in question, on the common-sense view that any anticipated economic value is more uncertain the farther into the future it is.

Like expected inflation, price-level uncertainty discourages money holding. As noted above, this has favorable and unfavorable economic consequences. Unlike expected inflation, however, price-level uncertainty damages the economy by subjecting the real yields on all assets and contracts denominated in the money unit, particularly those of longer maturity, to higher uncertainty. A simple example characterizes the problem. Suppose the expected inflation rate for the coming year is 60 per cent, but everyone attaches a 95 per cent confidence interval of 20 percentage points on either side of this expectation. Prospective lenders will then seek interest rates that compensate not only for the expected inflation of 60 per cent, but also for their risk that the inflation rate will turn out 10 or 20 points higher than 60 per cent. Prospective borrowers, in contrast, will seek interest rates that compensate less than the expected 60 per cent, because they lose to the extent inflation turns out less than expected. There is no *a priori* reason to suppose this market would compromise by incorporating the 60-per-cent expectation in the interest rate as a fair medium. Where the market interest rate turns out, and which side of the market therefore bears more risk, is determined by which side has the superior market power—that is to say, by which side is prepared not to transact rather than to bear the risk.

In any credit market where price-level uncertainty mattered this much, some participants would conclude that the market was too risky and withdraw to markets of shorter maturity, for which the anticipated price-level rise would be less uncertain. This is why inflation tends to wreck longer-term fixed-rate financial markets—it makes them too risky. Price-level uncertainty shortens contract maturities for the same reason: it becomes too risky for purchasers and sellers of contracted services to enter into long-term contracts. Shortening of asset and contract terms is an unfortunate development for an industrial economy's productive efficiency. Certain economic activities—particularly the capital formation required by modern industrial processes—are far more difficult to carry on without long-term finance and contracts. Frequent financing and contract negotiations are a nuisance, and impose real costs and uncertainties on productive processes.

Inflation rates characteristically vary considerably over the course of any episode of inflation. This is what generates surprises and induces price-level uncertainty. The experience of Argentina, a nation that has undergone several decades of chronic inflation (see Chapter 9), indicates the orders of magnitude involved. Over the years 1971–88, Argentina's consumer price index rose at a month-over-month average rate of 9.1 per cent; the standard deviation of the monthly increases was 7.1 percentage points. (This excludes 1989, during which Argentina had two episodes of hyperinflation.) The average monthly inflation rates in each year were generally correlated with higher standard deviations (although using the calendar year as a unit in this way is arbitrary). Years of relatively low inflation were generally, but not always, years of lower standard deviations: the monthly average was 2.8 per cent in 1971, with a standard deviation of 3 percentage points; consumer prices rose at a relatively steady 8.3 per cent rate in 1977, with a standard deviation of 1.8 percentage points. In mid-1975, Argentina came near hyperinflation: over that year monthly inflation averaged 13.4 per cent with a standard deviation of 9.1 percentage points. In mid-1985 a price freeze staved off hyperinflation: monthly inflation averaged 14.7 per cent over the year with a standard deviation of 11.8 percentage points.

One means that has been suggested and occasionally used to keep price-level uncertainty from affecting contracts has been "index-linking" (see Chapter 8). Strictly defined, an index-linked financial asset or contract is one whose unit of account is purchasing power rather than money. An index-linked 1000-*peso* one-year promissory note, for example, promises to pay a quantity of money at the end of the year whose purchasing power equals that of 1000 *pesos* today. Unfortunately, index-linking does not necessarily make price-level uncertainty less of a problem. It only changes the precise way such uncertainty affects contractual relations and enters into people's calculations. True, lenders might prefer not to acquire assets denominated in money units if they do not know how much purchasing power they will receive; but borrowers might also be reluctant to issue purchasing-power liabilities: unless the purchasing-power value of their own future income streams were highly certain, they could not be sure that they could cover a purchasing-power commitment.

Price-level uncertainty has an associated aspect with similar consequences. Not only is the inflation rate over any future period uncertain at any moment; different people have different expectations and uncertainties at any given moment.[9] That is, inflation is characterized by "dispersion of inflation anticipations." As in the case of price-level uncertainty, the higher the inflation rate, the more severe this dispersion is likely to be, since there is wider scope for divergent opinions. It is probably also more severe, the longer is the future time period in question. It disrupts markets for fixed-rate longer-term credit and other contracts in much the same way as price-level uncertainty. For example, if a would-be debtor expects inflation of 50 per cent over the coming year, but would-be creditors expect 70 per cent, it could prove impossible to reach agreement on a yield, even if—in this case, particularly if—both parties hold their expectations with perfect certainty. The problem may be made more or less complex to the extent they hold their anticipations with uncertainty.

5   RELATIVE-PRICE DISPERSION

The fourth reason why inflation is a bad thing is that it tends to increase the "dispersion" of an economy's relative prices of goods and services. Relative prices shift over time in any economy, even where inflation is negligible, as conditions of supply and demand change. Experience suggests, however, that larger relative-price shifts accompany inflation, and, more important, the shifts have less to do with conditions of supply and demand. This is a bad thing, first, because misaligned relative prices provide signals to market participants that are inconsistent with current supply and demand conditions; and second, because it makes future relative prices more uncertain, complicating the task of planning.[10]

The precise nature of the relative-price dispersion problem is subtle. According to familiar neo-classical value theory (summarized in this and the following three paragraphs, which some readers may prefer to skip), the price of each good and service is determined by its scarcity—that is, by people's *disposition to purchase*, or "demand," in combination with people's *disposition to sell*, or "supply," at each possible price. For each good and service market there presumably exists a price at which the quantities in demand and in supply are equal. At higher prices, some would-be sellers find no purchasers; they offer lower prices in hope of persuading "marginal," or closely persuadable, purchasers. Symmetrically, at lower prices, some would-be buyers find no sellers; they offer higher prices in hope of persuading marginal sellers. Only at that "equilibrium" price are supply and demand equilibrated, and the market thereby "cleared."

In an economy with many different goods and services, demand for and supply of each depends not only on its own price, but also on the prices of all other goods and services available in the economy—including money.[11] Imagine that the price of apples suddenly doubled through some mistake, in the absence of any change in people's disposition to sell and purchase them. If no other price changed at the same time, demand for apples would fall and supply would increase, disequilibrating the market for apples until the price is bid back down by sellers unable to find buyers. In the meantime, however, other markets would be disequilibrated as well. For example, people who previously purchased apples but now find its price too high might find the price of peaches more acceptable, and so increase demand for peaches.

What matters here is the price of apples relative to the price of peaches, as well as to the prices of other goods and services. Suppose that at the same time the price of apples doubles, all other prices in the economy, *and* the total quantity of money, double as well. In this case demand for and supply of apples should not change, and nor should any other demand or supply in the economy. Or, suppose the money supply and all prices *except* the price of apples doubled suddenly. Now demand for apples should increase and supply decline, disequilibrating this market. At the same time, however, demand for peaches should fall as consumers are attracted to apples.

If production conditions or tastes for particular goods and services change, the economy's price array should change. Otherwise some markets will be stuck in disequilibrium, with some amount of unsatisfied demand or supply. If production conditions and tastes for goods do not change, however, the price array should not change. If it does, some markets will go inappropriately into disequilibrium. Note that for these purposes, a change in the total money supply amounts to a change in "the market conditions" of a particular good, money. If the disposition to hold purchasing power in the form of money remains unchanged, an increase in the quantity of money should induce disequilibrium in no particular market, as long as all money prices in the economy increase neutrally by precisely the amount of the increase in the money supply. Tacking one zero on to the end of each price figure, bill and coin should have no effect on any real economic relation, for example: prices rise by a factor of ten, but all prices would remain the same relative to one another. If the quantity of money increases by some percentage x but nothing changes in the real economy, then, if some prices increase by more or less than x per cent, some other markets are likely to become disequilibrated.

This is the essence of the relative-price dispersion problem. Inflation induces changes not only in the money prices of goods and services generally; it seems also to induce changes in relative prices that have nothing to do with changes in fundamental demand and production conditions. That is, in severe inflation different money prices rise at different rates, apart from differences reflecting changing real market conditions.[12]

Part of the reason inflation increases relative-price dispersion is that money prices are frequently made "sticky" by price controls, including those established by law, institutional relations, and custom. Some prices are costly to change, and are therefore changed infrequently. Advertising and catalogues might have to be changed, for example. As a result, a money price may remain fixed for a relatively long time, but then rise suddenly and sharply; the relative, or "real" price slides over time, with occasional jumps. Firms facing no heavy competitive pressure or "inelastic" demand—i.e., demand insensitive to price—may find it easiest simply to set their output prices at relatively infrequent intervals in this way, thus establishing a rough average real-price and cash-flow pattern over time.

Another cause of money-price stickiness is the existence of contracted money prices. Prices fixed by legal or implicit agreement ordinarily cannot change until the agreement terminates. Some prices may be sticky because the costs underlying them are fixed under contract. If a firm's labor costs are fixed under a one-year contract, it will be under less pressure to raise its own output price over the course of the year: it can maintain a competitive advantage by selling at a lower price. That is, as noted above, the existence of "old" contracted prices affects current price setting.

Money-price stickiness apart, there are various reasons why fully flexible prices would rise at differing rates. At any moment, not only are future inflation rates uncertain, the *current* inflation rate is uncertain as well. Since people may not be aware precisely what the current price level is, they estimate it differently. They may take account of their uncertainty about it in determining current behavior. Since people set and respond to prices on the basis of different guesses about the current price level, it is not surprising that prices rise at different rates.[13]

For any given inflation rate, the associated relative-price dispersion could be of any magnitude: money prices could move relatively closely with the price level, or at very different rates. For a given inflation rate, there ought to be less dispersion in an economy that is competitive, flexible, and well-integrated, and more in an economy that is oligopolized, unresponsive, and segmented. "Speculative" activity in particular markets may either mitigate dispersion by moving relative prices more swiftly to their market-clearing values, or aggravate dispersion by generating "unnecessary" price swings. There will be more dispersion, the larger is the quantity of controlled prices in the economy, the higher the cost of price adjustment, the larger the number of old contracts in existence, and the deeper the problems people have obtaining current information.

It is reasonable to suppose that an economy's relative-price dispersion and inflation rate are positively correlated over time. The higher the inflation rate, the more the controlled, sticky, and contracted prices will diverge from the price level, and the more such prices must then "jump" when they finally must. Moreover, the wider will be the scope for miscalculation, and the wider the scope within which prices can be set.

One might expect dispersion to be lower for longer time intervals— that is, relative prices should change *less* from year to year than from month to month, because the competitive forces that drive real prices toward mutually appropriate scarcity values ought to operate more reliably over longer time periods. This is probably more true for relatively "moderate" inflations. On the other hand, severe inflation may cause the price system to malfunction so severely that inflationary dispersion may actually be higher for longer time periods.

The rates at which an inflationary economy's prices change over any given time period are apparently not distributed randomly around the average inflation rate. Price changes over any time interval appear to fall in a leftward-skewed pattern around the average: more prices rise less and fewer rise more than the average.[14] That is to say, the average inflation rate in any given period tends to be led upward by a relatively small proportion of all prices. It is probable that the degree of skewness is higher, the shorter is the time interval in question. That is, over short time-intervals most prices move little or not at all; a few prices rise sharply, leading the general price increase.

Relative-price dispersion, particularly in combination with price-level uncertainty, causes problems for allocative efficiency and economic growth. Divergence of relative prices from appropriate scarcity values disequilibrates markets, and the unpredictability of relative prices complicates business planning. Real cash and profit flows are difficult enough to predict even with price stability; dispersion and uncertainty make predicting them harder still. For the short term, producers find it harder to determine optimal output and employment levels. For the long run, they find it harder to evaluate capital-formation projects. Since capital formation is the fundamental basis of real economic growth, aggravation of relative-price dispersion is an important way in which inflation diminishes real economic growth.

6   HYPERINFLATION

One of the "bad" things about severe inflation not mentioned thus far is the possibility of its running out of control and becoming "hyperinflation." What occurs in hyperinflation, while in many respects similar to but worse than what happens in severe inflation, is so grotesquely worse that it is qualitatively different from "merely severe" inflation. In a hyperinflation expectations cannot be formed for any time horizon, and as a consequence there is no question of meaningful surprises. Uncertainty becomes so extreme that it demolishes even short-term contracting. The price system and the currency unit effectively cease to function as such, severely disrupting production and distribution.

Although qualitatively different, the precise point at which severe inflation becomes hyperinflation is unclear. It is unreasonable to say, for example, that monthly inflation of (say) 49.999 per cent is severe inflation and 50 per cent is hyperinflation. The distinction is imprecise, and should properly be taken to depend on the symptoms: thus, whatever the rate, if expectations formation, financial contracting, the price system, production and the use of the currency unit are breaking down, then the inflation has become hyperinflation. In economies like Argentina and Brazil that have developed means of living with inflation, monthly inflation of 25 per cent would be merely severe, whereas in economies without such mechanisms it would be hyperinflation.

A number of analyses of economic behavior under hyperinflation, and also some important analyses of what it takes to stabilize hyperinflation, have been published in recent years.[15] Some of the lessons from these analyses inevitably apply to "merely severe" inflation, and have influenced the lessons economists have drawn about inflation in general. Nevertheless, apart from the observation that the danger of its becoming hyperinflation is one of the bad things about any severe inflation, hyperinflation *per se* is taken to lie beyond this book's scope.

7 CONCLUSION: WHY "IDEAL," "SEMI-IDEAL," "NEUTRAL," AND REAL-LIFE INFLATIONS ARE "BAD"

Even a hypothetical "ideal" inflation—in which the price level never surprises anyone, there is no uncertainty about future price levels, and all prices rise at the same rate (except for changes reflecting real market conditions)—would impose welfare costs on an economy, through the effective tax on money balances. A still-hypothetical "semi-ideal" inflation would add the costs of disagreeable surprises. A "neutral" inflation would add the costs of price-level uncertainty, which makes the purchasing-power value of future money transactions uncertain. In sum, real-life inflation is costly because it involves all the costs of neutral inflation plus those arising from worsened relative-price dispersion. Although some good things can result from people holding less money than they otherwise would, and from happy surprises, the bad things that result from inflation are significant, and worse, the higher is the inflation rate. Inflation's unpopularity is perfectly understandable.

In explaining why inflation is "a bad thing," this chapter has been deliberately taxonomic. A drawback of this approach is that it conveys too segmented a sense of why inflation is so damaging. The combination of inflation's consequences is worse than their simple sum.

A high inflation rate generates massive economic waste. To carry out the additional planning, forecasting, bargaining, and transacting required by high inflation, an economy must expend energy that could otherwise be used productively. Argentines and Brazilians spend appreciable amounts of time in such activities as visiting the bank, shifting wealth between assets, revising budget calculations, and disputing fair prices and contract values. They absorb repeated surprises, some happy, some unhappy, with inevitable, damaging consequences for people's views about the relation between genuinely productive enterprise and real income. With market distortions rampant in a severe inflation, people able to do so concentrate on seeking fortunes by "arbitraging the distortions."

Inflation devastates the concept of economic value, demoralizes people, generates resentment and cynicism, and sets continuing incentives for unethical business behavior. Inflation catalyzes purchasing-power shifts that have no political nor business sanction. The longer it goes on, the more inflation devastates the ethical bases on which business and even political relationships are based. Once the value of money becomes relative and ever-changing, it becomes easier to "relativize" the other values that make civilized society possible. This is the most important reason why inflation is "a bad thing."

3 Inflation Feedback

1 MONETARY ABUNDANCE

In neo-classical monetary theory, the purchasing-power value of money falls when the money stock exceeds what people wish to hold. People bid down the value of money by offering it for other things, just as stockholders bid down the value of a stock by offering it for sale. This is an incomplete explanation of inflation, however, because it fails to explain why the money stock remains excessive. Any theory of inflation must explain why presumably equilibrating decreases in the monetary unit's purchasing power fail to equilibrate— that is, why money continually returns to abundance.

At any instant, an economy's "money demand" is the amount of money the economy desires in the aggregate to hold. Each money unit's purchasing power is the number of "baskets"—each containing an economy's commodities in proportion to their general availability— it can purchase at current prices.

At any instant, "excess demand" for money is the difference between money demand and the outstanding money supply; "excess supply" is the difference between supply and demand. Prices of things in excess demand tend to be bid up; prices of things in excess supply tend to be bid down. When money is in excess supply, by definition, people wish to exchange it for "other things"; in doing so, they bid down the monetary unit's purchasing-power value. If everyone taken together in an economy tries to exchange some money for other things, all other things come into excess demand. Thus, when money is in excess supply, "all other things"—goods, services and non-money financial assets—must be in excess demand.

There are various ways in which excess money supply *cum* excess demand for other things can arise. Money creation by the banking system or a decline in the public's disposition to hold money directly generate excess money supply—and excess demand for everything else. "Aggregate demand" for goods and services can increase in any of several categories used by economists—e.g., private consumer-goods demand, capital-goods demand, government expenditure, foreigners' export demand. (Excess demand for goods and services *could* be accompanied by excess supply of non-money financial assets, in which case the excess supply of money could be zero or even negative; there would be no price rise to explain then.) "Aggregate supply"—the economy's disposition and ability to provide goods and services—may decline, generating excess aggregate demand. This could happen because production costs—labor charges, finance charges, materials costs—increase, or because the efficiency with which factors of production are "combined" in production processes diminishes.

2   MONEY CREATION[1]

A modern economy's "money supply" is its banking system's "monetary liabilities," that is, currency or checking-account deposits whose ownership can be transferred rapidly and conveniently.[2] "Money" may be defined "narrowly" in this way, or more "broadly" to include "less liquid" commercial-bank obligations, such as savings accounts and time deposits.

A "commercial-banking system" comprises various "commercial banks" and a "central bank." A commercial bank's basic business is to provide commerce and working-capital loans, which "bridge" the interval between the time firms incur costs and the time they earn revenues. Thus, dress merchants take bank loans to purchase inventory, repaying from sales proceeds; dress manufacturers take working-capital loans to pay labor and materials costs, similarly repaying from sales proceeds.

Commercial banks provide such loans by *creating* money, crediting the loans provided directly to borrowers' checking accounts. Banks' ability to create loans and money, and so to generate interest revenues, is limited by the reality that checking deposits are "sight" obligations. A bank must pay cash "on sight" of any account holder's request to do so. Failure to honor such a request presumably amounts to failure of the bank. Because modern economies generally use checks for significant transactions, and prefer to hold most of their money in checking accounts rather than cash, bankers have learned that over any time interval they will be asked to provide cash for only a small fraction of their deposit liabilities. Modern monetary authorities set the minimum fraction of deposits that commercial banks must hold in cash reserves, but this minimum is typically higher than the "technical" ratio bankers would hold to ensure that they could meet withdrawal requests.

In principle, a central bank is a commercial bank with two special features: it may create "legal tender," i.e., cash that by law must be accepted if offered to settle a debt; and it lends only to the government and commercial banks. Since it creates cash, unlike commercial banks, a central bank need not hold a reserve in domestic cash.

Historically, the first central banks—notably, the Bank of England, founded in 1694—were private banks chartered on the understanding that they would lend to their governments, and they received a monopoly of legal-tender issue to facilitate this. The relationship of commercial and central banks evolved over the eighteenth and nineteenth centuries in retrospectively inevitable ways.[3] Since they could not create cash, commercial banks sought central-bank loans when their cash position tightened—that is, when they faced sharp withdrawal demands or their credit demand rose sharply. Although then-private central banks saw the chance to profit on such loans, they understood the importance of limiting cash issues, keeping them scarce to preserve their purchasing power. They provided loans to commercial banks at a reduced interest rate, the so-called "rediscount rate."[4] But they also restricted banks' access to such credit, making it available only for instances of severe liquidity tightness. Central banks also set conditions that banks would have to meet to qualify for loans: after some experimenting, one basic condition came to be that the commercial banks maintain a minimum ratio of cash reserves to deposit liabilities.

In the course of their operations, central banks naturally came to acquire gold and foreign exchange. Exporters, importers, and other people who acquired foreign exchange found it convenient to use it to purchase domestic currency. The central bank, for its part, sought to maintain sufficient gold and foreign exchange to sell to whomever needed or wanted it—and to back its own cash issues. Over time, banking systems evolved the basic structure they now generally possess: the central bank backs its monetary issue—the so-called monetary base—with gold and foreign exchange, claims on government, and claims on commercial banks. Commercial banks in turn back their deposit liabilities with a mix of claims on the private sector and central bank, the latter including cash.[5]

A commercial-banking system has essentially the balance-sheet structure (in national currency units) shown in Table 3.1. Bank reserves (R) include vault cash (issued by the central bank) and checking deposits at the central bank. Currency in circulation (C)—i.e., held by the non-bank public—excludes currency held by banks, which is included with bank reserves. The consolidated system's liability stock is the money supply ($M = C + D$). Its assets comprise its

Table 3.1   The basic balance sheet structure of a banking system

Consolidated commercial banks	
Bank reserves (R)	Demand deposits (D)
Loans to the private sector (L)	Rediscount credit (H)
	Net worth (W)

Central bank	
Loans to the government (F)	Monetary base (B)
	$=:$ Currency in circulation (C)
	$+$ Bank reserves (R)
Rediscount credit (H)	
International reserves (A)	Net worth (V)

Consolidated banking system	
Total loans ($L+F$)	Money supply ($M = C + D$)
International reserves (A)	Total net worth ($V + W$)

claims on the private sector (L), the public sector (F), and the rest of the world (A). If A^* represents the value in US dollars of international reserves and e the exchange rate (currency units per dollar), $A = e A^*$. The central bank's claims on the commercial banks (H) and the commercial banks' claims on the central bank (R) disappear in the consolidation. Thus, an economy's money supply "is backed by" the banking system's claims on public and private entities and on the rest of the world. In creating money, a banking system provides credit and takes on claims to these entities.

Over the late 1800s and early 1900s, monetary authorities came to set rediscount rates and minimum required-reserve ratios not only to ensure safe bank operations, but also as policy instruments. They regulated the money supply, constantly seeking the razor edge at which credit availability was adequate without the money stock being excessive. This role of central bank boards of directors as the national "monetary authorities" became increasingly clear and accepted. Through their lending to governments and to commercial banks they influenced the size of the monetary base. They learned to set, or at least to influence, exchange rates, and hence to influence the size of their foreign-exchange reserve along with the monetary base. Through minimum reserve ratios they then influenced the size of the money supply. In industrial economies, central banks' holdings of government obligations became the basis of a particularly powerful means of monetary control: by selling government obligations, central banks absorbed cash; by purchasing such obligations, central banks injected cash.[6] Because these direct, flexible transactions are performed in "open" financial markets, rather than in "closed" stock markets where only members may transact, they are called "open-market" operations.

The "policy levers" a monetary authority can use to "set" the dimension of the money supply may be understood from the balance sheets above. First, it can influence the size of the monetary base. The central bank can purchase or sell government obligations in open-market operations: if it purchases (sells), it increases (reduces) F and B. It can lend reserves to commercial banks (and receive repayment of previous rediscount credit); if it lends, H and B (more precisely, R) increase. Finally, by setting the national-currency price of foreign exchange e relatively high (i.e., devaluing domestic currency), the authority encourages people and firms to sell foreign exchange and discourages their buying it. The central bank tends thereby to accumulate international reserves, and to maintain the values of A and B relatively high. *Vice versa*, of course, if the national-currency price of foreign exchange is kept low.

Second, the monetary authority can influence the money multiplier, that is, the ratio of M to B. Let k represent the maximum of (i) the minimum reserve ratio the monetary authority allows banks to maintain, and (ii) the reserve ratio that the banks themselves prefer to maintain. Suppose the monetary authority knows the approximate value of z, the ratio of currency to bank deposits the public likes to maintain. Finally, let m represent the "money multiplier." Since

$$z = C/D, k = R/D, \text{ and } m = M/B,$$
$$m = (C + D) / (C + R)$$
$$= [(C/D) + (D/D)] / [(C/D) + (R/D)]$$
$$= (1 + z)/(k + z) \ [> 1 \text{ since } k < 1].$$

This expression shows that the higher is the value of k, the lower the money multiplier will be, hence the lower the value of M will be for a given value of B. For example, if the minimum reserve ratio is 20 per cent and the currency-demand deposit ratio is 30 per cent, the money supply would be $m = 2.6$ times the monetary base. Therefore, for a given monetary base, the monetary authority can set the money multiplier and the money supply by manipulating the minimum reserve ratio.

A monetary authority accordingly possesses the means to limit its economy's money supply to whatever total it considers appropriate. A monetary authority's basic mission is to keep the money supply sufficiently small (i) to preserve the monetary unit's value, but also sufficiently high, (ii) to constitute adequate domestic credit supplies, and (iii) to maintain adequate international-reserve holdings. It is the monetary authority's task, that is, to find a compromise position on all these three criteria—each of which matter differentially to different social and economic constituencies.

3 "MONETARIST," "STRUCTURALIST," "DEMAND-PULL" AND "COST-PUSH" APPROACHES TO INFLATION

Any price-level rise must, tautologically, result from, indeed, *be*, an excess of money supply over money demand—which is also to say, an excess of demand for over supply of all other things. Broadly speaking, the "monetarist" view is that (i) money demand is relatively "stable," so that price-level rises result mainly from excessive money-supply growth; and (ii) the most common cause of money-supply growth is money creation against government borrowing from central banks.[7] At this writing, throughout the world, this view appears to have become a virtual truism, having "proven itself" against "structuralism" and other theories of the causes of inflation.

The debate about monetarism is, in some senses, centuries old, but the modern debate dates from the early part of the twentieth century when economists developed the money-demand concept. Money-demand stability became an aspect of the debate: monetarists asserted that money demand grows slowly over time with economic growth and evolution of transactions techniques. Once theoretical and empirical research established, however, that money demand is not literally stable in any economy, monetarist analysts retreated to the position that at least the mathematical rule through which economic activity, interest rates, and expectations determine money demand is relatively stable. It is now broadly accepted that money demand rises with economic growth, and that it falls when rates of return rise on competing financial assets. Indeed, the point that money demand falls when inflation expectations worsen is considered a contribution of monetarist analysis.[8]

Monetarist analysis takes the view that money-supply growth and (hence) the inflation rate, are, or should be, the monetary authority's responsibility: the monetary authority has, or should have, the means to limit the money supply to any magnitude it considers appropriate. This argument is theoretically defensible, but often difficult to apply in practice. Monetary authorities must often permit money-supply growth higher than they would if price stability were their exclusive objective.

"Structuralist" approaches, which have competed since the 1940s with monetarism to explain Latin American inflation, have slipped out of fashion in recent years. Structuralist analyses maintain that certain aspects of developing economies' "structures"—including inefficient agricultural sectors unable to respond to higher demand, rapid urbanization, inadequate availability of foreign and domestic inputs, distorted industrial structures, and monopolized markets—cause aggregate supply to lag chronically behind aggregate demand.[9]

In their debates in the 1950s and 1960s, monetarists sometimes noted that it was illogical to blame cost pressure for inflation: cost pressure might raise *particular* costs and prices, but money supply must exceed money demand for costs and prices to rise *generally*. Structuralists have replied, *inter alia*, that particular cost and price rises can create powerful pressures to permit money-supply growth. A monetary authority may find that it must "validate" particular cost and price increases—i.e., make it possible for such increases to take place without other prices having to fall. By allowing credit to flow to firms facing higher prices and costs, the monetary authority expands the money supply by enough to generate a price-level rise sufficient to accommodate the higher prices and costs.

As noted, any excess money supply must be accompanied by—indeed is equivalent to—excess demand for all other things. Increased excess demand for all other things may occur through increased demand for or decreased supply of goods and services. This suggests that, in theory, monetarist explanations of price-level increases could be consistent with structuralist explanations—or indeed with any explanation involving excess aggregate demand.[10] Excess demand

means both that demand exceeds supply—i.e., "demand-pull inflation—and that supply is less than demand—"cost-push" inflation:
saying that aggregate demand exceeds aggregate supply is indistin-
guishable from saying that aggregate supply is less than aggregate
demand.

Since the mid-1950s, economic analysts have devoted considerable
energy to determining whether particular inflation episodes were
demand-pull or cost-push in character. Such diagnoses would have
presumable policy implications: in a demand-pull inflation, policy
would concentrate on restraining aggregate expenditure (in particular, on limiting monetary expansion); in a cost-push inflation, it would
seek to restrain wages and otherwise encourage production. Unfortunately, however, this distinction is quite arbitrary. One analyst may
argue that aggregate demand is excessive relative to aggregate supply,
another that aggregate supply is insufficient relative to aggregate
demand. One analyst might observe a sharp rise in aggregate
expenditure; another might reply that production ought to have risen
to meet the higher demand. Objective, scientific criteria are difficult,
probably impossible, to set. The arbitrariness of the distinction is
complicated by the fact that growth rates of goods-and-services
demand and supply are never independent. For instance, suppose
"demand-pull" inflation is diagnosed where aggregate demand grew
10 per cent and supply grew 5 per cent; it is possible that if demand
had grown only 8, not 10, per cent, supply might have grown only 3,
not 5, per cent.

Some analysts might reply that, even if the distinction is arbitrary
for relatively low rates of demand growth, there can be no question
when goods-and-services demand rises by, say, 25 per cent a year or
more: no one could reasonably argue that aggregate supply ought to
grow so fast, and so the resulting price-level increases must indis-
putably be demand-pull in character. This argument misses the point
that, as inflation proceeds, expectations align themselves with experience and with anticipated consequences of "real" events and policies.
If people expect prices to rise by x over a given time-interval, they
calculate in terms of a money unit whose purchasing power will decline
accordingly. Thus, suppose the money supply rose sufficiently "to
validate" this expectation. The supply of money would equal the
demand for money based on people's expectation that prices would
rise by x. Prices would then rise by x, as anticipated. *Real* excess
aggregate demand would be zero; *nominal* excess aggregate demand,
measured as the difference between aggregate demand at the inflated

prices and aggregate supply at the initial prices, would be positive. There would be no basis to claim, however, that real aggregate demand is excessive or supply deficient: their difference would be appropriate for the anticipated price-level rise.

People formulate plans and set contracts in terms of a money unit with some expected purchasing power. To judge whether aggregate demand is "excessive," the economy's expectations must therefore be taken into account. If aggregate demand exceeds (falls short of) aggregate supply, prices will rise faster (slower) than expected inflation; if prices rise faster (slower) than expected inflation, one may conclude that aggregate demand has exceeded (fallen short of) aggregate supply.

Once prices have risen in response to excess money supply *cum* excess demand for all other things, excess money supply and excess demand for everything else should then fall to zero, leaving no further pressure for prices to rise. The price rises themselves ought to have removed any disequilibrium, simultaneously increasing the amount of money people want to hold, reducing demand for goods and services and stimulating their supply. The questions remain, Why is the equilibrating process overcome by renewed inflationary pressure? Why are excess money supply and excess aggregate demand recurring?

One possible answer is that inflationary shocks are recurring. For example, suppose an economy's real willingness to hold money grows at some constant rate—say, at the rate of real output growth—and the money supply grows at another constant rate—say, to finance a continuing government deficit or as a result of a continuing balance-of-payments surplus. The price level ought then to grow at a rate roughly equalling the difference between the latter and the former rates.[11] This is possible, but it still misses essential aspects of the reality of inflationary experience. If the money supply growth and inflation resulted from a balance-of-payments surplus, self-correcting forces— described below—should tend to reduce the surplus. Otherwise, the question remains: Why would an economic society arrange its affairs so that money supply grew faster than money demand, thereby producing inflation?

It has become a truism that inefficient, oversized public sectors cause inflation: their financing requirements tend to be financed, directly or indirectly, through money creation. Precisely because this argument has become so widespread, it must be applied with care. First, wherever there is inflation, it is always true that the money-supply increase would have been smaller if the central bank had provided less net financing to the public sector—or if the public sector were running a larger surplus and placing the proceeds on deposit with the banking system. Second, a public sector's deficit may not be an entirely "exogenous" development: if prices rise, the government's own costs may rise, and its tax collection may diminish—again, for reasons described below. The government and monetary authorities ought to have taken corrective policy steps, one may argue; nevertheless, the authorities' ability to act rapidly may be limited in the short term. Third, the way in which the authorities limit the public-sector deficit, or limit money issue to finance it, may prove inflationary over the longer term. For example, if they raise taxes or public enterprise prices, they may reduce aggregate supply; if they borrow at high interest rates rather than issue money, they may increase their future interest bill.

Having noted these caveats, the reality is that nations that have inflation problems tend to have inefficient or heavily indebted public sectors. Reform programs, incorporating civil-service reorganization, better taxation, and better public debt management are likely to help over the medium term. Moreover, large public borrowing requirements tend to reflect a society's disagreement about taxation burdens and spending priorities. The public sector is, inevitably, an arena in which a society and its creditors carry on disputes over income allocation that "the market" has not resolved to everyone's satisfaction. Observers may feel this is inappropriate, that public sectors should only provide essential public services. Public sectors inevitably deal with income allocation, however, and are expected to do so even by people who profess to think otherwise (e.g., the government's creditors). Once an inflation gets going, whatever its initial causes, it catalyzes shifts in—and intensifies disputes over—purchasing-power allocation. This sustains inflationary pressure; intensifies the demands on the market system, the banking system, and the public sector to help resolve the disputes; and makes it harder to rationalize the public sector.

4 INFLATION FEEDBACK

Since a price-level increase should restore macroeconomic equilibrium, continuing inflation, it would seem, could only occur through repeated "shocks"—new money-supply increases, continuing slippage in money demand, aggregate-demand increases, renewed supply pressures. The "inertial-inflation" approach holds, in effect, that price-level rises may themselves constitute such repeated shocks. Such increases may be equilibrating in some ways, but disequilibrating in others, in the sense of generating new excess money supply and excess aggregate demand.

An "inflationary shock" may be defined as an event that generates excess money supply, thereby inducing a price-level rise. The "inflation-feedback process" may then be defined as a cycle in which price-level rises repeatedly constitute new inflationary shocks.

A price-level rise may constitute a new inflationary shock in several ways. First, obviously, the experience of a price-level rise inevitably alerts people to the possibility of future inflation; increases in expected inflation constitute inflationary shocks. Increases in price-level uncertainty also constitute inflationary shocks. A price-level rise directly reduces the purchasing-power value of credit denominated in the money unit. To the extent credit is required for efficient production, this may reduce aggregate supply of goods and services. The monetary authority might be pressured into reconstituting the lost credit, thus generating a further inflationary shock. A price-level rise can shift relative goods-and-services prices haphazardly, that is, in a way unrelated to true market conditions. This could disrupt aggregate supply, and so constitute an inflationary shock. Finally, a price-level rise can affect the allocation of purchasing power in such a way as to constitute an inflationary shock.

To the extent people form expectations as extrapolations of experience—i.e., "adaptively"—a price-level rise induces expectations of further rises. To the extent people form expectations by evaluating available evidence about reality—i.e., "rationally"—the experience of a price-level rise might or might not serve to increase expectations.[12] People who form inflation expectations rationally would only increase them if they believed the policy settings and economic conditions would generate continuing inflation—i.e., if their "implicit economic model" indicates inflation. Note, however, that a price-level increase should influence even people who form their expectations rationally, to the extent they believe the price-level rise will increase other people's expectations, or that a price-level rise will generate future inflationary pressure in other ways. In any case, even if expectations formation is largely "rational," a price-level rise would call attention to the causes of inflation that rational people would incorporate in their calculations.

Little is known about how people really form inflation expectations. Although some researchers have literally asked people what their expectations are and how they form them, most people articulate anticipations too hazily to enable economists clearly to describe them.[13] Researchers generally apply statistical analysis to economic time-series data to infer the expectations that people have been holding.[14] Unfortunately, the statistical methods require strong *a priori* assumptions. Most probably, people form their expectations—and uncertainty—through a mix of adaptive and rational procedures.

Having increased their inflation expectations, people act on them by reducing their money demand, contributing to excess money supply. Unless interest rates quickly rise sufficiently to compensate for anticipated inflation, they may also save less and consume more, contributing to aggregate-demand pressure. Would-be consumers who expect their purchasing power to diminish try to purchase durable goods sooner rather than later, bidding their prices up. At the same time, however, if interest rates rise, they discourage money demand.

Higher inflationary expectations may encourage firms to spend more on capital formation, although this is unclear. It depends on how the price rises would affect a constellation of management anticipations, including the cost of borrowed funds, costs of and availability of productive inputs, and prices of and demand for the firm's output. The higher relative-price dispersion and price-level uncertainty associated with higher inflation are likely to discourage expenditure for capital formation. All other things being equal, however, higher anticipated inflation reduces the anticipated real cost of borrowed funds, and increases consumer demand. To this extent higher anticipated inflation should increase firms' expenditure on capital formation. In the short term higher capital-formation expenditure contributes to aggregate demand and hence to inflationary pressure; in the longer term, once the capital is in place, it contributes, in greater or lesser degree, to aggregate supply and helps diminish inflationary pressure.

Finally, a price-level rise and an increase in anticipated inflation both induce suppliers of factors of production to demand higher wages, rents, interest rates, raw-materials prices, and so on. To the extent these rise more than the anticipated price-level rise, production is discouraged and aggregate supply declines, contributing to inflationary pressure.

If a price-level rise surprises people, their price-level uncertainty is likely to increase. Price-level uncertainty is, if anything, harder to observe or measure directly than expectations: the ways people "form" uncertainty are at least as mysterious as the ways they form expectations.[15] It seems fair—though debatable—to conjecture that price-level uncertainty rises as a consequence of any unforeseen price-level change, whether up or down, but is generally higher when expected inflation is higher, and so probably rises more with any unforeseen price-level rise than it would for an equivalent price-level fall.

Higher price-level uncertainty reduces people's money demand. It also reduces the disposition to save, because it makes the purchasing-power yield of savings instruments denominated in the money unit less predictable. People may try to keep their real savings up, however, since higher price-level uncertainty makes the purchasing power of future income less predictable. Some of the inflationary effects of higher price-level uncertainty resemble those of higher price-level expectations, but there are additional effects. One is that price-level uncertainty reduces the contract durations to which people are willing to commit themselves (see Chapter 2). This can be inflationary in a number of ways. One is its effect on production, hence on aggregate supply. A firm may need financing for the length of its productive cycle, but creditors may be unwilling to supply funds for that long; this discourages production.

A "price-level bubble," or a "bear market in money," may form part of an inflation-feedback process. As each price-level rise sustains or increases people's expectations of and uncertainty about future price levels, willingness to hold money diminishes continually, and the cycle continues—that is, money diminishes in value in part because people observe it to be diminishing. Such a process is closely analogous to "bear" and "bull" cycles in stock markets, in which demand for equities falls (rises) because people observe their prices falling (rising). A bear market in money that continued until it completely consumed the money unit's value is probably impossible; nevertheless, bear markets in money assuredly account for some of the feedback pressure in any inflation.[16]

The reduction in the purchasing-power value of assets serves in some ways to stabilize and in some ways to destabilize the price level. As real asset holdings diminish, people tend to spend less, partly because their aggregate purchasing power is diminished, partly because they try to maintain savings stocks. This would be stabilizing. To the extent firms still have "old" contracts with workers, financiers, and suppliers, a price-level rise increases unit profits, thus encouraging production and aggregate supply; this too would be stabilizing. At the same time, however, a price-level rise reduces the value of money-denominated obligations. This has at least two inflationary effects. First, to the extent people's liabilities turn out to be worth less than they had anticipated, they are wealthier, and will tend to spend more and save less. Second, as a financial system's real resources diminish, it can provide less real credit, and this reduces aggregate supply.

Paradoxically, although any price-level rise presumably results from excess liquidity, it tends to generate banking-system illiquidity. This may create a dilemma for the monetary authority. On the one hand, fearful of further inflation, it may prefer to limit money-supply growth. This could sustain the illiquidity, perhaps deepen it to the point of reducing aggregate supply: if the banking system is illiquid, at least some credit requests must be denied. Depending on how much is refused, and to whom it is refused, recession, bankruptcies, unemployed resources, and financial panic could result. Facing this prospect, the monetary authority may prefer to allow a few additional points in the annual inflation rate.

To the extent a price-level rise is associated with higher dispersion of relative prices from the equilibrium values that would clear markets, production incentives are distorted. Aggregate supply might increase if relative prices shift in certain ways, but it is more likely to diminish, particularly as the price system becomes less stable and harder "to read"—i.e., more uncertain. Rising relative-price dispersion accompanying a price-level rise may therefore reduce aggregate supply, and so contribute to a new price-level rise.

Finally, shifts in the purchasing-power allocation are bound to accompany any price-level rise. Such shifts may be stabilizing or destabilizing. To the extent purchasing power shifts toward people and firms with higher propensities to spend on consumption and investment and lower propensities to save, the price-level rise is less stabilizing, more destabilizing.

5 INFLATION FEEDBACK THROUGH THE PUBLIC-SECTOR BUDGET

Any price-level increase is likely to affect various aspects of a government budget. In some ways it may drive the budget toward surplus. To the extent it drives the budget into deficit, however, the budget becomes a channel for inflation-feedback pressure. For example, prices of goods and services the public sector purchases may rise with the general price level. The authorities might elect to purchase less, but they are likely to have to maintain some minimum flow of real purchases.

Whether higher inflation will generate a higher deficit depends partly on how public-sector revenues respond to higher prices. If taxes are levied as percentages of money prices and incomes, tax revenues should rise. For various reasons, however, inflation tends to reduce tax revenues. One reason is that inflation may induce resentment, and this may encourage tax avoidance and evasion. In the short term, revenues may decline as a result of the "collection lag," the time that elapses between the "taxable event" and the time the government receives the revenue. Inflation erodes the real value of tax revenue over the collection lag: the higher the inflation rate, the lower the real tax revenue will be. This is called the "Olivera–Tanzi effect," after two analysts whose papers discussed the problem.[17]

Public-sector productive enterprises present a parallel problem. Their costs often rise before the authorities raise their prices—partly because political pressure against raising public-enterprise prices is inevitably powerful. These prices often figure significantly in economies' cost structures, since public sectors often provide electric power, transportation, fuel, and other important commodities and services. This often creates a peculiar dilemma for policy-makers. If they raise prices, they increase cost pressure; if they fail to raise them, they reduce the enterprises' profitability, hence maintain the public-sector deficit and aggregate-demand pressure. This exemplifies the policy dilemmas inherent in the inflation-feedback process: policy-makers may sometimes be able only to choose the transmission channel of inflationary pressure, rather than whether there will be such pressure.

Public-sector budgets often incorporate stabilizing features. The Olivera-Tanzi effect is offset to the extent there are lags in public-sector payments for goods and services, and to the extent wages and prices paid by the public sector are fixed under contracts. One well-known example of a stabilizing feature in public budgets is "progressive" income-tax schedules, which impose higher percentage tax rates on higher money incomes. Unless the tax brackets are index-linked (see Chapter 8), personal incomes drift into higher tax brackets as inflation lifts them. In this way price-level rises tend to produce real tax-revenue increases. Higher taxes also reduce households' real "disposable" income, which reduces aggregate consumption, hence aggregate demand. This feature of progressive income-tax systems has often been called an "automatic stabilizer," because it reduced consumption and public deficits in response to inflation without specific policy actions. Where prices were still drifting up but an economy remained in recession, however, it was often called "fiscal drag." In any case, "bracket drift" has been viewed as unfair and inefficient, since, as long as the brackets remained unadjusted, average income-tax rates tended to rise with the price level. Bracket drift affects aggregate supply over time: as wage earners' incomes float into higher brackets and take-home pay becomes a smaller proportion of total pay, firms come under pressure to pay higher wages, raising the cost structure.

Income taxes produce limited amounts of revenue for most Latin American nations, and those with severe inflation have introduced indexation to relieve bracket drift (see Chapter 8). Moreover, the Olivera-Tanzi effect is a significant but not overwhelming channel of inflation-feedback pressure; unless the inflation rate rises sharply, the change in tax receipts as a proportion of GDP is relatively limited: if annual inflation rises suddenly from zero to 100 per cent in an economy whose tax-collection lag is 30 days, the average tax rate should fall about 5.5 per cent—e.g., if it had been 20 per cent of GDP, it would fall to 18.9 per cent of GDP. Nevertheless, tax revenues have fallen sharply in Latin American nations with significant inflation problems over the 1980s; avoidance, evasion, the collection lag, and recession probably all figure among the reasons.

In recent years, external and internal interest bills have constituted powerful short-term inflation-feedback channels in Latin American public budgets. Since nominal interest rates tend to rise with expected inflation and price-level uncertainty, and since these rise in response to inflationary experience, inflation tends accordingly to swell public-sector interest bills. Financing a public-sector interest deficit presents a policy dilemma. If the authorities sell obligations to private financial markets, they pressure (real) interest rates upward, widening the deficit; if they sell obligations to the central bank, they pressure the money supply to increase, leading to inflation and higher interest rates, widening the deficit.[18]

Price-level uncertainty can have nasty consequences in this context. Private financial markets are likely to insist on higher real rates of return on longer-term obligations to compensate for price-level uncertainty. The authorities may elect to issue shorter-term obligations to reduce their interest charges. Public-sector debt would then roll over more frequently: if inflation worsens and market interest rates rise with expected inflation, the public sector's average interest rate rises more rapidly, since the proportion of outstanding obligations at older, lower rates diminishes more rapidly.

In some nations, the central bank's role in this process has become more intricate than elementary monetary theory would indicate. In most economies, bank reserves pay no interest. Central banks tend accordingly to earn operating profits, since their assets typically yield interest while their liabilities do not. More recently, however, some Latin American central banks have come to pay interest on bank reserves. They did so mainly because high reserve requirements would otherwise have decapitalized commercial banks or forced them to charge high interest rates on their loans, particularly where high reserve ratios deprived commercial banks of a significant part of their lending capacity.[19] Moreover, several Latin American central banks have issued interest-bearing non-monetary obligations to absorb money—in part, because central-bank obligations happened to be easier to sell in domestic financial markets than government obligations.[20] As a consequence, central-bank operating profits have diminished, and in some instances turned into losses—so-called "quasi-fiscal" deficits. Central banks that accrued more in interest owed than interest receivable tended to become more deeply indebted and decapitalized; to the extent they actually paid out more in interest on liabilities than they received in interest on assets, they created money.[21]

Public-sector external debt can also contribute to inflation-feedback pressures. Rising domestic prices reduce the international competitiveness of exports and encourage imports, and this creates pressure for devaluation. External borrowing may avert the need to devalue. A number of governments (notably Argentina and Chile between 1978 and 1982) borrowed so heavily that they sustained relatively high exchange values for their currencies—i.e., their goods and services became expensive in dollars. When creditors restricted new lending, however, devaluation became unavoidable. Devaluation increases the local-currency value of external debt, hence the local-currency value of external interest and amortization payments. Thus, by inducing devaluation and thereby in turn higher external debt-service charges, inflation tends ultimately to deepen public financial deficits.

To the extent inflation reduces the real value of outstanding public-sector debt, the government effectively secures revenue. The reduction in the real value of outstanding debt should be subtracted from the measured public-sector deficit in order to obtain a better indicator of the deficit's economic significance.[22] Otherwise, since nominal interest rates implicitly incorporate a component that compensates for the erosion of the debt principal by inflation, the deficit would be overstated as a proportion of GDP. Since this interest is paid to the private sector, private saving would be correspondingly overstated. The public-sector deficit so adjusted has come to be known as the "operational," or "real-basis" deficit. The argument for using the operational deficit *to measure* the pressure of the deficit on the macroeconomy is sound.[23] Nevertheless, the "inflation component" (i.e., the rest) of the deficit matters for inflation feedback. The full deficit must be financed: as the previously outstanding debt matures and new government debt is created, wealth-holders must decide whether to renew their financing of the public sector. To the extent "voluntary" sources of finance for the deficit prove reluctant, the authorities must choose, as always, between raising interest rates to encourage voluntary financing or securing financing from the central bank.

6 INFLATION FEEDBACK THROUGH THE EXTERNAL ACCOUNTS

Powerful inflation-feedback processes operate through an economy's external accounts. Given conditions in the rest of the world, the response of the external accounts to a domestic price-level rise depends largely on how the authorities manage the exchange rate. A central bank could either fix the exchange rate, promising to buy and sell foreign exchange for domestic currency at that rate, or, alternatively, allow the exchange rate "to float," i.e., be determined freely in the foreign-exchange market; the central bank might buy or sell in this market, or not do so. Some economies have fixed exchange rates for specified kinds of transaction and allow, or tolerate, "parallel" exchange markets for others.

In theory, if the exchange rate is fixed, the external accounts should respond to a price-level rise in a way that ultimately stabilizes the price level. As exports become uncompetitive and the propensity to import increases, the trade account would move into deficit. The central bank would then be selling international reserves and absorbing money. As the money supply diminishes, domestic prices decline. This adjustment process may entail unacceptably large reserve loss, however, impairing the economy's ability to carry on external transactions. The authorities then face two disagreeable alternatives. Either they borrow foreign exchange to rebuild reserves, thus incurring a foreign-exchange debt which will have to be serviced at some later date; or they devalue the currency. Devaluation tends to be inflationary, first, because it directly raises foreign goods-and-services prices, and indirectly pressures up prices of goods and services into which foreign goods are inputs; and second, precisely because it interrupts the process of money-supply contraction. If the exchange rate is flexible or floating, it may depreciate in response to any condition of excess demand for foreign exchange that emerges, particularly if the central bank elects to limit sales or increase purchases of foreign-exchange; this may pressure the price level up.[24]

A monetary authority that devalues to protect its international-reserve position after a price-level rise risks setting off a vicious cycle in which inflation gives rise to devaluation and devaluation to a new round of inflation. Such a cycle could converge or explode, depending on whether each round of devaluation gives rise to proportionally less or more inflation—which depends in turn on whether each round of inflation induces other kinds of feedback effects.

The exchange rate also figures in at least two other related inflation-feedback channels. The first operates through the parallel exchange rate, while the second operates through the use of foreign exchange as a unit of account in domestic transactions.

Consider a nation whose price level has just risen sharply, but whose monetary authority has elected not to devalue, preferring instead (say) to allow international-reserve loss to diminish inflationary pressure. Suppose the financial markets believe, however, that the monetary authority will prove unable to control the reserve loss and that devaluation will soon become unavoidable. Expected devaluation—likely to be coupled with expectations of subsequent inflation—can have powerful inflationary consequences. Expected devaluation may induce people to shift their wealth into foreign exchange. As they shift out of domestic currency, they pressure its purchasing-power value down; to the extent they hoard foreign exchange, less foreign exchange is available for imports. As the scarcity value of foreign exchange rises, "parallel" or "black" foreign-exchange markets may take on increasing importance, with foreign exchange commanding a (one-way) speculative premium. To the extent foreign-exchange transactions occur in the parallel market, it is as though devaluation has already occurred, because in many markets the parallel exchange rate establishes costs and competing prices. Such circumstances can force a monetary authority to devalue, because people who earn foreign exchange prefer to sell it in the parallel market rather than to the central bank. Accordingly, the central bank tends all the more to lose reserves, hastening devaluation.[25]

Some nations permit their financial systems to denominate assets and liabilities in foreign exchange. The purpose is to forestall "capital flight": people who fear devaluation often place their funds in foreign exchange. To the extent anticipated devaluation—rather than security from taxation or confiscation—is the motive for placing wealth abroad, people are willing to hold wealth within the nation if it can be protected from devaluation. The problem is that existence of assets denominated in foreign exchange augments the inflationary consequences of both anticipated and actual devaluation. Availability of legal, liquid devaluation hedges within an economy makes it easier for people to move their wealth out of domestic currency into a form of wealth protected from devaluation. The economy's willingness to hold domestic money may therefore diminish by more than it otherwise would in response to a higher expected devaluation rate. More important, banking-system issues denominated in foreign exchange ("dollar deposits"), are virtually part of the economy's money supply. Devaluation therefore directly increases the money supply.

7 INFLATION FEEDBACK THROUGH AGGREGATE SUPPLY

Inflation discourages aggregate supply in various ways, and to this extent contributes to the inflation-feedback process. In other ways, inflation increases aggregate supply, and so promotes stabilization. The views that inflation and aggregate supply are positively associated, that inflation and economic activity are positively associated, and that inflation and unemployment are negatively associated are often referred to in economic literature as "the Phillips curve." The Phillips curve—a downward-sloping locus drawn on a graph diagram with unemployment on one axis and the inflation rate on the other—is a broad notion encompassing a wide range of ideas, but the one that matters most for present purposes is that aggregate supply responds positively to inflation or to inflationary expectations. This is true in many respects, but inflation also discourages aggregate supply in various ways, thus constituting yet another inflation-feedback channel.

Worldwide experience indicates that increases (decreases) in inflation rates and increases (decreases) in economic activity are positively correlated. Economic research since at least the 1950s has verified and attempted to explain this.[26] The expression "Phillips curve" derives from a 1957 paper by A. W. Phillips, which discussed statistical verification for a negative association of wage-rate growth with unemployment rates. The argument's premises were that unemployment rates measure excess supply in the labor market, and that the cost of labor services ought to rise less or fall more, the higher is the excess labor supply—an application of supply-demand analysis to the labor-services "market." Later writers suggested that the Phillips "curve" could describe the inflation-economic activity correlation. On the one hand, low unemployment and high economic activity came to be regarded as practical synonyms; on the other hand, "wage growth" and "price inflation" came to be seen as related, since wages form the bulk of prime cost and prices are formed on the basis of prime cost.[27]

By the mid-1960s, after an influential paper by Paul Samuelson and Robert Solow (Samuelson and Solow 1960), economists established a basic Phillips-curve paradigm. Its essence was that active fiscal and monetary policy could increase aggregate demand and hence economic activity. Past a certain level, as excess labor supply disappeared, wages would be bid up and push prices up. The Phillips curve was presented as a "menu" of paired choices available to policy-makers: depending on society's "preferences," they could select higher inflation and lower unemployment, or lower inflation and higher unemployment.

In the late 1960s this view came under vigorous critique by the increasingly influential (University of) "Chicago School."[28] The critique has several distinct aspects, but its basic thrust was as follows. Granted, any generally *unanticipated* increase in the inflation rate is likely to generate increased economic activity, for two basic reasons. First, businessmen cannot easily distinguish increases in prices they receive from general price-level increases, and may be "fooled" into believing their *real* prices are rising. Second, output prices rise while labor wages and other costs remain fixed under contracts negotiated earlier on the basis of inflationary expectations lower than the inflation actually occurring; this temporarily improves enterprises' cash flow and profits. Having been surprised by inflation, however, people will try not to be fooled again. Workers will seek to revise contracts as soon as possible, not only to "catch up" to the higher cost of living, but to compensate for anticipated future inflation. If no further unanticipated increase in the inflation rate occurs, economic activity is likely to subside to its previous level.

The Chicago reasoning implies that the Phillips-curve trade-off can only be temporary. Once policy-makers exercise the option to increase economic activity and hence the price level, the curve effectively shifts "upward and outward" in subsequent periods—that is, a higher inflation rate is needed to sustain the new activity level. In the medium to long term, the Chicago argument runs, since economic activity will be determined by fundamental market forces regardless of the inflation rate, the Phillips curve comes to be a vertical line rising from the economy's "natural" unemployment rate.

The Chicago critique and the analysis deriving from it center on the response of aggregate supply to inflation and inflation expectations. Once inflation comes to be expected, "fundamental" economic forces will re-assert themselves and render inflation irrelevant to aggregate supply. The consensus of the economics profession now appears to be that "expansionary" policies can stimulate both economic activity and inflation in the short term, in a mix that depends on the short-term response of aggregate supply to higher inflation, so that a short-term Phillips curve policy "trade-off" is a reality. Past the short term, however—and the short term is shorter in nations whose inflationary experience is longer—the Chicago critique is valid. That is, aggregate supply may respond positively to the difference between actual and expected inflation, but this difference tends to diminish as societies become accustomed to inflation.

The argument that inflation may be in some degree self-stabilizing through its positive effect on aggregate supply is therefore suspect at best. On the other hand, there are many reasons why inflation tends to discourage aggregate supply, and why higher inflation rates tend more deeply to reduce aggregate supply, encompassing almost everything discussed in Chapter 2. Higher inflationary expectations and uncertainty discourage enterprises from holding the money balances they require for efficient operations; inflation reduces the stock of real financial resources available in the economy, not only for longer-term investment but also for short-term working capital; inflationary uncertainty makes the contracts required for modern industrial processes harder to negotiate; and the relative-price dispersion that accompanies inflation implies that the price system malfunctions, with inevitable negative consequences for aggregate supply. The aggregate-supply channel of inflation feedback, accordingly, operates through all the different ways in which inflation disorganizes and disrupts productive processes.

8   CONCLUSION

The observation that an economy's price level rises if and only if the money supply exceeds what the economy as a whole wishes to hold is a tautology, by no means a theory of inflation. A theory of inflation must explain how the money supply tends to become excessive again, in spite of a presumably stabilizing price-level rise. This chapter has argued that a price-level rise itself may constitute, or contribute to, an inflationary shock. By changing people's price-level expectations and uncertainty, by reducing the economy's real liquidity, by increasing relative-price dispersion, by changing the allocation of the economy's purchasing power, by widening the public-sector's deficit, and by creating pressure for devaluation, a price-level rise can generate renewed inflationary pressure, reducing money demand and pressuring the money supply to increase. In this way an inflation can be self-perpetuating.[29]

4 Inflation Feedback and Competition for Purchasing Power

1 INTRODUCTION

By definition, any true monetary "authority" possesses legal and operational means to limit the economy's aggregate money and credit to any quantity it deems appropriate (as explained in Chapter 3). In reality, however, political, social and economic realities circumscribe monetary authorities' powers, in greater or lesser degree. The tighter the credit supply, the harder it will be for firms to do business and meet contracted commitments. Monetary authorities always have three fundamental missions. One is to maintain the value of the currency, by limiting its supply. The others are to maintain credit conditions adequate for "normal" business and an adequate international reserve stock. Over the longer run these objectives coincide: stable currency is essential for sound credit, while business stability and reserve adequacy are essential for a sound currency. On a day-to-day basis, though, the monetary authority's peculiarly difficult task is to set the money supply small enough to meet the price-stability objective but large enough to meet the credit- and reserve-adequacy objectives.

The need to ensure adequate credit availability often makes monetary policy less "autonomous," or more "endogenous," in the inflationary process than theory implies. A monetary authority may be reluctant to limit economic entities' access to credit, not just because it would seem unfair to do so, but because denying credit to one entity could affect other entities through intricate networks of business relationships. Thus, although in principle a monetary authority could rapidly stop an inflation by strictly limiting money creation, it may prefer to work circumspectly in practice.

Political and institutional realities matter in this context. In particular, it matters very much who the true monetary authority is. In some nations, such as the United States and Germany, central-bank directors are the monetary authority: they have the means to determine the money supply and are not subject to government instruction. The directors of the British and Italian central banks are subject to ministerial instruction, but their prestige is such that governments usually permit them to be authorities in practice. In Brazil, in contrast, monetary policy is set by a National Monetary Board, comprising the "economic" ministers and presidents and directors of key publicly owned financial institutions, including Central Bank directors. The Finance Minister chairs this Board, and in practice wields the basic monetary power.

Many analysts consider systems in which the central bank is subordinate to the finance ministry to be inherently inflationary, because a finance minister unable or unwilling to control the government deficit can direct the central bank to finance it, or to set financial market conditions to make it easier to finance. Political considerations are more likely to enter into a minister's instructions to a central bank. Economists generally recommend the German Bundesbank system of independence. It is only realistic to recognize, however, that even independent directors are subject to powerful "real-world" pressures.

Monetarist analysts often use a metaphor involving an island whose inhabitants produce a fixed quantity of coconuts. A helicopter periodically flies over the island and drops money. Since the money supply continually increases, the price of coconuts continually rises. The metaphor would more closely approximate reality if the helicopter were employed collectively by the islanders, and if individual islanders tried to influence the flight plan. If the island produced bananas as well as coconuts, the relative price of the two commodities would matter in the dynamic process. It would matter, for example, how much money fell on people who prefer coconuts, or on people who produce coconuts.

Other metaphors also help to understand inflationary processes. Children's games like Old Maid or Musical Chairs, in which players compete in each stage not to lose, characterize aspects of the inflation-feedback process. (Keynes cited these games as metaphors in his celebrated characterization of equity markets; see *The General Theory*, p. 156.) Just as in Musical Chairs there are always more players than chairs to sit in when the music stops, in an inflation people's purchasing power continually exceeds what is available for purchase.

2 THE MONETARY SYSTEM IN THE INFLATION PROCESS

A banking system backs its money supply with a "portfolio" of private loans, credit to the public sector, and international reserves, less its total net worth. (See the simplified balance sheet in Chapter 3.) A monetary authority can manage the money and credit stocks (as explained in Chapter 3) by manipulating such policy "instruments" as commercial banks' minimum reserve-deposit ratios, central-bank credit to commercial banks, open-market sales and purchases of government securities for the central bank's own account, and the exchange rate. Suppose for the moment that the system's net worth is given and fixed. Since assets identically equal liabilities plus net worth at any moment, any increase in banking-system assets (apart from changes in asset valuation) must be accompanied either by a money-supply increase or a decrease in other assets, as part of the same transaction. Similarly, a net increase in banking-system assets must accompany any money-supply increase.

A monetary authority that "tightens" money-supply growth must therefore simultaneously "tighten" growth of the banking system's total claims. If the banking system is acquiring foreign exchange reserves and providing loans to the government, the monetary authority can hold money-supply growth to zero only by forcing a reduction in private-sector credit. This explains why monetary authorities often respond ambivalently to inflationary pressure. If they fight inflation by "making room" in the banking system for loans to the government or for foreign-exchange inflows, they work against their "credit-availability" objective.

Commercial banks forced to limit lending operations are likely to do so somewhat arbitrarily and unfairly. The level of credit already outstanding, or even personal relationships, may matter as much as profitability or creditworthiness considerations. Credit limitations may force firms to scale back operations, perhaps lay off workers and reduce inputs purchases to cut variable costs. Firms that had recently invested in plant or inventory might find their circumstances precarious following banks' unanticipated refusals to renew working-capital credit. Widespread complaints may incline monetary authorities against reducing private-sector credit "to make room" in the banking system to finance a government deficit; instead, they may permit some monetary expansion.

This is the "monetary" reason why government borrowing from the central bank tends to be inflationary. The same phenomenon may be interpreted slightly differently. By running a deficit, the government "unilaterally" increases its purchasing power. It finances the deficit by borrowing in some combination from (i) external lenders, (ii) private domestic lenders, or (iii) the central bank. Private domestic lenders transfer purchasing power to the government voluntarily, in exchange for the interest on the bond issues. If the government borrows from the central bank or from foreigners, however, the central bank creates money—in the first case, to purchase the government's obligations, in the second, to purchase the foreign-exchange loan proceeds. Either way, the government would have more purchasing power, but the private sector would not have relinquished any.

If the monetary authority allows no increase in the money supply, it effectively forces a transfer of purchasing power from the private sector to the government: the monetary authority would have to reduce private-sector credit to hold the money supply constant. If the monetary authority allows the money supply to increase, on the other hand, the extent of purchasing-power transfer is uncertain. Total purchasing power in the economy increases initially. If the aggregate supply of goods and services remains unchanged, prices must rise to cut back aggregate purchasing power. If the government makes its purchases before the price rise, it secures all the purchasing power its deficit implied. To the extent prices rise before the government makes its purchases, they erode the government's purchasing power, and diminish the transfer of purchasing power from the private sector to the government.

Whenever anyone, not only the government, receives credit, the purchasing-power allocation changes. This implies that, in reality, monetary authorities are something like umpires in societies' determination of the purchasing-power allocation. When they allow no overall money-supply increase after some entity receives net additional credit, they force a purchasing-power allocation favoring that entity. To the extent they allow some money-supply increase, they decline to act as umpire, and instead provide the means with which different sectors compete for purchasing power.

3 COMPETITION FOR PURCHASING POWER

To understand how a private sector can pressure a banking system to inflate, imagine a simple economy that produces and consumes only bananas and coconuts. There is a monetary authority and commercial-banking system, but otherwise no government. (Without government credit, the central bank manages the money supply with the minimum reserve ratio and rediscounting operations.) Merchants specialize in bananas or coconuts. They receive supplies under contracts with producers which are negotiated monthly. Commercial banks finance merchants' wholesale purchases by discounting thirty-day promissory notes. To simplify, assume that wholesale prices are set by competitive bidding the first of every month. On this day each merchant completes orders and concludes borrowing arrangements with his bank. Also to simplify, suppose initially that consumer tastes for and outputs of both bananas and coconuts are invariant in the short run, but that this fact is not generally known in this economy.

Suppose that one month the coconut merchants, each acting independently, decide to purchase 5 per cent more coconuts than the previous month because they—incorrectly—anticipate higher sales. To do so, they attempt to borrow 5 per cent more from their banks. Banks might prefer not to lend, but, as in any other business, they might be swayed by the prospect of larger business volume, or by fear that merchants denied credit might take their business to competing banks.

Banks must now either reduce total lending to banana merchants, or else persuade the monetary authority to allow money-supply growth. If the monetary authority allows no money-supply increase and credit is reduced to banana merchants, purchasing power would effectively flow from banana to coconut merchants. If the monetary authority does allow a money-supply increase, total purchasing power increases. The monetary unit's purchasing power may then be bid down. Either way, the wholesale price of coconuts should be bid up, as the coconut merchants bid against one another for available supplies.

If the money supply remains unchanged and banana merchants' credit falls, their demand for bananas should fall; so then should the wholesale banana price. The higher coconut price and lower banana price should about average out, so the wholesale-price level should not significantly change. If the money supply increases, however, the banana price could remain unchanged while the money supply rose by the full amount of the credit increase to coconut merchants, since credit to banana merchants will remain roughly unchanged. Since the wholesale coconut price should increase under demand pressure, the wholesale price level should rise.

Either way, things will not have worked out as the coconut merchants had hoped. They will be paying more for their coconuts, but, because coconuts are in fact in fixed supply, they will be unable to purchase more. They may try to recover their profit margins by raising retail prices. Once this happens, though, some consumers may find the coconut price too high and refrain from purchasing, pressuring it back down somewhat. To the extent this demand shifts to bananas, banana retail prices should come under upward pressure. As long as consumer tastes and the relative availabilities of the two goods remain unchanged, whether or not the money supply rises, the *ratio* of the retail prices of the two goods should tend back to its original value. If the money supply remains unchanged, the *money* retail prices of the two goods should return to their original values. The coconut merchants will find themselves squeezed between higher wholesale prices, higher credit charges, and unchanged retail prices.

For at least some time, in contrast, coconut *producers* should find the situation agreeable. Regardless of whether the money supply increases, they receive a higher real wholesale price. They may have to pass some on to workers, landlords, and so on: skilled workers, for example, might offer their labor to other producers if they fail to receive some part of the price increase. Nevertheless, once the retail price of coconuts turns back down, the wholesale price to be negotiated next month will be under pressure to fall. The windfall to coconut producers, workers and landlords would then be only temporary.

The process began when coconut merchants tried to increase their business. The banking system provided the means—additional credit—to carry out this attempted "coup." Eventually, however, with consumer tastes and output invariant, their effort would tend to fail. Output invariance clearly matters here, for coconut producers might otherwise have responded to the higher wholesale price by increasing output. This might have pressured the price downward—a case of incipient inflation stimulating production and so stabilizing itself.

The process need not have begun with the merchants, of course. Coconut producers, for example, might have demanded a higher wholesale price. Merchants might then conclude that, rather than resist producers' demands, it would be easiest to ask their banks for additional credit and then raise their retail price. Or the process might have begun with coconut workers demanding higher wages; producers might decide that raising the wholesale price was the way of least resistance. Such purchasing-power "coups" could succeed at least temporarily, if merchants acceded and persuaded banks to finance wholesale purchases at the higher price.

The general point is that any part of an economic society may attempt to lay hold of additional purchasing power. The issue is likely to end up sooner or later at the commercial-banking system, in the form of a request to provide additional credit to merchants or producers (or to the public sector). If commercial banks shift financing to one group of economic agents away from another, they effectively favor a group in the competition. If they increase credit to one group without reducing credit to others, the money supply must increase.

This example also suggests why increased relative-price dispersion is likely to accompany a general price rise. Once the coconut merchants receive additional purchasing power, the ratio of the wholesale prices of coconuts and bananas tends to shift. Assuming no change occurs in relative demands for and supplies of coconuts and bananas, however, the ratio of their prices should be pressured back to its initial value.

4   INFLATION FEEDBACK AND PURCHASING-POWER COMPETITION

In the story thus far, the price level should rise if the money supply grows, but nothing more should happen thereafter: if tastes and output remain invariant, the economy should re-establish the original relative-price equilibrium. The price-level rise need not become an inflation. For inflation, the crucial moment is "the first day of the following month," when new wholesale supply contracts are negotiated. Assume that by this time the price array has settled at its new equilibrium: could the price-level rise recur?

Although the coconut merchants increased their real credit balances, they failed to increase their real business volume. At the same time, coconut producers, and possibly their workers, enjoyed an initial real-earnings increase, but this increase tended to decline as "fundamental" market forces re-asserted themselves. Meanwhile banana producers', and possibly their workers', real earnings declined, but the same market forces reversed these losses. By the start of the new month, all concerned may have reason to be disappointed, confused or apprehensive. An economist with a bird's-eye perspective might, after appropriate research, conclude that the initial and final prices were proper scarcity prices, but the economy's participants may view matters less disinterestedly.

Having failed to raise their real business volume during the first month, coconut merchants might conclude that their attempt was an error, and simply continue to do business as before. In this case there should be no subsequent inflation. On the other hand, they might believe that persistence and determination would eventually be rewarded, and so request another increased quantity of real credit for the new month. If people's perceptions and attitudes remain unchanged, the second month's events could resemble the first month's. The banking system would again provide increased credit; the monetary authority would decide again between allowing and not allowing money-supply growth; there would be an incipient shift of real earnings flows toward the coconut business, away from the banana business, followed by restoration of the initial price relationship.

The experiences of the first month are likely to change people's perceptions, attitudes and expectations, however. Coconut producers may argue that the higher real wholesale price they received was, at long last, the proper price for their produce, and demand its restoration. Coconut workers may feel that the higher wages they received were appropriate. If merchants accede to a higher wholesale price, they must seek additional bank credit even to maintain the same real business volume.

Banana merchants, producers, and workers may also make demands. Having seen their real retail price diminish the previous month, having lost some of their real credit supply, and fearing similar events in the coming month, merchants are likely to petition their bankers for more credit. Banana producers, following the coconut producers' example, might unilaterally demand higher prices, thus giving banana merchants further reason to seek additional credit.

In general, in the wake of an attempt by one part of an economy to lay hold of increased purchasing power, *all* of the private sector, including the original "aggressor," can be expected to act, either to recover or protect its purchasing power. The larger and wider the pressure to increase the commercial-banking system's credit balances, the more intense the pressure on the monetary authority to allow money-supply growth. The inflation-feedback process operates through competition of this kind over purchasing-power allocation. Having few objective criteria to work with, a monetary authority is likely to allow credit increases, particularly if these are based on verifiable cost increases, and leave it to the private sector to determine, through inflation, how the purchasing power is to be divided up.

Such a competition could be resolved sensibly, it would seem, if real wages, real wholesale prices and real retail prices moved flexibly to reconcile availabilities and tastes. Neo-classical general-equilibrium theory suggests that trial-and-error convergence could find the appropriate price array. The outcome would be stable, would employ all available resources, and would equilibrate supply and demand in all markets—coconuts, bananas, credit, and money. An important reason why the appropriate price vector is hard to reach, however, is that credit *cum* money creation is subject to the judgment of commercial banks and the monetary authority. The monetary authority knows neither the relative-price structure nor the socially acceptable income allocation at any moment, and cannot be sure how far prices and incomes are from "equilibrium." It therefore cannot decide on this basis whether to allow the credit supply to increase. If it did allow the credit supply to increase, it cannot be certain that the credit would go to the "appropriate" clients.

5   THE "PEAKS-AND-VALLEYS" METAPHOR FOR CONTRACTED PRICES UNDER INFLATION

As the price level rises, any stream of contracted money payments steadily loses purchasing power. When the contract is renewed, the payments will probably rise to reflect both accumulated and anticipated inflation. The purchasing power of such a stream has a characteristic profile of "peaks and valleys," with purchasing power at a peak just after and in a valley just before contract adjustments. The higher the inflation over the period, all other things being equal, the steeper the slope will be from peak to valley, and the wider the variation in the real value of flows over the contract duration. The rise from the valley floor to the peak, in contrast, is a vertical leap with the step up to a new contracted price. For a given rate of price-level rise, the shorter the contract duration, the smaller the variation in purchasing-power flows.[1]

If future inflation were certain and neutral ("semi-ideal" as defined in Chapter 2), a money contract could easily be negotiated with a pre-determined purchasing-power value. Price-level uncertainty and rela-tive-price dispersion make the negotiating problem more intricate, however. The purchaser, fearful that prices will rise less than expected, will bargain for lower contracted payments; the seller, fearful that prices will rise more than expected, will bargain for higher payments (see Chapter 2). Higher price-level uncertainty encourages the parties to reduce the contract length, accepting the cost of more frequent contract negotiations.

This "peaks-and-valleys" reasoning elucidates the problem that inflation causes for wage negotiations. Imagine that an economy has a single annual labor negotiation, which determines the contracted wage for one year. The purchasing power of the national payroll will be at a maximum for the year just following, and at a minimum just prior to, the negotiation. The difference of total income and total wages is non-wage income—for simplicity, call it "profit" income. Real profit income will be at a minimum for the year just following, and at a maximum just prior to, the negotiation.

In such a simplified system, once a national nominal wage has been set under contract, the output price determines the income allocation. The faster it rises, the more it moves against labor and in favor of profits. The output price would rise, of course, to the extent higher wages raised demand pressure. Such pressure would be at a maximum immediately after the contract is signed, when real wage income jumps sharply and real profit income drops correspondingly. The pressure would be the greater, the sharper is the wage-income jump, and the more power firms have to set the output price. The inflation-feedback mechanism comes into play in each round of contract negotiations: the higher the price level has risen, and the higher inflation expectations become, the higher the new wage labor will demand.

Once labor costs rise, firms either reduce their employment or seek additional working-capital credit from their banks. Unless they could force an offsetting contraction, additional credit would require the monetary authorities to permit monetary expansion. In this way the monetary authorities would effectively "validate" the wage increase. If they allow credit to expand by less than what is required to validate the wage increase, economic activity might diminish, because some firms would receive less credit than they need to carry on at the new wage level.

In reality, most economies' wage negotiations occur asynchronously in different industries and firms. Each group of wage earners' negotiating stance is influenced by earlier and concurrent negotiations. The same is true in any complex economy, with or without price stability. Inflation makes such wage negotiations more difficult, however, because price-level uncertainty and relative-price dispersion deepen uncertainty attaching to labor and management calculations.

Inflation tends to engage many interest groups in what is characteristically a leap-frog struggle. Imagine that at the end of month t the n groups of wage earners have a particular purchasing-power distribution, summing up to some total purchasing-power aggregate, and that at this point some subset of the n entities has its purchasing power increased through new contracts. Unless wage earners generally save their new purchasing power, expenditure will exceed available product by more than previously. A price-level rise is then required "to dilute" the excess. The new contracts improve the directly affected wage earners' relative standing within the purchasing-power allocation and worsen unaffected wage earners' relative standing. In the next month, a different subset of wage earners will have its purchasing power revised and will recover some of its standing in the purchasing-power allocation. And so the process continues, either toward higher inflation or toward a more generally accepted purchasing-power allocation.

6   AN ECONOMIC ENTITY'S CAPACITY TO ENGAGE IN INFLATIONARY COMPETITION

An entity or group's capacity to participate in inflationary competition depends on its ability (i) to raise prices and quantities of goods and services sold; (ii) to resist increases in prices of inputs and final goods; (iii) to secure credit on reasonable terms; and (iv) to secure government support, through subsidies, tariff protection, favored tax treatment, debt relief, and the like. At any moment, a group may be deficient in one or two of these, but may possess the others in sufficient degree to assure its capacity to compete effectively. Not surprisingly, an economic entity's capacity to participate in inflationary competition is related to its capacity to engage in market competition, although some entities may compete quite effectively through non-market or semi-market means—that is, through calls on the government or on the banking system.

If the "entity" in question is an identifiable group, it may or may not be sufficiently cohesive to carry out a price increase; a price rise may be harder if group members compete against one another. An unregulated monopolized or oligopolized industry can raise its prices more easily than a competitive industry. An industry protected by trade restrictions from external competition can more easily raise its output prices. A group may be able to increase its earnings by increasing its output. In general, this would be less inflationary, because additional supplies would require lower prices. In the short term, however, an industry working at full capacity may be physically unable to increase output.

An entity's ability to maintain or increase its earnings depends on (a) the amount by which the entity could raise product prices before falling demand diminished earnings; and (b) the amount by which the entity could increase output before the price drop required to sell it pushed earnings down. In technical terms the issue is the "elasticity" of demand: demand may be elastic to a price cut and inelastic to a price increase, or *vice versa*.[2] Clearly a firm facing "upward inelasticity" and "downward elasticity" of demand in its markets is in the best possible competitive position. To the extent firms face inelastic demand—i.e., demand that varies little with price increases—the economy's inherent tendency is inflationary, because firms can increase revenue flows only by raising prices.

An entity's capacity to resist cost increases negatively mirrors the market powers of entities from whom it purchases. The more elastic an entity's demand for inputs and final goods—in part, the more able or willing an entity is to do without particular inputs—and the more easily suppliers can increase output in response to increased demand, the greater is the entity's capacity to control its costs.

7 CONTRACTS AND CREDIT CREATION

Contracts, which are fundamentally necessary in industrial economies, can play an important role in the inflation-feedback process. Suppose that in a given economy workers are customarily paid on the first day of each month for work done under contract the previous month, and that merchants customarily pay producers at the start of each month for shipments made the previous month. If prices never varied, it would matter little whether merchants and producers paid before, during or after receiving their respective month's goods and services. It does matter, however, if prices fluctuate.

Suppose that during June workers demand a 10 per cent wage increase effective in July, and that producers, figuring they can pass it on to the merchants, accede. As a consequence, contracts between producers and workers for July (to be paid August 1) incorporate a 10 per cent wage increase. At the same time, suppose the producers try to pass on their cost increase by demanding a 10 per cent increase in wholesale prices. This price rise will be paid on August 1.

Under the assumed contract customs merchants need not raise retail prices during July to maintain their current margins. They pay for July's output on the first day of August. Particularly if merchants compete with one another for sales, this delay in the effective payment date of the higher wholesale price would tend to hold down the retail price through July. (This is one reason why retail price increases often lag behind wholesale prices.) Through July, however, merchants will be preparing additional commercial-bank credit requests for August 1. In their discussions with bankers, merchants will note that, since they are taking deliveries through July, they will have a contracted commitment on August 1, just as the producers will have a contracted commitment to their workers on the same date. Should they fail to receive increased credit on August 1, the merchants would have to cover their higher obligations from their own capital. Merchants in tight circumstances might default instead, either to commercial banks for July credit, or to producers for July shipments.

Such contractual arrangements pressure banks to accommodate, hence validate, cost increases. If this economy operated strictly on a "pay-as-you-go" basis, with workers paid each day and shipments paid on receipt, then, if producers raised their price, merchants would either have to seek new credit immediately or reduce their purchases. Lower demand by merchants could even oblige producers to rescind price increases. Pay-as-you-go, however, is an inconvenient basis for any actual economy's exchange relations. Thirty-day deals are inevitably more efficient than daily orders and payments, and contracted business operations always make planning easier. Since payment for a thirty-day deal can be made in advance, in the middle, or at the end of the month, one party or the other is under contractual obligation to provide a good or service for money already paid, or to pay for a good or service already provided; hence the possibility of default. This possibility is often an explicit or implicit argument that a bank should provide credit as necessary, if only to reduce the risk on the bank's previous loans.

Because a modern financial economy is a network of obligations, one default can induce an unpredictable chain reaction of defaults. A cautious, conservative monetary authority, not knowing how far such a chain reaction might go, may prefer some inflation to the risk of severe trouble when a large default has just occurred or seems imminent. Walter Bagehot, the nineteenth century English writer who first described central banks' "lender-of-last-resort" function, made a celebrated argument (Bagehot 1873) that in situations of imminent, widespread default a central bank ought to make rediscount credit easily available, but at a high interest rate, so that only banks genuinely needing it would take it. While this remains a fundamental central-banking principle, a monetary authority following it can nevertheless rapidly increase the monetary base substantially.

As use of contracts and credit has widened and deepened, many economies' inflationary propensities have intensified. Hyman Minsky has argued persuasively in various papers that, on several occasions since World War II, threats of widespread default have obliged the US Federal Reserve to permit inflationary money-supply expansion.[3] Had it not permitted expansion more widespread bankruptcies might have resulted. Since World War II the United States' financial obligations grid has become increasingly intricate. As a result, the Federal Reserve has expanded credit in response to imminent defaults that have been further and further from the banking system— "further," that is, from being debts to commercial banks' debtors, or to their debtors, rather than debts directly to commercial banks.

Minsky has also made the intriguing argument that United States corporate credit once tended to be provided against assets maturing— i.e., reaching their "pay-out" period and yielding their return—more or less at the same time as the credit. Since World War II, and particularly in the 1980s, such credit has tended increasingly to mature before the assets for which the credit was used. This implies that the firm in question must either sell assets or, more likely, take on new credit in order to pay off the initial credit. That is, the availability of future credit has become a standing basis for a large proportion of current credit. This may in turn mean that some credit is premised on at least the possibility of future inflation.

Price-level uncertainty shortens contract and financial-asset terms. The pay-out periods of most real economic activities have no reason to shorten in response to price-level uncertainty, however; there is no reason why inflation should significantly affect the time it takes to grow a wheat crop or to build a factory. As financial terms shorten, credit tends increasingly to be provided for shorter terms than necessary—on assumptions, or prayers, that the credit will be rolled over as necessary, and that the monetary authority will set credit conditions as required to make such rollovers possible.

8   INFLATIONARY COMPETITION AND THE PUBLIC SECTOR

Many people now reason that, if there is inflation, public-sector borrowing must be excessive. This idea accompanies an increasingly widespread view that the operations of governments and public enterprises are inevitably inefficient, because they run without private incentives. Precisely because this view has become so widespread, it is important to remember that public-sector budgets do not result exclusively from public officials' vision—misguided or not—of the public interest. Private sectoral interests—including people on the public payroll, contractors to the public sector, users of public services, taxpayers, recipients of transfers and subsidies, and people who earn interest on public debt—figure heavily in the determination of any public budget. Relationships between the public sector and the various private interests are set through various arrangements made by executive, legislative, regulatory, judicial, or bureaucratic entities. "Arrangements" include laws, executive instructions and decrees, contractual agreements, entitlements, expenditure programs, tax incentives, regulatory rulings, privileges, understandings, and corruption.

Where a public sector has a borrowing requirement large enough to require significant inflationary financing, it may be difficult, and in some degree arbitrary, to say objectively who is "responsible." Private-sector entities may consider it perfectly appropriate to pressure the public sector politically for the best possible arrangement. A government is presumably supposed to limit its borrowing requirement in the interest of society at large, but political or organizational deficiencies may limit its ability to do so. The private sector may be unwilling or unable to pay adequate taxes. External or domestic lenders may be unwilling or unable to lend at reasonable interest rates. Or the public sector, having borrowed excessively in the past, may now face an uncontrollably growing contractual claim.

Latin American nations expanded their public sectors' administrative, productive and financial activities in the 1960s and 1970s, partly in response to the need for infrastructure and social expenditure arising from rapid urbanization and industrialization (see Baer 1990). After the 1973 oil-price rise, international commercial banks took on a "recycling" function, making oil exporters' surpluses available to oil-importing developing economies determined to sustain the pace of industrialization. Even oil exporters like Venezuela and Mexico borrowed in hope of industrializing more rapidly. The large size of the financial surpluses pressured international interest rates down. Latin American public sectors generally borrowed heavily, since real interest rates were low or even negative. When both oil prices and interest rates surged in the early 1980s, however, higher interest rates on floating-rate debt sharply increased debt-service charges, precisely at a moment when foreign creditors became reluctant to lend.

As a result, in the 1980s virtually all Latin American public-sector budgets became the foci of deep crises. The issue was which elements of society would surrender purchasing power to permit public expenditure to go to debt service and to reduce the overall public-sector borrowing requirement. Purchasing power lost by particular groups has often placed public budgets under further pressure by narrowing the tax base. Latin American nations have managed these crises differently, according to their circumstances. Chile's military regime, at one extreme, could effectively decide who would lose in order to reduce the deficit and make room for external-debt service. It effectively assumed the bulk of its private sector's external debt, and renegotiated its external debt without missing a contracted payment. To stifle its 1985 hyperinflation, Bolivia's government placed its public accounts on a daily cash basis, averting deficit by the crude expedient of spending only cash revenue actually in hand; the experience of hyperinflation made this politically possible. After 1982, Mexico's government, which enjoyed the advantage of a well-entrenched political party and public administration, as well as the special political attention of the United States, gradually but steadily reduced non-interest public expenditures in order to manage its debt.

On the other hand, the constitutional regimes of Argentina, Brazil and Peru—which replaced military regimes whose external-borrowing policies, among others, had discredited them politically—found it harder to control public borrowing, and took on substantial amounts of domestic debt in addition to their external debt. Pressures to remunerate fairly, to subsidize, to develop, and to service domestic and external debt have intensified the pressure on these nations' public budgets. The deepening difficulty of raising revenue and the diminishing disposition to hold public obligations have compounded the problem. A particularly important point is that Argentina's and Brazil's public sectors have relatively few export activities; Mexico's and Chile's governments, in contrast, own oil and copper exporting enterprises that earn foreign exchange directly.

Observers often ask why the authorities cannot raise taxes, or cut excessive employment, subsidies, and tax incentives, in order to cover their debt service. In broad terms, the answer must be that governments—especially constitutional governments—cannot easily pick and choose among their political, legal, or moral commitments to constituents and creditors. It seems wrong to default on public obligations; it seems indecent to dismiss public servants who have poor prospects in a narrowing economy; it seems wrong to deny pensions to people who vested their rights over years of work at the moment of their greatest vulnerability; it seems wrong to cut subsidies to businessmen who invested on the presumption that these subsidies—however misconceived—would continue. Indeed, to the extent an elected government's leaders feel their "mandate" requires that none of its constituents explicitly lose, they set a disposition to deficit and inflation—which, whatever its other drawbacks, allows the authorities to manage without explicitly reneging on commitments.

Some observers assume that more independent central banks would help, at least to prevent monetary financing of public deficits. Where a public sector runs a substantial deficit but cannot borrow in external or domestic financial markets, something must give: the deficit must diminish or the central bank must provide financing. Independent or not, the central bank is likely to have to give in. Central bank directors cannot easily oblige a government to fire civil servants or default on contractual obligations. As inflation continues and deepens, of course, the public may be more prepared to support a determined central bank. Nevertheless, it is unrealistic to suppose that an independent central bank can easily force a government rapidly to make the difficult choices that, in effect, amount to choosing among responsibilities and commitments.

9   "INFLATIONARY COMPETITION"

Inflationary expectations, uncertainty, and relative-price dispersion intensify the competition over the allocation of purchasing power, and contribute in this way to the inflation-feedback process. An economic entity that expects or fears that its purchasing power will diminish will compete more vigorously to acquire more purchasing power. The word "compete" is used here in a broader sense than neo-classical economics usually uses it. "Inflationary" competition for purchasing power includes not only exploitation of market power, but also securing public-sector support and additional credit.

Inflationary episodes typically start with some economic entity's attempt to obtain and exercise additional purchasing power. Unless additional goods and services sufficient to satisfy this demand are forthcoming, it must be satisfied either by someone else's surrender of purchasing power, or through the competition of claimants asserting their purchasing power in the form of newly created money. The money supply increases and the value of the money unit diminishes in the course of, in function of, such a competition. The monetary authority is a reluctant referee: if it restricts the money supply, it stifles the inflation, but forces a resolution of the competition in a way that may be unacceptable to someone or everyone; but if it allows money-supply growth, it sanctions inflationary competition.

5 Inflation and Financial Systems

1 INTRODUCTION

There is an argument that financial systems can function and develop reasonably well despite high inflation, as long as rates of return are not "repressed"—that is, as long as rates are either market-determined or set by authorities aiming roughly to equilibrate supply of and demand for financial resources. In particular, "neo-liberal" analysts argue that financial rates must be permitted to exceed the inflation rate, to stimulate saving and to allocate credit to genuinely profitable uses.[1]

Although many practising economists consider this argument a truism, it must be applied with care in both analysis and policy-making. Financial markets can generally find ways to circumvent interest-rate controls if private interests consider it desirable to do so; in certain circumstances they may not. Indeed, where inflation and uncertainty are high, *market-clearing* money interest rates may be less than expected inflation. In any case, inflation expectations, inflation surprises, price-level uncertainty and relative-price dispersion all damage financial markets, and, even if not "repressed," financial markets cannot entirely neutralize the effects of inflation. At the same time, financial systems can be powerful inflation-feedback channels. Rising inflation rates tend to pressure both money and real interest rates upward, particularly in a confused context of inflationary expectations and uncertainty. Capitalization of high interest flows into financial asset stocks can propagate powerful inflation-feedback pressures.

2 "FINANCIAL REPRESSION"

People presumably make financial plans according to real, not money, interest rates. Lenders who expect the money unit to lose purchasing power over a given time interval will seek compensating money interest before agreeing to lend (as explained in Chapter 2). Borrowers should consider it fair to repay the quantity of purchasing power borrowed, plus interest, and, moreover, should be able to pay as long as the purchasing power of their income streams maintains pace with inflation. On this reasoning, as long as rates of return can rise appropriately, inflation should cause financial markets no problem.[2, 3]

Financial markets are often burdened with regulations that keep rates from rising with expected inflation. Some have ceilings for interest rates on legally contracted loans, so-called "usury laws" Financial markets can be trammelled by various kinds of interest-rate control and regulation. Taxes on financial operations and high unremunerated reserve requirements raise financial intermediaries' costs, and force them to set wider "spreads" between asset and liability rates: loan rates tend accordingly to be too high, deposit rates too low, or both. They make the volume of financial transactions lower than it would otherwise be. Finally, by narrowing the field of competition, barriers to the entry of new financial enterprises also keep deposit rates low and loan rates high. Neo-liberal financial analysts characterize such practices as "financial repression," and urge their elimination.

In addition to government regulations affecting interest rates, operations, and competition, "financial repression" also includes some governments' practice of borrowing heavily in their financial markets. Some governments even require financial intermediaries to lend to them, through such devices as required reserves or Treasury bond holdings. Nevertheless, because they are far less likely than other borrowers to default on domestic debt, governments—even financially undisciplined governments—tend to be preferred borrowers, partly because they retain the ultimate option of financing their obligations through money issue. Excessive government borrowing takes up resources that could be used by the private sector, however, thus "crowding out" productive commercial and productive purposes and bidding up real interest rates in the process.

3 CIRCUMVENTION AND ACCEPTANCE OF REPRESSIVE CONTROLS ON INTEREST RATES

On the reasoning that rational people would never deliberately lend money at a loss, it seems a matter of common sense that market-clearing real interest rates must exceed zero. Where nominal interest rates are below expected inflation, economic analysts characteristically conclude that some law, regulation, custom, tradition or institutional inertia must be "repressing" them. In such circumstances, it is likely that financial transactions are occurring through other channels. Financial markets are generally capable of circumventing repressive controls, albeit at some cost, when market participants find doing so in their interest.

There are various ways around repressive controls, depending on their precise nature. In Argentina, for example, over the long periods in the 1970s and 1980s when bank interest rates were subject to ceilings, a voluminous "inter-firm" credit market emerged. While this "disintermediation" permitted certain vital transactions that might otherwise not have occurred, it was costly, because it lacked many of the specialized capabilities, risk pooling, legal protection and economies of scale that financial intermediaries could provide. Moreover, only established firms could participate; small, unproven firms had no access to this market.

To circumvent controls on deposit rates, financial intermediaries can offer depositors various kinds of special facility. Instead of taking conventional deposits, they may issue "certificates of deposit" at a discount, thereby raising the effective interest rate. In the 1950s and 1960s some Brazilian financial intermediaries evaded interest-rate controls by legally defining longer-term deposits as "participations" and the payments they made as "dividends." Rather than charge high rates on loans, financial intermediaries may charge "commissions and fees." Lenders may urge borrowers to maintain "compensating balances."[4] Where private financial intermediaries are willing and able to operate illegally, of course, they can do virtually anything: in some economies, extensive financial operations are carried on outside the legal framework. The essential problem is usually the lack of legal recourse.

Interest-rate ceilings may be nothing more than simple administrative directives to government-owned financial intermediaries. Where government-owned intermediaries are large, they may exert a powerful "price-leadership" role in financial markets, and so may constitute the means by which governments make controls effective. Since public financial intermediaries are often perceived as safer than private intermediaries, and since they have access to government deposits, they often have adequate resources to carry on their operations even at relatively low interest rates.

Although controls discourage financial operations, private financial intermediaries often find that controls serve their interests. Their profits are based on spreads between lending and borrowing rates. If controls apply to both rates in such a way that the spread between income and outgo remains high, intermediaries can profit even on relatively low transactions volumes—possibly more than they would if lending and borrowing rates were market-determined. Even if controls apply only to one side of a financial intermediary's balance sheet, the markets may still allow it to set the other rate so as to maintain a positive spread, particularly if the financial-market structure is concentrated. All other things being equal, financial managements prefer lower interest-rate levels because they make loan default less likely; this may further incline them to accept controls.

Interest-rate ceilings on demand deposits remain the norm in most economies, although there has been a gradual worldwide tendency to offer interest on such deposits. Again, commercial banks often find this kind of control convenient, as long as the public is willing to maintain adequate amounts in checking accounts for transactions purposes. Checking accounts are costly to operate, in any case, and bankers may prefer not to pay for deposits they might receive for free anyway. Nevertheless, as the section following argues, interest-rate controls on demand-deposit accounts—on money generally—are the core of the financial-repression issue. Even in the absence of all other financial controls, ceilings for interest rates on demand deposits amount to financial repression. Neo-liberal analysts have always emphasized this point (see McKinnon 1973). Where controls on deposit rates are effective, the neo-liberal argument goes, the banking system attracts fewer resources than it potentially could. The resources attracted then command higher rates to borrowers because of their scarcity, and are inefficiently rationed among borrowers. At the same time, interest-free demand deposits set a lower competitive standard for other financial assets.

4   NON-POSITIVE MARKET-CLEARING REAL FINANCIAL RATES

Market-clearing real interest rates may fall below zero in certain circumstances, even in the absence of significant regulatory controls. This is possible, first, because "old" financial assets may still exist whose real interest rates have turned out less than zero, and second, because money, which pays no interest, exists. Even if money pays a fixed interest rate, this basic point still holds.[5]

Suppose inflation rates have recently turned out higher than previously expected, but many "old" financial contracts remain outstanding with interest rates that reflect the earlier, lower expectations. A competitive financial intermediary that has borrowed money under such "old" contracts may still be able to lend money at low, even negative real, rates, because it would still have a sufficient positive spread. For example, an intermediary that had locked in time deposits at an annual rate of 20 per cent for six months could earn a positive spread by lending at 25 per cent during those six months, even if inflation expectations rose meanwhile from 15 to 30 per cent. True, the intermediary might be able to set higher lending rates, and so earn a larger positive spread. But if it operates in a competitive market, struggling to hold clients against other intermediaries that have also locked in time deposits at low real interest rates, it may find it has no choice but to charge its borrowers a non-positive real interest rate. If inflation expectations remain high, of course, depositors will insist on higher rates, and perhaps shorter terms, when they renew their time deposits; consequently, the market-clearing lending rates should drift up.

The competition of (interest-free) money itself can relax the pressure to raise interest rates in response to expected inflation (as noted in Chapter 2). If money offers no higher interest rate when the expected inflation rate rises, wealth-holders will tend to move out of money and into other assets in response to higher expected inflation. In doing so, they bid up the values of those other assets, and so bid their yields down. This offsets the upward pressure on interest rates resulting from the higher inflation expectation. That is, higher inflation *expectations per se* may pressure *real* interest rates downward.[6]

The competitive pressure of money can suffice to drive real interest rates below zero. To simplify the discussion, imagine (if possible) an economy whose non-financial price "distortions"—i.e., prices significantly different from market-clearing values because of controls or other distorting influences—are insignificant. Assume initially that money pays no interest. If people expect some inflation, and if expected real rates of return on an economy's primary (productive) assets are depressed, or so uncertain that their "certainty-equivalent" expected returns[7] are non-positive, (i) borrowing demand will be low, (ii) the propensity to save will be strong, and (iii) risk aversion and liquidity preference will induce people to hold wealth in shorter-term applications. These circumstances could combine to make market-clearing interest rates non-positive.

The point that needs to be explained is how there could be positive saving flows in spite of zero or negative expected real interest rates. In depressed economic conditions, people may effectively be willing to pay to accumulate financial savings and to maintain them in relatively liquid forms. For example, individuals who lack access to credit, or who prefer to avoid debt because they are uncertain about their future income, may save either to make a large future purchase or to build up a precautionary wealth stock. Businesses may accumulate liquid savings from their profit flows even when the prevailing rate of return is zero or negative, because managers consider the alternatives—investment projects—too unprofitable, too uncertain, or both. In any economic climate, creditors may insist that businesses accumulate "equity" savings to qualify for credit. The essential point is that it is by no means inevitable that an economy will simply consume at moments when the future seems to offer no positive return: uncertain business conditions may induce individuals and firms to build precautionary and speculative asset balances. If at the same time depressed conditions diminish the disposition to apply the savings in investment, the excess supply of savings resources can drive real interest rates below zero.

One might suppose that, however deficient demand might be, the supply of financial resources could never bid real financial rates below zero: holdings of real goods presumably have a non-negative real rate of return, and this sets a non-negative lower bound to real rates. Relative-price dispersion makes this assertion doubtful. A complete, weighted basket of everything that has a price is never genuinely available as an asset. Even if it were, it would be highly illiquid: to acquire or to sell it would entail considerable transactions costs. Moreover, the price array includes prices of services, which cannot generally be "held." Relative-price dispersion implies that over any time interval real prices change at different rates, with some rising and some falling; inflation widens the scope for the random behavior of real prices. Since the inflation rate is the average rate of price increase, at least half an economy's prices—possibly more—rise by less than the inflation rate over any time interval (see Chapter 2). No subset of all goods and services can be a guaranteed inflation "hedge." Since holdings of goods may have uncertain, possibly negative certainty-equivalent, yields in real terms,[8] they may fail to set a non-negative competitive floor for real interest rates.

Index-linked or dollar-denominated financial assets are available in some economies. These presumably would set a competitive floor of zero for other real rates of return. Marketable index-linked financial assets are, however, subject to risk of capital loss, in the event real interest rates rise. A more important point is that any economic entity that issues index-linked assets assumes a risky "open" balance-sheet position, unless it can back them with (i) a weighted basket of everything in the price array, (ii) someone else's inflation-proofed asset, or (iii) the capacity to inflate. Not surprisingly, inflation-proofed assets are almost always issued or guaranteed by governments, who back them with their capacity to inflate rather than with holdings of baskets of goods. (These points are discussed in Chapter 8.) Ironically, then, to the extent index-linked assets set a competitive floor for real rates of return, it is based on potential inflation, not on the real supply of and demand for financial resources. As for dollar-denominated financial assets, their comparative rate of return is a function of the exchange rate, hence of exchange-rate policy. Foreign exchange is as capable as any other asset of declining in real terms over any given time period.

A prospective negative return on money allows competing assets to carry low or non-positive real rates of return. Interest-bearing assets need only offer a positive nominal, not necessarily a positive real, interest rate to make them competitive with money. Indeed, since inflation causes equal real losses on each *peso* of money and each *peso* of interest-bearing bonds, the choice between holding bonds and money should not depend on anticipated inflation. Since shorter-term money-denominated fixed-return assets share liquidity and risk characteristics with money, their real rates of return tend to be bid close to that of money. Commercial banks may also play an important role in holding down real market-clearing interest rates. To the extent their deposits pay zero or low fixed interest rates, they cost commercial banks less than nothing in real terms in an inflationary context. The more competitive the banking system, the more of this cost advantage will be passed along to borrowers. Real lending rates will tend toward or below zero, placing competitive downward pressure on other financial rates. The scarcity of funds may offset this in whole or part, since low real deposit rates encourage people to minimize their deposit holdings. The scarcity of loanable funds would then pressure banks' real lending rates back upward, or encourage credit-rationing practices.

The discussion has thus far assumed that there are no significant non-financial price "distortions." In reality, certain market distortions can contribute to reducing market-clearing real interest rates. The distortions may worsen the prospects of particular sectors, and so cause their credit demand to be lower than it would otherwise be. The distortions may also be such that they cause income to flow excessively to higher-saving economic entities. Consider the familiar example of a small, open economy with an overvalued fixed exchange rate. Exporters will be pessimistic about future profitability if they believe the policy will persist. Importers may also be pessimistic, however, either because they fear the policy will persist and foreign exchange will become increasingly scarce, or because they fear a sharp devaluation. Such pessimism could reduce exporters' and importers' credit demand. Interest rates should weaken and possibly fall below anticipated inflation; this is the means by which financial intermediaries discourage people from providing them resources they cannot profitably lend.

Note that if a distorted economy's real interest rates are non-positive, it would be incorrect to infer that there had to be excess demand for financial resources: the non-positive real interest rates could *result from* excess supply of financial resources. In the case of exchange-rate overvaluation, devaluation should revive exports and at least reduce uncertainty for importers. As credit demand revived, interest rates would then come under upward pressure. This example illustrates a related point: a low saving rate and financial rates below the inflation rate do not necessarily imply that financial repression *per se* is the essential problem. Low saving may result from depressed national income, possibly resulting from non-financial price distortions. Low interest rates that result from pessimistic anticipations could be helpful: by encouraging credit demand, they help turn the business cycle upward.

The arguments thus far all require that money itself carry a negative real interest rate, and so do not fully contradict the neo-liberal argument regarding financial repression. Neo-liberal analysts have argued that money (ideally even currency, but in practical application checking deposits) ought to yield positive real interest rates, to encourage people to hold it and to ensure that high credit rates allocate resources to profitable uses (see McKinnon 1973). If money pays a positive real yield, demand for short-term assets should not exceed zero at any negative real rate, because the real return from holding liquidity in the competing form of money would exceed zero.

The problem with this argument is that if money paid interest at m per cent, the public might expect the money supply to increase at a minimum rate of m as the interest was credited to checking accounts.

People might then expect inflation to be m percentage points higher than it would otherwise have been. Consequently, even if all *money* interest rates incorporated additional interest of m percentage points, the *real* interest-rate level might be no different, and could still be non-positive.

That is, all other things being equal, when interest is credited to deposit-holders' accounts at the end of each time period, the money stock would be $(1 + m)$ times the stock at the end of the previous period. The price level should accordingly be under pressure to grow at a similar rate. Indeed, since everyone *knows* that money pays interest, people might even raise prices automatically by m per cent—perhaps even anticipating the interest payment. (This would be an application of rational-expectations reasoning.) The disposition to hold money should then grow as well at m per cent, to meet increased nominal transactions requirements. Since the growth rates of money demand and supply should both be higher by m percentage points than they would otherwise have been, interest payments on money should have little more real consequence for the economy than, say, dropping zeroes from the money unit. Interest paid on money could be financed in a way that took *pesos* out of the economy—for example, taxation, or higher interest charges for bank credit. Even so, however, paying interest on money should still be regarded as inflationary *in itself*: the taxation would then amount to an offsetting anti-inflation policy.

Paying interest on money effectively changes the money unit from, say, the *peso* to the "interest-bearing *peso*." Whatever previously caused inflation by forcing up *peso* prices could just as well produce inflation measured in units of interest-bearing *pesos*.

5   THE CONSEQUENCES OF INFLATIONARY EXPECTATIONS, VARIABILITY, UNCERTAINTY, AND DISPERSION FOR FINANCIAL MARKETS

Chapter 2 named four broad characteristics of inflation that affect real economic activity, mostly for the worse. These are (i) inflation expectations—i.e., people anticipate purchasing-power losses on the money unit and behave accordingly; (ii) inflation surprises—the price level can turn out different from people's expectations; (iii) price-level uncertainty – people are uncertain about future price levels and behave accordingly; and (iv) higher relative-price dispersion—real prices fluctuate haphazardly and unpredictably. These characteristics of inflation all affect financial markets, mostly in debilitating ways, even in the complete absence of financial repression.

A) Inflation Expectations

Assume for simplicity that the inflation in question is "ideal"—that is, neutral and correctly anticipated (as defined in Chapter 2). If money pays no interest, expected inflation should cause real financial rates to be lower than they would otherwise be. Suppose expected inflation surged suddenly from zero. Wealth-holders would exchange money for other financial assets and for real goods and services, and so bid down the real value of money. At the same time, with money now in excess supply and other financial assets in excess demand, real rates on other assets should decline. As the value of money falls and people arrange their affairs to make do with relatively less of it, commercial banks' deposit base would decline, leaving them fewer real resources to lend. If they are not allowed to attract deposits by offering (higher) interest, they must ration loanable resources by raising real lending rates or in some other way. All other things being equal, even an "ideal" inflation might therefore diminish the real volume of commercial-banking business.

Commercial banks compete heavily for deposits in inflationary circumstances, because inflation enables them to increase their profitability. For example, suppose a "simple" commercial bank derives its resources entirely from checking deposits yielding no interest, and that it holds its reserves in cash yielding no interest. If its nominal lending rate precisely equals the inflation rate—so that it earns real interest of zero—its spread would equal the inflation rate divided by $(1 - k)$, where k represents the reserve-deposit ratio. That is, net bank operating income tends to be related positively to the inflation rate. A bank can be profitable even if the money interest rate on its loans is at, or even below, the inflation rate. While high expected inflation reduces banks' deposit base, it encourages them to compete for deposits by whatever means they can, because they can lend profitably at interest rates at or even somewhat below expected inflation.

Bank credit may have to be rationed, and downward pressure on non-bank real lending rates might be offset by the credit-demand pressure from would-be borrowers denied bank credit. Nevertheless, the competitive pressure of relatively low commercial-bank rates helps reduce other real lending rates. To the extent people shift out of bank deposits into foreign assets or real goods, however, downward pressure to reduce interest rates is attenuated. In the 1980s, the vigorous competition of international financial markets placed all nations' domestic interest rates under upward competitive pressure. This pressure has been particularly strong in inflationary, indebted economies, which are considered to be subject to "country risk," and where wealth-holders could often augment high international interest earnings through real devaluation.

B) Inflation Surprises

Suppose now that the inflation is "semi-ideal"—people hold their expectations of future inflation with perfect certainty and the inflation occurs neutrally, but the inflation rate may turn out different from what people had anticipated. Financial operations may accordingly yield windfall gains and losses: if inflation turns out higher (lower) than originally expected, lenders receive and borrowers pay less (more) purchasing power than originally anticipated. Where inflation rates are generally high, they are likely to vary more; surprises are accordingly more frequent and quantitatively more important. Under high inflation, financial systems come to operate, and to be seen to operate, like casinos, as savers puzzle over and virtually bet on which placements will yield the highest real return.

Financial intermediaries that effect "term transformations"—i.e., whose assets have longer maturities than their liabilities—are vulnerable to fluctuations of inflation rates and inflationary expectations. Suppose a financial institution offers one-year loans at 10 per cent on the basis of resources obtained from six-month deposits yielding 5 per cent. If the expected inflation rate surged suddenly from zero to 5 per cent, the intermediary's depositors might find 5 per cent inadequate; other financial intermediaries might offer more. The institution then faces a dilemma. If it failed to raise its deposit rate, some depositors might withdraw when the six-month deposits mature. Its deposit base would diminish: even as loans were repaid the institution could neither renew them nor provide new ones, since it would have to use the funds to pay withdrawals. Its lending volume and profitability would diminish. On the other hand, if it raised the deposit rate, the spread between its asset and liability rates would narrow or even turn negative while its older loans remained outstanding. To retain all deposits, the institution might have to raise its deposit rate toward 10 per cent, far above its asset rate, and run an operating loss.

Depending on its competitors' responses, a financial intermediary in such circumstances might compromise, raising deposit rates somewhat (say, to 7.5 per cent) and accepting some deposit loss. If the intermediary has a cash-flow problem on account of the withdrawals, it might raise cash by selling some of its loans at a discount—hence a loss—to other financial intermediaries.

During the 1970s many United States' savings-and-loan institutions slipped into problems of this kind. These intermediaries provided long-term mortgages financed by passbook savings accounts, which the institutions treated as sight deposits (even though they could legally require 90 days' notice for withdrawals). In the 1960s, annual inflation ran, and was expected to run, around 3 per cent. These intermediaries could hold deposits at 3–4 per cent a year and provide mortgages at about 6 per cent, thus earning a 1–2 per cent spread from which to pay overhead and profit. In the 1970s, however, as annual inflation drifted toward double digits, depositors found 4 per cent inadequate, especially when higher-yielding alternatives appeared. The savings-and-loan institutions held too many old mortgages provided at lower rates. Unable quickly to redeploy these assets to increase their yields, they could not pay higher yields on deposits without incurring losses. Many accordingly suffered withdrawals, illiquidity, and decapitalization, even before the disastrous developments of the 1980s.

Term-transforming financial intermediaries have often experienced analogous difficulties over the short term in Latin America. Many intermediaries effectively provide one- to six-month credit on the basis of funds committed for weeks or even days. They are therefore vulnerable to surges in short-term interest rates: they may have to pay sharply higher rates to roll over their liabilities or sell loans to raise cash to pay deposit withdrawals.

One might suppose that a decline in expected inflation leading to lower interest rates would be a happy surprise for a term-transforming financial intermediary: deposit rates could fall while rates on old loans remained high, providing a period of higher spread and profits. While this is generally true, there are at least two important caveats. First, where deposit rates remain controlled, declining inflation expectations may only reduce lending rates, and therefore simply reduce commercial banks' spreads. This was a problem for Argentine and Brazilian banks in the late 1980s, when heterodox stabilization programs reduced expected inflation suddenly. Second, borrowers who took loans at earlier, higher rates may have expected higher inflation than actually occurred, and could encounter repayment difficulties.

C)   Price-level Uncertainty

Experience of surprises gives rise to price-level uncertainty. Price-level uncertainty may persist even after an inflation rate has stabilized: even if people *expect* the inflation rate not to change much, they may perceive a possibility of change, and act on the basis of this possibility along with the expectation.

Price-level uncertainty may prevent financial rates from responding to expected inflation according to the Fisher equation, and reduce the volume and terms of financial-market operations (as described in Chapter 2). Risk aversion may prevent even borrowers and lenders who have the same inflation expectation from agreeing on a real interest rate: lenders would seek higher rates than the Fisher equation would imply, to cover the risk of inflation turning out higher than expected, while borrowers would seek lower rates. Borrowers' and lenders' differing risk aversion and relative market power determine where the money rate of return turns out, but in any case the quantity transacted is lower than it would otherwise be, since market participants tend to withdraw to shorter-term markets characterized by lower price-level uncertainty.

In general, lenders can move their wealth into short-term markets more easily than borrowers can move their demand, since borrowers try to match their term to the purpose of their loan. Thus, a firm borrowing to finance an aging wine stock may require a loan lasting many years. It could borrow for half the aging period, and hope to secure financing for the latter half, but this is risky, because the second loan's interest rate could exceed that of the first loan; funds at reasonable terms might even prove unavailable. Lenders, on the other hand, can be quite certain of having something to do with their wealth if they deploy it in short-term applications.

Severe price-level uncertainty can shrink longer-term financial activity to the point of extinction. This is unfortunate, for without long-term finance, large-scale capital formation and residential construction become far more difficult. Maturities can shrink to the point that financial assets effectively become interest-bearing money. Brazil's "overnight" financial market, which operated through the 1980s, is a case in point. Financial intermediaries in this market financed portfolios of government obligations by borrowing overnight, with the obligations serving legally as collateral. The obligations paid floating interest rates based on the overnight rate, so that the intermediaries earned the spread, facing only the risk of a capital loss. Many financial institutions offered to sweep outstanding checking balances at the end of the business day into overnight accounts.[9]

D) Relative-price Dispersion

The essential reason why relative-price dispersion damages financial markets is that it makes loans to the private sector riskier. To the uncertainty about what the price level will be when a given loan term concludes, relative-price dispersion adds uncertainty about relative prices. Relative-price uncertainty makes prospective cash flows and profits, and hence real rates of return on investments in capital and inventory, more uncertain. This discourages both lending and borrowing. It also discourages purchases of equity shares. In particular, the uncertainty attaching to real income streams discourages mortgage credit for housing, because it makes would-be borrowers and lenders less confident that borrowers' income streams will cover their commitments.

Relative-price dispersion disrupts financial markets in much the same way as inflationary variability and price-level uncertainty. Because inflation is not neutral, final borrowers cannot assume their prices will keep up with the overall price level. Even if there were no uncertainty about the price *level*, a borrower who feared his or her own price would lag behind the price level would be reluctant to borrow at an interest rate that incorporated expected inflation.

6 FINANCIAL MARKETS AND INFLATION FEEDBACK

Once an inflation has been under way for an extended period, not only do people form expectations, but financial contracts—indeed, contracts generally—come to rely on inflation. Contracts come implicitly to assume not only rising future price levels, but also that sufficient "means of settlement" will be available when the time comes to "validate" them. "Means of settlement" may mean either money or disposition of lenders to renew credit. The total means of settlement available is related to the total money supply: lenders will be unwilling or unable to renew credit if there is insufficient money in the system and they need means of payment for themselves. Accordingly, to the extent the monetary authority is likely to restrict money creation, contracts generally are riskier.

On any given date, maturing contracts incorporate expectations of the current price level held in earlier periods. A monetary authority will be under pressure to set the money supply to ensure that all contracted payments can be met. In this way old expectations can be self-fulfilling. Contracts maturing on a particular date may be said together to require some aggregate means of settlement, hence some money supply—the "minimum-contract-validation" money supply. All other things being equal, on a given date, the higher inflation expectations have been in the recent past, the greater this magnitude must be, and the higher the money supply would have to be to ensure validation of "most" maturing contracts.

An "expectations-driven" inflation, in which inflation occurs mainly because it has been expected and so is required for contract validation, is a possibility, and may be an important aspect of "inertial processes." The key "rational-expectations" idea—that transactors anticipate monetary-authority behavior and form expectations accordingly—is perversely turned on its head: monetary-authority behavior is forced by the expectations previously held by transactors. A monetary authority could presumably suffocate such an expectations inflation by creating less means of payment, but at a risk of widespread bankruptcy.

Price-level uncertainty further complicates matters. If lenders have the greater market power in a given financial market, price-level uncertainty can raise the market-clearing money interest rate above what it would otherwise be. Unless the higher interest rate discouraged financial transactions and diminished the volume of contracts requiring subsequent validation, this would worsen an expectations-driven inflation. If price-level uncertainty encourages lenders and borrowers to move to short-term markets, the problem deepens further. Shorter maturities mean that a larger proportion of existing financial contracts come due on any given day. This makes the financial system more vulnerable, because on any given day the money supply required to validate contracts coming due is larger. The need to settle and to renew financial contracts more frequently makes financial markets more tense. Financial intermediaries find themselves competing each day to renew larger proportions of their obligations portfolios. If means of settlement are in short supply, or if managers merely fear that they might be, interest rates can be bid up rapidly.

An inflation driven largely by its own expectation perversely traps an economy: lenders demand adequate compensation for expected inflation; borrowers are compelled to accept lenders' conditions; the monetary authority must then validate the expectations or force bankruptcy and recession. The process is especially perverse if the government itself is the main borrower, since it can force inflation as long as the monetary authority is either "accommodating" or subject to ministerial instruction. Suppose a government has a borrowing requirement, but private lenders insist on protection for the inflation they anticipate (or fear), and discount government obligations accordingly. The government must either accept the discount, committing itself to higher future debt-service payments, or else borrow from the monetary authority. In the first case the government implicitly accepts the market forecast that the monetary authority will inflate; in the second the monetary authority inflates directly. So much the worse if the government's current borrowing requirement arises entirely or predominantly from debt-servicing needs based on previous high interest charges.

Interest rates on government obligations may be high because financial markets fear the government will inflate or even default on its obligations. These circumstances may be understood as a game with two players, a government and would-be lenders. If the markets are confident that the government will honor its commitments without inflating, interest rates on government debt should incorporate a low risk premium and so be relatively low; the government is therefore more likely to meet its obligations without inflating. If, on the other hand, the markets believe the government will inflate or default, interest rates on government debt should incorporate a high risk premium; the government is therefore more likely to inflate or default.[10] Governments in such circumstances try to "signal" their intention to honor commitments. A government incapable of persuading the markets may prove incapable of avoiding inflation or default. The problem is further complicated by the fact that the "financial markets" comprise many decision-makers, each of whom worries not only about the government's intentions but also about other market participants' perceptions. A single market participant might, for example, be persuaded that the authorities intend to honor government obligations, but might also believe that other market participants remain unpersuaded. This person, and others similarly placed, might therefore reason that the government is still likely to be forced to inflate or default.

In this kind of inflation, price-level uncertainty makes decomposition of interest rates into "real" and "expected-inflation" components almost futile and irrelevant. There may be no way to tell *ex ante* which part of any money interest rate is "real." Indeed, the fact that financial-market participants cannot easily guess the real component of an interest rate is an important aspect of the problem—not only a source of confusion to any transactor trying to use interest rates for price information, but a policy-maker's nightmare as well. Suppose a monetary authority forces up interest rates in order to reduce aggregate-demand pressure. Financial-market participants cannot know whether interest rates are rising on account of (i) the monetary authority's real restriction or (ii) rising inflationary expectations. If all participants assume the latter, they are likely then collectively to increase their inflation expectations, and to continue to enter into new contracts. Paradoxically, then, tightened monetary policy and higher interest rates in the present may then imply larger money issue in the future.

6 The Dilemmas of Inflation-Stabilization Policy

1 INTRODUCTION

Inflation-stabilization efforts can fail in at least two ways. First, they may generate excessive recession, bankruptcy, and unemployment. Second, they may suppress inflation only temporarily, or not at all, with resurgent inflation following or even preceding relaxation of the stabilization policies.

Under the pressure of external debt, Latin American nations have had to stabilize inflation at the same time as they have adjusted their external accounts, which has severely complicated policy management. This chapter sidesteps the issues of external adjustment to focus on the problem of stabilizing inflation *per se*. It discusses such stabilization approaches as "tightened" monetary policy, "tightened" fiscal policy, and price and wage controls. Chapter 7 considers the problems of simultaneously stabilizing inflation and the external accounts.

Economic analysts distinguish "orthodox" and "non-orthodox" stabilization approaches. Orthodox policies are those characteristically favored, and non-orthodox policies are those not favored, by the IMF, international bankers, developed nations' bureaucrats and "mainstream" academic thinking. Orthodox approaches include restrictions on money-supply growth, higher interest rates, greater reliance on market mechanisms, public-sector expenditure cuts, and tax increases. Non-orthodox approaches include price and wage controls as well as contract revision.

Orthodox stabilization is often called "austerity," although many people experience it as privation. People inclined to orthodoxy suggest that, following the indiscipline that engendered inflation, austerity is necessary to "discipline" the economy. Some analysts argue, however, that austerity may unnecessarily debilitate the economy: Why, they ask, is it necessary that an economy produce less than it could in order to stabilize prices? The appeal of unorthodox approaches is partly the hope of diminished pain. Policy packages combining both

is Argentina's unsuccessful June 1985
itively successful July 1985 program, and
ary 1986 "Cruzado" Plan were described
August 1985 stabilization program (like
stabilization program) exemplified the
ous fiscal restraint ended runaway infla-
c activity severely depressed.
policies generate recession largely by design.
They work by reducing the purchasing power of income and wealth,
thereby reducing excess aggregate demand. Once inflation turns out
sharply lower than previously expected, people and firms that owe
money under contracts premised on higher inflation find it harder to
meet their obligations, leading to bankruptcy and declining incomes
and wealth.

2 "GRADUALIST" AND "SHOCK" APPROACHES TO STABILIZATION

Broadly speaking, inflation stabilization can be carried out as (i)
"shock" or (ii) gradual programs. "Shock treatment" carries a higher
risk of recession, but should produce a sharp, rapid drop in the
inflation rate. Orthodox shock programs consist of some combination
of rapid expenditure cuts, tax increases, and tightened monetary
policy, typically with a forceful "announcement" intended to reduce
people's inflationary expectations. "Heterodox" shock programs may
include freezing prices, wages, interest rates and the exchange rate.
They may even include revision of previously existing contracts, to
modify the inflation anticipations they implicitly incorporated.[1]
Gradual programs reduce expenditure, raise taxes and tighten monetary policy gradually over time; they may also incorporate less
dramatic controls on prices, wages, interest rates and exchange
rates. They are intended to produce a slow, less traumatic decline in
the inflation rate.

Bolivia's 1956–7 stabilization program was an example of relatively
successful orthodox shock treatment. Partly because Bolivia's economy was relatively small and uncomplicated, tight fiscal controls under
an IMF-supported austerity program took only a few days in
December 1956 and January 1957 to work.[2] After rising 157, 93,
138, and 84 per cent in 1953, 1954, 1955, and 1956 respectively, the
GDP deflator rose only 7, 14, and 15 per cent in 1957, 1958, and 1959.

Nevertheless, Bolivia apparently underwent stabilization recession: real GDP, which had fallen 6 per cent in 1956 after growing 5 per cent in 1955, fell another 3 per cent in 1957. Three decades later, in August 1985, after three years of high inflation degenerated into hyperinflation, Bolivia resorted again to shock-treatment stabilization. Again inflation ceased rapidly (although it flared briefly in December 1985). Again, real output and real income declined and remained low through the remainder of the decade—although both had been falling sharply since 1980.[3] Inflation remained just barely above international levels through the remainder of the 1980s, however.

Brazil's stabilization effort of the mid-1960s was an example of a relatively successful gradualist program—perhaps the first stabilization program conceived as such. The program was carried out under a military regime that had taken power in April 1964. Under the "Government Economic Action Program," the public-sector budget deficit fell gradually, largely through gradual public-enterprise price increases and subsidy reductions that induced what the economic authorities described as "corrective inflation." Wage-setting rules, buttressed by 1965 legislation limiting the right to strike, reduced real wages in the public and private sectors: by 1968, real wages were 25 per cent below their 1964 levels.[4] Not only did the deficit diminish, an increasing proportion of it was financed through sales of index-linked obligations rather than money creation. (Chapter 8 discusses the role index-linked government bonds played in this program.) Annual inflation fell from nearly 100 per cent in 1964 to 25–35 per cent in 1968 and 1969. Real economic activity grew slowly from 1964 through 1968, and brief "stabilization recessions" occurred in 1965 and early 1967. Nevertheless, gradualism brought inflation down without hurling the economy into deep, prolonged recession, and set the basis for the 1968–73 "miracle" years, when real annual GDP growth rates were of the order of 10 per cent.

An important risk of shock approaches is that, if they fail and need to be repeated, the economy could slip into a cycle of shock stabilization and inflation. Public cynicism unfailingly deepens with each repetition. People stop reducing their inflation anticipations when new shock announcements are made, and take on a postponement psychology as the economy recovers from one "policy package" and awaits the next. Repeated shocks tend to slow real economic activity: private and public investment projects are postponed, activity diminishes generally, and bankruptcy and unemployment worsen. Many observers believe orthodox shock programs fail because the authorities are unwilling to clamp down long and hard enough: restrictive policies, the argument goes, must be maintained a long time until they smother inflation definitively. Part of the problem, however, is that a tightly restrictive monetary policy maintained sufficiently long may cause many firms to disappear through credit starvation. The economy may then become less inflationary, but may also become decapitalized and less productive as well.

The argument for gradualism is that it spreads the pain of stabilization over time. This may help policy-makers maintain political support to see it through. By minimizing the output loss and softening the shock to production and demand, it may be possible to sustain consumers' and entrepreneurs' confidence, and so sustain the propensity to form capital. The problem of gradualism is that it may fail to break inflationary momentum; inflation-feedback processes are more likely to work against it. Brazil's gradualist effort broadly worked, however, at least until inflation revived in 1973, first as a consequence of imbalances in the productive structure created by the rapid 1968–73 growth and then as a result of the October 1973 world oil-price increase. Brazil's subsequent efforts to control inflation gradually have generally been disappointing, largely because of the persistence of powerful inflation-feedback mechanisms.

3   RESTRICTIVE MONETARY POLICY

If inflation is a matter of persistently over-abundant money, restriction of monetary growth would seem a logical policy prescription. Unfortunately, tight monetary policy tends to imply tight credit, which disrupts commerce, production, investment, and entrepreneurship.[5] Credit restriction can make monetary restriction not only painful, but—perversely—inflationary, to the extent restricted credit diminishes aggregate supply.

When a central bank tightens monetary policy, it changes not only the total credit stock but its allocation as well. In theory, as tight monetary policy forces up credit costs, credit is reallocated to business enterprises that have the most profitable projects, use credit more "efficiently," or use credit more intensively in their operations. Unfortunately, the nature of credit markets makes it difficult for them to carry out this reallocation effectively. Businesses that already owe large credit balances tend to have preferential access to credit, since creditors will want to ensure that they maintain their debt service. As real interest rates rise, heavily indebted firms may slip into "distress cycles," in which debt stocks mushroom through borrowing to finance mushrooming interest bills. Riskier, innovative projects are less likely to receive funding. Financial intermediaries are more apt to "ration credit," providing less than clients demand at prevailing interest rates, because high interest rates themselves make full debt service less likely. Haphazard patterns of credit deprivation may generate haphazard business cutbacks and failures, possibly inducing chain reactions of cutbacks and failures.

Credit restriction is anti-inflationary, in part, because it deprives economic entities of the means to participate in the purchasing-power competition. Credit-starved businesses may either carry on operations less efficiently or scale them down.[6] To the extent they scale down operations, they reduce their own participation in the competition, but to the extent they reduce their output, they leave the competition more acute. Once the restriction relaxes, however, economic entities not driven from the competition may seek new credit and attempt to recover. In this regard monetary restriction resembles price controls: in some degree it "represses" inflation. If disagreement over the underlying purchasing-power allocation remains unresolved, inflation is likely to revive once monetary policy relaxes and economic entities acquire means of competing.

The arbitrariness in the effect of credit restriction on production results partly from the unrealized inflation anticipations embedded implicitly in outstanding contracts (see Chapters 2 and 5). Contracts implicitly assume that means of payment sufficient to honor them will be available, but monetary restriction may mean that aggregate means of payment are less than the contracting parties had implicitly assumed. The likelihood that all contracts can be honored will accordingly be lower. The more severe the restriction, the more likely it is that any particular contract will fail, or that firms must decapitalize themselves to honor commitments they might have met by securing new credit.

The "overhang" of old contracts and persisting inflation expectations can be particularly troublesome for gradualist programs. Shock programs can incorporate contract revision, and should in any case have more rapid effects on expectations and uncertainty. Under gradualist programs, the inflation anticipations embedded in new contracts are likely to remain on the same orders of magnitude as those embedded in older contracts. This works against gradualist programs because validation of contracts may still require substantial subsequent growth in means of payment. The authorities will constantly have to choose between rolling back inflation and preventing widespread bankruptcy. One might imagine a gradualist monetary restriction gradually rolling back inflationary pressure by restricting means of payment each month to, say, only 98 per cent of what is necessary fully to validate an economy's contracts. If firms in the aggregate had to use their profits to make up the remaining 2 per cent, aggregate-supply disruption might be minimized. Even so, the allocation of such credit restriction is unlikely to be fair and efficient.

An important destabilizing consequence of tight monetary policy is that, as it drives up interest rates, it raises the interest bill on public-sector debt, and to this extent increases the non-financial public sector's borrowing requirement. With high real domestic interest rates, a heavily indebted public sector may itself face "distress," in which its real debt stock mushrooms under the pressure of the borrowing requirement created by a mushrooming interest bill. (Sargent and Wallace (1981) treats this possibility, which is often referred to by this paper's title, "unpleasant monetarist arithmetic.") Such public-sector "bankruptcy" may itself constitute a macroeconomic crisis, in which the authorities find themselves under pressure to default on public debt, through (i) "debt consolidation" at reduced interest rates, (ii) inflation (using money growth to finance the higher borrowing requirement and the consequent price-level increase to deflate existing debt), or even (iii) outright default.

4   RESTRICTIVE FISCAL POLICY

Successful fiscal control permits a public sector to reduce its call on the monetary authority for finance,[7] and to limit its future interest bill. The role fiscal deficits play in inflationary processes was more controversial in the 1950s, 1960s, and 1970s; at this writing, however, public opinion is increasingly convinced that inflation is caused largely, if not entirely, by public-sector deficits, and that public expenditure must be permanently cut, by firing staff, closing public offices, concluding unnecessary subsidies, and so on. Raising public-sector revenues, while perhaps acceptable as a temporary expedient, would be sub-optimal for the longer term, since it does nothing to reduce the public sector's scope and absorbs resources that the private sector might apply to investment and production.

At least three broad points are essential to maintain this view of fiscal policy in perspective. First, notwithstanding the widespread view that public sectors are self-serving bureaucracies, any public sector serves a wide range of legitimate private and foreign interests as it purchases goods and services, pays interest, subsidizes, pays pensions, and taxes more or less heavily. Some public-sector activities—for example, security and emergency services, public health and education services, infrastructure maintenance and investment, and so on—are evidently vital. Second, the inflation-feedback process operates partly through public-sector accounts: inflation itself widens public-sector deficits and these deficits renew the inflationary pressure. Third, at any given moment, fiscal pressure may not be the only source of inflationary pressure; even if it is, fiscal contraction may fail, at least initially, to reduce inflation rapidly.

By definition, "fiscal policy" is the manipulation of public-sector revenue and expenditure flows for macroeconomic objectives. It includes any measures that affect public-sector revenue and expenditure flows, including changes in public-sector goods and services prices and public-sector wage rates, as well as specific appropriations and tax rates. In macroeconomists' taxonomy, "fiscal policy" determines the non-financial public-sector borrowing requirement (NFPSBR).[8] The financing of the NFPSBR, however, is largely an aspect of monetary policy: if it can buy and sell Treasury obligations, a monetary authority can ultimately determine the proportion of its own financing of a NFPSBR.

In any economy whose inflation and public-sector debt are significant, the NFPSBR measured on a "real" (or "operational") basis—that is, the full NFPSBR less the *ex-post* inflation component of public-sector interest charges—best indicates the NFPSBR's pressure on the macroeconomy, and should be used as the basic policy indicator (see Chapter 3). In a shock program, since inflation should presumably drop rapidly, the difference between the full and real-basis deficits should drop rapidly. In a gradual program, a steadily tightening real-basis deficit should help gradually ease down the inflation rate. A practical argument for using the real-basis NFPSBR rather than the full NFPSBR to guide policy is that the authorities have more direct control over the real-basis NFPSBR; financial charges are previously contracted payments due.

Public-sector consumption and capital formation are components of aggregate demand. As such, all other things being equal, higher public-sector expenditure is more inflationary. One caveat here is that if public-sector capital formation is inadequate, aggregate production costs may increase, reducing aggregate supply over the medium term. Higher taxation, on the other hand, may be either stabilizing or inflationary in the short term. It draws purchasing power out of the economy, and so reduces aggregate demand; to this extent it should be stabilizing.[9] Higher tax rates may discourage economic activity, however, and so reduce the tax base, diminishing the resulting revenue increase. To the extent they discourage production, higher taxes and higher prices for public-sector goods and services reduce aggregate supply; this effect—emphasized by so-called "supply-side" economists—is inflationary. Moreover, to the extent higher taxes are paid at the expense of private saving and wealth, they reduce the resources available to financial markets. Real interest rates may rise as a consequence, reducing aggregate supply and possibly increasing the public sector's interest charges as well.

That is, diminished government expenditure should unambiguously reduce inflationary aggregate-demand pressure, but higher taxes might not. Reasoning from the view of inflation as purchasing-power competition leads to the same point. To the degree a government reduces expenditure, it withdraws from competition, thus mitigating the competition's intensity. To the degree a government raises taxes, it draws income and wealth from the rest of the economy. This reduces the rest of the economy's capacity to engage in the competition, which is stabilizing; but it may intensify the rest of the economy's determination to engage in the competition to recover purchasing power lost to the taxes.[10]

Such "indirect" taxes as sales levies, tariffs, export taxes, and the like, constitute a large proportion of the tax structure, particularly in developing nations. Although economists frown on them because they distort relative prices, developing nations often find them rapid, efficient ways to gather revenue. The temptation to rely on such indirect taxes is particularly strong for a government under pressure to cut a deficit quickly. While higher income taxes may fail to increase revenue for several months, higher gasoline taxes can increase revenue within a week. Moreover, indirect taxes are less subject to the "collection-lag" problem (see Chapter 3): when prices and incomes rise generally, income-tax revenues take longer to reflect the fact than indirect-tax revenues. Similarly, where governments own productive enterprises, they can rapidly raise public-sector revenue by raising the relevant prices—an effect that is enhanced if the goods and services in question are also taxed.

Such price and tax increases directly increase the price level, and this may provoke a feedback response. In recent years, Latin American stabilization programs have often incorporated heavy increases in indirect tax rates and in the prices on which they are levied. Peruvian stabilization policy packages since 1975, for example, have often incorporated sharp public-sector price increases.[11] In the mid-1960s Brazil's government justified its gradualist approach partly by noting that, in order to restore public-enterprise profitability, it had to raise public-enterprise prices that had been repressed before March 1964, and this would induce "corrective inflation." Two decades later, in November 1986, when the Cruzado Plan was failing, the Brazilian government tried to revive it through higher sales taxes on automobiles, liquor, tobacco, and other "luxury" items, for a revenue increase then estimated at 2 per cent of GDP. These and similar experiences had mixed results. Brazil's program in the mid-1960s worked, albeit slowly over half a decade; in contrast, the Peruvian policy packages and the Brazilian November 1986 package[12] failed to prevent higher inflation. Raising prices and indirect taxes can work only if it improves public finances sufficiently to offset the feedback consequences of the immediate price rise.

Even if lower expenditure is preferable to higher taxes, expenditure may often be difficult to reduce. As a broad generalization, tax increases spread the burden wider; expenditure cuts fall heavily, perhaps unfairly, on particular recipients. Government expenditures comprise (i) wages and salaries of public servants and of the military, (ii) purchases of goods and services, and (iii) public "infrastructure" capital formation; in addition, the negative entries in governments' net-revenue accounts comprise (iv) domestic and external interest, (v) subsidies, (vi) regional transfers and (vii) other "transfer" payments.[13] A moment's reflection on this list indicates the difficulties inherent in reducing public expenditure. Dismissals, wage cuts, suspension of contracts, and cuts in transfers and subsidies heavily affect individuals and firms, and are likely to lead to political contention with the people most directly affected. Reducing "entitlements" (e.g., veterans' pensions) and contractual commitments (e.g., interest due, or tax breaks to private firms that fulfilled regional-investment commitments) may damage the state's standing as a reliable contracting party. Societies have minimum standards for police protection, health services, sanitation, and so on that make it difficult to reduce expenditures in these areas.

Moreover, a government's scope to control expenditure in the short term may be more limited than is generally realized. Significant personnel or wage cuts may be difficult not only politically, but legally as well; the judiciary, for example, have sometimes ruled against policy-makers' attempts to limit public-sector wage increases. In any case, delaying cost-of-living increases precisely when prices are accelerating may seem deeply unfair. Public-sector debt service and obligations to suppliers are contracted payments: most governments, understandably, prefer not to fail to meet contracted commitments.

Like banking systems forced to cut back credit rapidly, governments under pressure to cut expenditure rapidly often do so haphazardly and arbitrarily. Hiring freezes, limits on pay increases, and budget cuts interfere with public-sector operations and managements. The pressure of real needs inevitably forces exceptions, then further haphazard and arbitrary increases in expenditure as the government struggles to cope. Pressure to cut expenditure often leads the authorities to reduce capital formation: projects often seem postponable, and construction firms and workers are accustomed to work on a temporary basis. Some postponement may be justifiable, but some projects are essential, and excessive postponement may seriously constrain output growth. Postponement of transport infrastructure investment, for example, is likely to complicate growth prospects; nations wrestling with food-supply problems may need to open new regions to cultivation. The reduction in public investment by Latin American nations struggling to reduce public deficits in the 1980s has dangerously reduced their potential aggregate-supply growth rates, and accordingly made them more inflationary.

Efforts to reduce state-enterprise expenditure often run into similar difficulties, particularly if their activities have significant "social" or "national" objectives such as employment, regional development, and so on. Again, when considering how best to reduce expenditure, it is important to take account of state enterprises' need to carry out capital formation and efficiently to provide the energy, communications, transport and other services for which they were established. Deficits arising from capital expenditure are more justifiable than deficits resulting from excessive costs or controlled prices.

These observations suggest that governments whose public sectors have undergone haphazard expansion and control efforts may need to restructure their public sectors quite thoroughly. Many Latin American public sectors expanded too rapidly and inefficiently through the 1970s, helped by the forbearing support of external finance and widening domestic financial bases. In the 1980s they began contracting, but again rapidly and inefficiently, under the pressure of diminishing external finance and narrowing domestic financial bases. Their best hope of adjusting for the long term, accordingly, is a thorough-going restructuring that would at least make them more efficient and effective within a narrower scope.

In recent years several inflationary economies have had to deal with deficits in publicly-owned financial institutions. Inflation tends to reduce longer-term financial institutions' profitability and to increase short-term financial institutions' profitability (see Chapters 2 and 5). As inflation makes longer-term credit more scarce, governments come under pressure to substitute for reduced private financial activity by increasing the activities of public housing and investment (development) banks. This tends to increase overall public-sector losses. Publicly-owned commercial banks, in contrast, benefit like any commercial bank from inflation, as well as from their evident government guarantee.

Central-bank operating losses are a special problem. They arise because central banks sometimes issue interest-bearing obligations, or pay interest on bank reserves to prevent high reserve ratios from driving up bank spreads. If a central bank pays no interest on bank reserves, banks would presumably have to charge higher rates on loans to compensate for what they fail to earn on reserves. There is a persuasive argument that central banks should never take on domestic interest-bearing liabilities: interest paid by a central bank is, by definition, a source of money expansion, even if such expansion could be offset in principle by tightening monetary policy in some other way. Even where a central bank has no interest-bearing obligations, monetary contraction reduces its earnings, since the central bank will have provided less in interest-bearing rediscounts or sold some interest-bearing government obligations. Ordinarily, the reduction in central-bank earnings resulting from monetary contraction is a second-order problem. To run significant losses, however, a central bank must have interest obligations (or exorbitant operating expenses). A central-bank deficit must be financed, through money issue, further increases in the central bank's interest-bearing indebtedness, or reductions in central bank asset holdings—i.e., reductions in the money supply's asset backing.

How far must a public-sector deficit be cut to relieve an inflation? In principle, this question can be answered quantitatively (see Chapters 3 and 7).[14] The determinants are the willingness (i) of external borrowers to lend to the government, (ii) of domestic borrowers to lend to the government, and finally (iii) of the domestic economy to increase its money holdings, after taking account of any money growth resulting from the balance of payments or from rediscount lending to commercial banks. The broad point is that, to achieve a given inflation rate, the public-sector borrowing requirement can be larger, the larger is the domestic economy's willingness to hold money and public-sector debt, and the more external lenders are prepared to provide to the nation.

5   THE CONSEQUENCES OF RAISING REAL INTEREST RATES

Maintenance of positive real interest rates is an important tenet of orthodox policy approaches, on several grounds. First, higher real interest rates encourage saving and discourage inventory accumulation and capital-formation expenditure; they accordingly reduce aggregate demand. Second, they encourage demand for government obligations, making it easier for the government to fund its deficit without creating money. Third, they discourage demand for bank credit, and thereby relieve this source of money-creation pressure. Fourth, to the extent demand deposits and saving accounts carry higher interest rates, the public is more inclined to hold these forms of "broad" money, which presumably have lower velocities of circulation. (A fifth argument for higher interest rates is that they forestall "capital flight," i.e., placement of wealth abroad; this is discussed in Chapter 7.)

These arguments all have important caveats. In circumstances of recession and uncertainty, substantial saving flows may occur even with non-positive interest rates (see Chapter 5). Analysts since Keynes have found limited empirical evidence that interest-rate movements significantly influence people's saving behavior; real income assuredly matters far more for saving determination. Moreover, analysts since Keynes have found only mixed evidence that interest rate levels significantly influence firms' decisions to build inventories or to install capital. Particularly in economies with lengthy inflation experience, financial operations are likely to be concentrated in the short term. Fluctuations in short-term interest rates are unlikely strongly to influence saving and investment flows—although severe interest-rate volatility and persistently costly working-capital credit are likely to discourage capital formation. Finally, it is at least possible that higher interest rates could discourage aggregate supply more than aggregate demand, and so be inflationary.

Several rapid points may be made in support of the orthodox view, however. First, while small interest-rate movements have only slight effects on saving behavior, sharply negative real interest-rate levels assuredly discourage saving; a policy change leading to much higher interest-rate levels might significantly increase saving. Second, relative interest rates assuredly influence the ways in which people choose to hold accumulated savings; the interest-rate structure helps determine whether savings will be made available for credit operations. Savings accumulated in the form of foreign exchange, for example, may remain outside the domestic financial system. That is, high interest rates encourage people to hold the economy's assets, and this should be stabilizing.

That is, higher interest rates encourage people to purchase and hold both private and government obligations. One important problem with this reasoning, however, is that the stocks of these assets grow over time as they accrue interest. The higher the interest rates and the larger the stocks of obligations outstanding, the larger the resulting increase in purchasing power will be. If exercised, this purchasing power may become a source of renewed inflationary pressure. Moreover, accumulating interest charges may increase private enterprises' credit needs more rapidly than it discourages credit use. Higher interest rates increase the government's interest bill, and increase the government's overall borrowing requirement.

Rates high enough to reduce aggregate demand significantly are likely to damage financial activity, in several ways. Deposit-taking financial intermediaries may attract more resources than they can profitably and safely place: they either attract resources on which they must pay but cannot earn high interest rates, or they turn away some deposits. Term-transforming financial intermediaries' funding rates may rise above the yields of their existing asset portfolios. If passed on to borrowers, higher interest rates increase the likelihood of bankruptcy and "distress" cycles. All other things being equal, higher interest rates make each particular piece of debt more difficult to service, hence more questionable—that is part of the way they work. They make it more likely that old debt will have to be written down, or that more debt will be issued in the future to refinance maturing debt. As noted earlier (and in Chapter 5), once interest rates have risen, the authorities may come under pressure to inflate to ensure that there are sufficient means of payment to validate contracts, to forestall decapitalization of financial and non-financial enterprises.

Recent stabilization programs have sometimes treated "positive real" interest rates as a policy objective. If market-clearing real interest rates happen to be non-positive on account of inflation expectations and pessimism regarding real economic performance, it may be a mistake to force them up. Positive real interest rates are best regarded by policy-makers as an objective to achieve, not to force; when inflation expectations diminish, and real credit demand revives on the basis of anticipations of genuine returns from investment, real interest rates should recover on a sound basis.

6   COMPREHENSIVE WAGE AND PRICE CONTROLS

Cost and price controls are a powerful temptation for policy-makers frustrated by stubborn inflation. Although the world's experience with wage and price controls has generally been disappointing, it often seems that the direct, no-nonsense approach to dealing with high inflation is to order it to stop. The problem has always been that, even before the inevitable day when controls are relaxed, pent-up inflation has tended to revive and overwhelm the controls. Neo-classical economic theory advises strongly against price controls: bad as inflation may be, interference with the price system is usually worse, and futile. Some economists, however, have accepted the possibility that temporary controls can be used to break an inflation's momentum, and that this may be worth the temporary distortions.

It is helpful to distinguish "comprehensive" from "selective" controls; they are associated, respectively, with "shock" and "gradualist" stabilization approaches. Comprehensive controls subject most or all costs and prices to maximum allowable rates of increase. Examples include the ninety-day freeze that President Richard Nixon imposed in the United States in August 1971, and the global freezes of the Argentine Austral Plan and the Brazilian Cruzado Plan.[15] In a regime of selective controls, only certain prices and costs are subject to maximum allowable rates of increase. This section offers some observations on comprehensive controls; Section 7 discusses selective controls, and Section 8 briefly considers wage controls (and controls on "prime cost" in general).

If supposedly "comprehensive" controls in fact miss significant subsets of the price array, people whose wages and output prices are effectively controlled may be resentful, and inclined not to cooperate. Furthermore, to the extent some prices and costs are controlled and others not, relative-price distortions are likely to arise. Incomplete controls can therefore contribute to relative-price dispersion. Assume for now, however, that controls can in fact be applied comprehensively. Experience suggests that comprehensive controls can stifle inflation briefly in a market economy, but that it is difficult, and inadvisable, to maintain such controls for periods longer than several weeks. If no other changes are made in the economy, inflation will most probably resume when the controls are lifted.

The basic reason comprehensive controls are ultimately futile as anti-inflation policy is that the "price level" is a price—the rate at which money and other things exchange. Like any other price, supply-demand pressures to increase it are ultimately irresistible, particularly if money creation continues and the condition of excess money supply persists. Seen this way, comprehensive controls amount to "repression" of inflation: in a "closed" economy a price-level increase is the only means by which an economy can resolve an excess supply of money. Once controls are lifted, if not sooner, a repressed price level may confidently be expected to surge.

This argument is unfair to the best case for comprehensive price controls, however; it should be obvious that inflation cannot be stopped by outlawing price rises. The best case for a price freeze is that, if carried out at an appropriate time, for just long enough, and with sufficient public support, it interrupts some channels of the inflation-feedback process. With some inflation-feedback channels temporarily blocked, a government can more easily set policy to deal genuinely with the underlying causes of inflationary pressure. In part, the point is to calm "inflation psychology," relieving near-term price-level uncertainty. With luck this can relieve some of the panicky, "bear-market-in-money" pressure before controls are lifted. A partial analogy is the practice some stock and commodity exchanges have of suspending trading when prices fluctuate excessively. This permits market participants to verify rumors and review their positions while trading is suspended; as panic subsides trading can resume on a sounder basis. The analogy is partial because "trading" is not suspended when price controls are imposed; the point, however, in both cases is that a temporary "time out" should help relieve disorder and uncertainty.

Announcement of comprehensive controls should reduce inflationary expectations and uncertainty, and so increase the quantity of money the public wishes to hold, as long as the public believes the controls will be effective. Furthermore, if prime cost—including wages and the exchange rate—and intermediate-goods prices are controlled, then price controls should reduce pressure to increase the credit stock.

Temporary repression of inflation may relieve some, but not all, of the force of the inflation-feedback process. In part, the problem is that ordinary economic developments generate powerful pressures on some prices to rise. If the prices in question are fixed, excess demand persists in the affected markets. Demand unsatisfied in these markets may "spill over" into other markets, broadening the pressure on the price level. True, just as some prices come under upward pressure, others come under downward pressure, but the consequences are not symmetrical. Firms selling in glutted markets may reduce supply, but it is always harder to increase supply in tightened markets, particularly if frozen prices imply low unit profits. In general, demand shifts more easily from one market to another than supply. Once removal of controls is imminent, inflationary expectations and uncertainty will revive in some degree, and willingness to hold money will fall. Once costs are again permitted to rise, credit requirements should increase, and the money supply may come under renewed pressure to grow.

Even over the period that controls can be made to work, they are likely to disrupt market functioning significantly. The severe relative-price dispersion that accompanies any serious inflation implies that only through inconceivably good luck will a freeze be imposed with relative prices anywhere near mutual market-clearing values. Most probably, the freeze will begin with some markets in excess supply and some in excess demand, although all markets taken together are in excess demand with respect to money. Even if controls are imposed with most goods and services markets close to balance, supply and demand imbalances may develop rapidly as tastes and production conditions shift.

A partial counter-argument is that even provisional re-establishment of price-level and relative-price stability should have favorable micro-economic consequences. Just after Brazil's Cruzado Plan began, the sudden reduction of inflation rendered a wide range of inflation-related activities—from contingent budgeting (in households as well as firms) to re-marking prices and frequent reallocation of financial portfolios—unnecessary. These activities used real resources. Even if comprehensive controls fix mutually inconsistent relative prices, these prices should at least be stable and more or less predictable for a time. Had the inflation instead been allowed to continue freely, unpredictable relative-price shifts might have generated worse market imbalances.

Thus, from a microeconomic viewpoint, comprehensive price controls present advantages and disadvantages: they freeze what is assuredly an inappropriate relative-price array, but relieve the variability and uncertainty of relative prices. Once the end of the price freeze is imminent, relative prices, however, return to being unstable and uncertain.

7   SELECTIVE PRICE CONTROLS

In a regime of "selective" cost and price controls, an authority continually sets maximum values for particular prices and costs. This is a different approach from comprehensive controls. Selective controls aim to slow rather than to break inflation-feedback processes. Many aspects of economic policy-making could broadly be described as selective controls—for example, any exchange-rate policy apart from freely floating exchange rates, or any policy limiting increases in the prices of goods and services provided by the public sector or regulated sectors. The expression is usually reserved for controls on prices of goods and services more customarily set by markets. The premise of selective controls is that monopoly power, uncertainty, and relative-price dispersion cause particular prices to rise excessively: these generate subsequent price rises through factor-cost increases and relaxation of the downward competitive pressure they provided before rising. In controlling—i.e., setting—output prices, price-control authorities limit firms' or industries' profit flows.[16] Controls are sometimes set with a view to generating a "fair" profit for the firm or industry, given its current costs (which may themselves be controlled or under contract) and projected sales.[17]

Brazil's governments, for example, maintained selective price and wage controls over several decades: between 1965 and 1979, for example, Brazil's military governments closely controlled growth rates of wages; from the 1950s Brazilian governments maintained controls on a wide range of industrial prices through an "Interministerial Price Commission." To *control* prices did not necessarily mean to *repress* them: the Commission exercised controls on a case-by-case basis, and, in principle, permitted firms to pass on much or all of their cost increases. Perhaps inevitably, however, the Commission had bitter disputes with affected firms, especially when inflation worsened. No less inevitably, the Commission's effectiveness and usefulness is debatable. It assuredly delayed, but could never entirely prevent, some inflationary pressure; on the other hand, it probably caused considerable resource misallocation. As is so often the case in economic analysis, it is impossible to know how Brazil's economy would have worked if had never applied such controls.

The best use of selective controls is to forestall overshooting price increases in particular sectors. Where inflation is a long-standing problem, markets are apt to be overly tolerant of excessive price increases. Accordingly, in sectors characterized by substantial monopoly power or in which prices respond very rapidly to excess demand, there is a case for controls, not only to limit inflationary pressure but also to limit relative-price dispersion, and to ensure that price increases reflect scarcity value rather than abuse of market power or over-shooting as a market gropes for equilibrium. Economists have long regarded price regulation as appropriate for monopolized sectors, particularly for "natural" monopolies (such as electricity or telephone service). The case for setting ceilings on prices that would otherwise be highly volatile is less respectable, though: overshooting steel prices or interest rates would presumably fall anyway under market pressure. Before falling, however, they might impart a burst of inflationary pressure in the economy, particularly in sectors in which these prices are costs. (Once that happened, of course, the measured degree of overshooting would diminish *ex post*.)

The problem is that, even as part of a gradualist program, selective controls are difficult to apply safely and effectively. The controlling agency must either take partly uninformed decisions or else gather and analyze voluminous cost data. Not all nations have the requisite data-processing resources; the resulting bureaucracy may, in any case, turn out to be the worst aspect of the problem. Even with adequate data, technical capacity, and respected staff integrity, the controlling agency's decisions will still be difficult judgment calls; small errors can easily produce significant distortions. Where selective controls are very incompetently managed, they make everything worse: they distort markets, exacerbate relative-price dispersion, and break down when the controlled prices must be adjusted sharply, clobbering the objective of inflation control.

An important problem of selective controls is the means by which they are enforced. The effectiveness of selective controls depends partly on whether the public perceives them to be sensible, fair, and broadly efficient, which is ultimately possible only if they genuinely are. Legal penalties may work, but even draconian penalties will fail if pressure against compliance is widespread. One approach is to reward firms for compliance. For example, decisions of Brazil's Interministerial Price Commission were not always legally binding, but compliance has generally been a condition of various government benefits, including credit from the state-owned commercial bank, the Bank of Brazil. This implicitly came to mean that the Bank of Brazil would provide credit to compliant firms. In the late 1960s and the 1970s this practically implied that if a Brazilian firm agreed to limit its price increases, the money supply would increase, because until 1986 the Bank of Brazil retained the power to create money without reserve requirements. This mechanism effectively substituted one inflation-feedback channel with another. This is analogous to the dilemmas that arise when a government considers raising public-enterprise prices or indirect taxes: doing so generates inflationary cost pressure; not doing so sustains the public-sector deficit.

8   WAGE CONTROLS

The preceding section's discussion applies, on the whole, to selective controls on prices of particular goods and services. Matters are no less complex for selective controls on "prime cost"—costs of primary factors of production, including labor, finance, residential and commercial rents, and imported products and inputs. This section summarizes some issues involved in controlling "prime cost" generally, and then offers some observations on adjustment of labor earnings in particular.

Arguments for controlling prime cost can be divided into two related groups. First are what might be called "static" arguments: increases in prime cost diminish aggregate supply and increase aggregate demand. The higher the cost of production, the less profit-motivated firms will be willing and able to produce. Changes in real production costs imply changes in income allocation. Wage increases presumably favor people with higher propensities to consume (i.e., lower propensities to save), and therefore tend to increase aggregate demand. Prime-cost increases generally, and wage increases in particular, are therefore likely to be inflationary, because they reduce aggregate supply[18] and increase aggregate demand.

A second set of arguments for controlling prime cost concerns the inflation-feedback process. In general, if real production costs rise, credit demand increases, and the banking system will come under pressure to meet this demand. If the credit stock expands, the money supply probably also will, and this would tend to be inflationary. In addition, increases in prime cost generate anticipations of further inflation, with inflationary consequences. Accordingly, an explicit or implicit aim of controls on prime cost in general, and on wages in particular, is to make the inflation-feedback process less robust.

Wage controls implicitly address the reality of price-level uncertainty. A labor-management contract negotiation determines three conceptually separable components of a prospective wage increase: (i) an increase to cover the unanticipated purchasing-power loss that occurred since the preceding wage adjustment; (ii) whatever increase workers can claim and management offer on the "real" bases of productivity increases or tightened labor supply; and (iii) an increase that covers the purchasing-power loss anticipated over the contract term. All three could present problems in the negotiation. Replenishment of unanticipated purchasing-power loss may be a problem if the negotiating parties cannot agree on how much of the loss had been anticipated in the last agreement—labor will presumably claim that less, management that more, had been anticipated. An inflation-fighting government may be tempted to use controls to limit the second component—e.g., where a labor union uses its power to exact a high wage from a firm or industry, which then uses *its* bargaining power with clients and creditors to exact high output prices. Price-level uncertainty complicates negotiation of the third component. Labor can be expected, of course, to base its claim on higher anticipated inflation than management. The deeper problem will be that each side is uncertain about future inflation: risk-averse labor negotiators will demand higher wages to compensate for the possibility that inflation will be higher than they anticipate; risk-averse management negotiators will offer lower wages for fear that output prices will rise insufficiently if inflation turns out lower than they currently anticipate.

In imposing wage controls governments are often seen to oppose workers' interests. This is undeniable in some instances—for example, the controls instituted by the Brazilian military regimes. Beginning in 1965, these governments' rules effectively enabled them to fix annual wage increases. In practice, they raised wages according to a productivity indicator and (systematically over-optimistic) anticipations of the coming twelve months' inflation. Beginning in 1968, they allowed wage increases to incorporate a "catch-up" component to reflect the unanticipated inflation that had occurred over the preceding twelve months—they had permitted no such adjustment until then. As government economists later argued (for example, Simonsen 1970), they aimed to set the *average real* wage over the coming twelve months equal to the average real wage over the preceding twelve months. In the terminology of Chapter 4, they hoped this would reduce inflationary pressure, so the "valley," hence the average, real wage would not fall so far below the "peak" real wage. All the same, they reduced overall Brazilian real wage levels about 25 per cent between 1964 and 1968. This helped the struggle against inflation, but real wage levels did not rise significantly until the latter part of the 1970s.

In general, governments engaged in controlling wages would plead that they are fighting inflation in the interests of society as a whole, and, regrettably, this requires sacrifices by workers; and that they are ultimately saving the purchasing power of workers' pay packets. Each round of wage increases in particular sectors might not have so powerful an inflationary effect; but different groups of workers carefully watch one another's pay settlements, and try not to slip behind. If one group secures higher wages, other groups are likely to insist more forcefully. This is why inflation-fighting governments try at least to influence wage negotiations. More recently, however, many governments, frustrated by the results of trying to influence wage negotiations and fearful that they were disrupting local labor markets, have resolved henceforth to stop trying to do so.

Conceptually, a wage negotiation could be carried out in a three-part agenda. First, labor and management would agree on how much of the inflation accumulated under the preceding contract had been unanticipated. Negotiations could then proceed from a wage base adjusted to incorporate accumulated unanticipated inflation. Second, labor and management would negotiate the average real wage they would consider appropriate over the coming period, based on the "real" issues conditioning demand for and supply of labor. Finally, the negotiation would adjust the negotiated wage for anticipated inflation in order to yield the negotiated average real wage. A government could help with any or all of these steps. It could umpire or regulate the "catch-up" and the "real" factors, and it could provide a guideline for expected future inflation. Unfortunately, whatever guideline the government offers will tend to become a minimum inflation expectation for the economy as a whole. Such a guideline could, however, minimize labor-management debate over anticipated inflation—which would help precisely because anticipated inflation is beyond the negotiators' control. The guideline could then be recalled in the subsequent round of negotiations to calculate the unanticipated inflation adjustment.[19] Alternatively, a government could permit wage "indexation," as the Brazilian government did beginning in 1979. This is discussed in Chapter 8.

9 CONCLUSION

Modern macroeconomic analysis is built around a "policy" paradigm, according to which macroeconomic stability is a matter of proper policy choice. This paradigm is perhaps inevitable, since macroeconomists' professional purpose is to provide advice on proper policy choice. Nevertheless, this chapter's observations suggest that this paradigm must be applied carefully. For example, the fact that one policy course is inflationary does not imply that the opposite policy would be stabilizing. Raising public-sector prices reduces public-sector deficits, but also increases cost pressure. In this case, inflationary pressure would probably result from either policy choice, but more pressure might result from one choice than from the other, depending on particular circumstances. That is, governments must often choose not between inflationary and anti-inflationary, but between more or less inflationary, policies. Some policy measures may be deflationary in the short term but inflationary over longer terms—e.g., permitting the currency to revalue in real terms, or general price freezes. A given policy may be inflationary in one set of economic circumstances and deflationary in another—e.g., tight monetary policy is more likely to be inflationary in contexts of credit scarcity and heavy public indebtedness than it would be in a context of credit abundance.

Successful stabilization policy must either reduce the quantity of "claims" on real goods and services or persuade people to limit the exercise of their claims—that is, successful policy must narrow aggregate purchasing power and persuade people to save rather than spend. Stabilization policy with a longer-term focus needs in addition to encourage capital formation as opposed to consumption. The point that claims, or exercise of claims, need to be reduced in order to control inflation indicates one basic problem of price-freeze approaches. Unlike tightened monetary and fiscal policy, simply freezing wages and prices does nothing to diminish the claims on the economy's output. Price freezes alone therefore fail permanently to secure permanent stabilization.

This said, it is important to emphasize that "non-orthodox" approaches ought not to be dismissed as entirely pointless. In combination with approaches that reduce claims, or exercise of claims, temporary price freezes can play helpful roles. By creating temporary stability—what may be described as "quasi-stability"—a price freeze can relieve price-level uncertainty, and provide a setting in which more orthodox economic policy approaches have a better chance of working.

7 Inflation Stabilization under External Constraint

1 INTRODUCTION: "IMF-TYPE" STABILIZATION PROGRAMS

This chapter considers the policy problems of stabilizing an economy that has both high inflation and an external payments deficit it is unwilling or unable to cover through borrowing. During the 1980s, under the pressure of surging debt service, many Latin American nations dramatically increased their trade surpluses in stabilization programs supported by credit from the International Monetary Fund. Their inflation rates, however, either responded disappointingly or increased significantly. This chapter discusses this experience. It first explains how "IMF-type programs" should work, emphasizing the role inflation plays in them. It then discusses the intricate reasons why inflation has been a stubbornly persisting concomitant of the "debt crisis."

An "IMF-type program" is a set of coordinated monetary, fiscal, and exchange-rate policies intended primarily to stabilize a nation's external economic relationships, in the sense of adjusting its external borrowing needs to a flow that foreign lenders should be willing to provide. When formalized as an IMF program, attainment of "performance targets" constitutes "conditionality" for a foreign-exchange loan by the IMF to the nation's central bank. The loan shores up the central bank's international reserves while the program policies operate to improve the balance of payments. In the 1980s "debt crisis," IMF programs have served simultaneously as conditionality for concerted financing provided by creditor banks.[1] Governments have also carried out what may be described as "IMF-type" stabilization programs independently from the IMF, sometimes in hope of avoiding recourse to the IMF where its involvement is politically problematic.[2] This chapter's observations apply both to "IMF" and to "IMF-type" programs, considered here as the basic "orthodox" approach to balance-of-payments stabilization.

The balance-of-payments accounts may be said to show how a nation's "resource deficit"—imports less exports of goods and non-factor services—is financed, through a flow of net external finance less net payments of interest and dividends. With external finance presumably limited, an IMF-type program aims to stabilize this deficit—that is, set policy to reduce it from an unsustainable to a sustainable flow and ensure that it remains sustainable. In theory, developing nations—certain oil exporters excepted—*ought* to run resource deficits: since their holdings of finance capital are limited, it stands to reason that developing nations should receive financing flows. Neo-classical economic theory implies that finance capital, hence real resources, will (and ought to) flow from where they are relatively abundant and less well remunerated, to where they are relatively scarce, hence better remunerated. Developing nations might justifiably run temporary resource surpluses, to pay down excessive debt and to rebuild international reserves following a crisis, but their "normal" longer-term resource flows are presumably in deficit.

To stabilize the resource balance, IMF-type programs have two broad instrumental objectives: to change relative-price incentives to favor exports; and to reduce aggregate demand generally, to reduce demand for imports and for goods and services that could be exported. IMF-type programs accordingly comprise a characteristic set of policies, including some or all of the following:

(i) *Currency devaluation*: The underlying reasoning is that, if imports are too high and exports too low, domestic-currency prices of internationally traded goods might be too low relative to prices of non-traded goods. Devaluation rapidly, if crudely, realigns these prices. No less—and perhaps much more—important, devaluation directly reduces the external purchasing power of income flows and wealth stocks denominated in domestic currency. This reduces aggregate purchasing power and aggregate demand, which might otherwise have to be satisfied by imports or potentially exportable goods.

(ii) *Public-sector expenditure reduction*: Public-sector expenditure contributes to aggregate-demand pressure, and is often financed through money creation. Money creation raises the price level, making import prices relatively more and export prices relatively less competitive. IMF-type programs seek to shift the financing of public-sector deficits away from money creation and toward private financial markets—if possible, to limit public deficits to what can be financed by foreign sources.

(iii) *Measures to increase public-sector revenues*, including tax increases, subsidy cuts, and increases in the prices of publicly-provided goods and services: Again, the point is to reduce both aggregate demand and the public-sector borrowing requirement. While the IMF generally advocates changing the structure of taxation away from "indirect" taxation (e.g., sales taxes), which distorts the price system, and toward "direct" taxation (e.g., income taxation), indirect taxes generate revenue faster, so that IMF programs seeking fast results often move the revenue structure in the direction of indirect taxation.

(iv) *Tightened monetary policy*: The point is to control domestic inflation and to reduce aggregate demand. In particular, IMF-type programs aim to reduce the economy's total supply of bank credit, although attempting in the process to leave the private sector relatively favored by comparison with the public sector.

(v) *Policies to raise market interest rates*: The objectives are to encourage saving, hence reduce aggregate demand; to discourage "capital flight"; and to rationalize credit use.

(vi) *Wage control* of one sort or another: This aims to reduce pressure on aggregate demand and to relieve production costs, thereby making goods and services produced in the economy more internationally competitive. It serves also to control wage-related government expenditure. Many economists believe free wage negotiation to be the most efficient approach to private-sector wage determination. Where this is not feasible, however, an IMF-type program may incorporate measures to limit wages under the existing wage-determination system.

(vii) *Trade liberalization*, including reduced reliance on tariffs, export subsidies and quantitative trade restrictions: This may at first seem contradictory, since tariff reductions reduce government revenues, diminished export subsidies discourage exports, and liberalization encourages imports. The basic objective, however, is to augment productive efficiency by thrusting national producers into external competition, and to enable domestic producers to use lower-cost foreign inputs.[3]

(viii) Finally, *Removal of price controls*: The point is to permit the government to reduce subsidies, ensure the financial soundness of public enterprises, and rationalize the functioning of the economic system. Where taxes are levied on goods whose prices are controlled, price increases help enhance government revenues.

In a formal IMF program, the nation commits itself to quantitatively specified macroeconomic performance targets. Over the duration of a program, IMF credit is disbursed at periodic (typically quarterly) intervals, conditioned on achievement of the previous periods' performance targets. Should the economy fail to meet one or more of the performance targets, the IMF may grant a "waiver," on the grounds that performance was close enough, or that failure was for reasons beyond policy-makers' control, and disburse anyway; or may require negotiation of new performance targets before resuming disbursements. Governments have sometimes been unable or unwilling to reach agreement with the IMF on new targets, and have chosen to discontinue programs. Where international commercial banks make disbursements conditional on an IMF program, termination of the IMF program implies forgoing commercial-bank disbursements as well.

Quantitative performance targets typically include the following basic four: (i) a *maximum* increase in public-sector external indebtedness; (ii) a *minimum* increase in central-bank international-reserve holdings; (iii) a *maximum* total amount the public sector may borrow; and (iv) a *maximum* increase in net central-bank domestic assets, including public-sector obligations.[4] The minimum net-international-reserve increase addresses the program's main purpose, to restore the reserve level to an adequate magnitude (sometimes gauged in months of imports; three to six months of goods and services is typically considered the minimum necessary, but particular programs may set different standards). The maximum increase in public-sector external debt ensures that the reserve increase will not come simply through external borrowing. With public external borrowing limited, the limit on overall public borrowing then limits public-sector borrowing from the central bank and domestic financial markets. Given the minimum reserve increase, the maximum increase in the central bank's net domestic assets then implicitly limits the overall growth of the monetary base.[5]

The quantitative performance targets are calculated on the basis of quantitative objectives for real GDP growth, inflation rates, the exchange rate, international-trade flows, policy settings, and other relevant domestic and external economic variables as agreed by the nation's government with the IMF staff. These projections are used to calculate the balance of payments, willingness to hold money, and the various components of the public sector's accounts; these are then the basis for formulating the performance targets and ensuring that they are feasible and mutually consistent.

2   INFLATION AND IMF-TYPE PROGRAMS: THE INHERENT "NEAR-DILEMMA"

The balance-of-payments shortfall is the IMF program's primary objective; the inflation rate is the program's secondary, indeed instrumental, objective. Where inflation is already severe, an IMF program may worsen inflation before improving it. This is a problem, because the feedback process may then keep inflation from diminishing as the balance of payments improves.

This may be understood as follows. The conceptual underpinning of IMF-type programs is "the monetary approach to the balance of payments," a long-standing paradigm that describes the relationships among an economy's price level, money supply and balance of payments. The paradigm originated in an essay by the philosopher David Hume (Hume 1751). All other things being equal, money-supply growth implies higher domestic prices; higher domestic prices encourage imports and discourage exports, and so imply a lower net inflow—or higher net outflow—of external payments. A smaller net payments inflow implies smaller foreign-exchange accumulation, hence smaller money-supply growth; a larger net payments outflow implies larger foreign-exchange loss, hence larger money-supply reduction. Either way, higher domestic prices cause the money supply to diminish through the balance of payments, and so cause prices to fall or to rise more slowly.

That is, an open economy should operate in a self-correcting way to reverse a price-level rise: higher domestic prices reduce the balance of payments, implying foreign-exchange loss but also a smaller money supply, hence reduced inflationary pressure. Note that among the "all other things" held equal in this simplified scenario are the exchange rate and foreign prices. Moreover, the economy is assumed not to borrow to maintain its foreign-exchange holdings.

An economy's "money supply" is its banking system's monetary liabilities (as described by the balance-sheet structure presented in Chapter 3). These monetary liabilities are backed by net foreign assets and net domestic assets. If a nation has both an inflation problem *and* a balance-of-payments deficit sufficient to warrant an IMF-type program, logically, the money-supply growth that presumably caused the inflation must have resulted from acquisition of domestic, not foreign, assets. That is, if central-bank liabilities are increasing but net foreign assets falling, the balance-sheet identity implies that net domestic assets must be rising. To the extent an IMF program succeeds in reversing the payments outflow, however, the central bank acquires foreign assets. To buy the foreign exchange, the central bank issues local currency. In itself, this increases the money supply and thereby renews the inflationary pressure.

In an economy with extensive inflation experience, the willingness to hold money is likely to be relatively small as a proportion of GDP (i.e., velocity is likely to be high). As a result, comparatively small increases in the money supply may powerfully affect prices. Rapid balance-of-payments improvement in such an economy can therefore induce substantial inflationary pressure. In fact, if the price level "overshoots" it can quickly reverse the balance-of-payments improvement, or require further adjustment measures. This "near dilemma" is an inherent problem for an IMF-type program. It is a "near dilemma," because there is a narrow way through, at least in principle: policymakers must contrive (i) to reduce the growth rate of net domestic assets and (ii) to increase the growth rate of net foreign assets in such a way that (iii) their combined growth rate diminishes.

If the banking system's domestic assets grow too rapidly along with external assets, the program can succeed only temporarily in accumulating external assets. Sustained money-supply growth would maintain excessive inflationary pressure, and rising domestic prices would then pressure the external payments inflow back down. Indeed, while the central bank may have accumulated sufficient net external assets on the program's official conclusion date to declare the program a success, rising prices may thereafter widen the balance-of-payments deficit; permanent stabilization will not have been secured.

In dealing with a balance-of-payments problem deriving from domestically induced inflation, an IMF-type stabilization program deliberately blocks the Hume mechanism. International-reserve loss having been deemed unacceptable, the program aims to reverse it through such measures as devaluation. This blocks the external mechanism that relieves pressure on domestic prices. To fight inflation, the program must therefore incorporate countervailing measures to ensure that net domestic assets grow more slowly than external assets. These include measures to control the public sector's borrowing requirement, and possibly wage restraint, credit tightness, and other austerity measures. Should the program fail adequately to control domestic causes of money-supply growth, and domestic prices rise so far that the reserve accumulation reverses, a new round of stabilizing policy actions may be required, including further devaluation. The economy could then slip into a spiralling inflation-devaluation cycle.

In their attack on inflation, IMF-type programs generally target the public-sector borrowing requirement—that is, the net flow increase in outstanding public-sector external and domestic obligations. The amount of public-sector obligations—money and government bills and bonds—a domestic economy can be persuaded at any moment to hold is limited. Accordingly, any attempt by the public sector to borrow more from the domestic economy must lead to some combination of higher prices and higher interest rates. In stabilization programs, governments are often advised to limit their overall net borrowing requirement roughly to the interest they must pay on external debt, and to finance this interest from external sources. Since the external borrowing inflow would finance the interest outflow, this aspect of the government's operations would produce no inflow of net external assets, hence no money creation. On balance the government would be creating no domestic financial obligations, and so should generate neither pressure on the money supply nor on interest rates.

The "Hume" relationship between inflation and external-payments inflows may be reinforced by the combined relationships (i) between inflation and economic activity and (ii) between economic activity and the external-payments flow. The Phillips curve implies that higher inflation tends to be associated with higher economic activity, at least in the short term. At the same time, higher economic activity tends— like higher domestic prices—to reduce exports and increase imports. This is partly because higher economic activity requires more imported inputs; the higher income levels resulting from higher economic activity also imply higher domestic demand, hence reduced exports and higher imports. To cope with balance-of-payments difficulties, policy-makers may act to reduce imports or promote exports. To the extent they increase "net exports," however, policy-makers increase aggregate demand.

Accordingly, an IMF-type program may be said to work within the context of a three-dimensional Phillips curve. The Phillips curve represents the notion that policy-makers must accept higher inflation as the "cost" of higher economic activity, or lower economic activity as the "cost" of lower inflation (see Chapter 3). At the same time, higher inflation and economic activity entail diminished international-reserve inflows. These trade-offs are for the relatively short term, however. By reducing inflation and economic activity policy-makers may improve the external accounts; improved external accounts then generate inflation and increased economic activity, at least partly reversing the external-accounts improvement. To maintain the external-accounts improvement, policy-makers may have to struggle continually to contain inflation, and may be forced to accept diminished economic activity. To improve these trade-offs and diminish the amplitude of the stop-go cycle, the program must ensure that external assets are substituted for domestic assets in the asset backing of the monetary base, and that exportable and import-substituting activities are substituted—sustainably and efficiently—for non-tradable activities in the composition of production.

In the conception of inflation as competition for purchasing power, the open aspects of an economy require taking account of particularly powerful economic entities, such as exporters, importers, entities that must service external debt, and foreign shareholders and creditors. Political struggles over the exchange rate are much like other struggles over prices and wage rates. Much as workers aim to increase or at least maintain the purchasing power of their wages, exporters aim to increase the purchasing power of their unit export earnings, while importers aim to reduce their real unit costs. Just as workers back their pay claims by threatening to withdraw, or actually withdrawing, their labor supply, so exporters back their claims by withdrawing from exporting activity—with the significant difference that they may profit relatively by selling domestically, while workers, or labor-union funds, may lose substantial amounts while on strike.

To summarize, while inflation unquestionably diminishes net exports, the inherent problem for IMF-type programs is that successful reversal of the external-accounts problem entails at least a round of renewed inflationary pressure. Once devaluation or other measures to improve the external accounts have intensified inflationary pressure, the inflation-feedback process may aggravate it. Policy-makers then face a difficult struggle to contain the inflationary pressure resulting from adjustment of the nation's external position. Accordingly, the fundamental challenge for a stabilization program undertaken in an economy beset both by inflation and by external-accounts problems is to counteract the inflationary pressure arising from improvement of the external accounts.

3 EXCHANGE-RATE POLICY

The dilemmas inherent in dealing simultaneously with balance-of-payments and inflation problems are encapsulated in the dilemma of exchange-rate policy. Devaluation improves the balance of payments at the price of higher inflationary pressure.[6] Once a foreign-exchange crisis develops, of course, the authorities may have little discretion about the pace of devaluation. Inflation itself worsens the balance of payments sooner or later; devaluation therefore cannot permanently improve the balance of payments without additional offsetting measures to reduce aggregate demand.[7] Finally, unless there is offsetting deflationary pressure, a balance-of-payments surplus itself augments inflationary pressure.

Persuasive arguments can often be made, depending on particular circumstances, for allowing exchange rates to float. Floating is inevitably "dirty," because the government and the central bank would be purchasing foreign exchange for external-debt service and for reserve accumulation—indeed, for the deeper reason that any fiscal or monetary policy action (or inaction) always affects exchange markets. The advantage of floating is that, at least in principle, exchange-rate depreciation need go no further than the government's and central bank's combined demand for foreign exchange requires. In fact a sharp increase in the trade balance would create pressure for exchange-rate appreciation.

The chief drawback of a floating exchange rate, particularly by comparison with a crawling-peg exchange rate that maintains a fixed "real-effective" exchange rate (see Chapter 8), is that it would make the exchange rate volatile and uncertain. To be sure, part of the problem of floating is precisely that, as the government applies recessionary policies and domestic demand for imports and exportable goods diminishes, exchange-rate appreciation is likely to result, which would discourage exporters. Fixed but flexible exchange-rate mechanisms can be used, if necessary, in favor of exporters and foreign creditors—that is, devaluation and inflation are available as means to generate purchasing power in favor of these interests.

4 INFLATIONARY CONSEQUENCES OF EXTERNAL DEBT

Latin American inflation rates rose sharply as the external-debt crisis deepened in the early 1980s. The two events are assuredly related, but the nature of the connection is controversial and intricate. The "debt crisis" resulted from a surge in nations' interest bills at the same time as external finance became virtually unavailable. As public-sector external debt service rose, public-sector budgets came under pressure. To maintain the same structure of non-interest expenditure and taxation, overall public-sector borrowing requirements would have had to rise; alternatively, to maintain the same public-sector borrowing requirements, taxation would have had to increase or non-interest expenditure diminish. Moreover, external debt service required foreign exchange. Not only did net export earnings have to increase, but governments had to purchase the proceeds, often at high real prices as a consequence of the stiff devaluation required to set the requisite export incentive. These changes inevitably produced realignment of the purchasing-power allocation, and generated inflationary competition.

External-debt accumulation is not inflationary *per se*, of course. A borrower that spent external-loan proceeds domestically might bid up domestic prices, and, upon exchanging the proceeds for local currency, would increase the money supply. The price rise should only be temporary, since it would induce higher imports and diminished exports. In any case, the borrower is more likely to spend foreign-exchange proceeds externally, for imports. No reserve accumulation, hence no inflationary pressure, would result in this instance.

The combination of higher interest bills and diminished credit availability meant that indebted nations had to force import compression to leave export proceeds available to pay interest. This amounted to an increase in domestic aggregate demand, as well as a reduction in the net resource transfer from external sources. Merchandise imports for Latin America as a whole were about a third lower in 1984 than in 1982; nations like Brazil that had run trade deficits for years shifted to large surpluses. Fewer resources were available as a result to apply in capital formation. Aggregate supply fell as a result, with inflationary consequences. Although most Latin American nations secured financing through concerted financing arrangements, the proportions of their interest bills financed through external borrowing diminished. The difference had to be covered through higher taxation, expenditure cuts, or borrowing in domestic financial markets. The cost of domestic borrowing increased in nations as their credit needs increased and their risk ratings deteriorated. Many nations' domestic interest bills and overall borrowing requirements surged sharply: by the end of the decade, for example, the public sectors of Argentina and Brazil had added domestic debt crises to their external crises.[8]

A heavy external-debt burden diminishes the effectiveness of devaluation as a balance-of-payments adjustment device. Devaluation works in part, as noted above, by making external purchases relatively more costly and by reducing the real income and real wealth from which they are made. Interest payments, however, are contracted payments, not discretionary external purchases. Devaluation cannot reduce previously contracted interest payments, but it does directly increase their domestic-currency equivalent. To the extent the public sector is indebted externally, devaluation therefore increases public-sector deficits. It also decapitalizes enterprises that have net foreign liabilities. Monetary authorities inevitably come under pressure to permit monetary expansion, not only to purchase export proceeds but to deal with higher public-sector deficits, deeper private-sector decapitalization, and the higher prices and costs of anything related to the exchange rate.

Indeed, Argentina's and Brazil's experience since 1985 demonstrates the difficulty of devaluing heavily and then using contractionary monetary policy to offset the inflationary consequences. (Chapter 9 discusses this experience.) To offset the inflationary pressure of a heavy devaluation, monetary policy may have to drive real interest rates to unprecedented levels—among other things, to compensate financial markets' fears of further devaluation. Quite apart from the damage sharp increases in interest rates normally cause, the interest payments themselves are significant in magnitude. They add to public- and private-sector borrowing requirements, and also add significantly to private-sector asset holders' wealth holdings. Private-sector purchasing power grows accordingly, and may become the basis for subsequent destabilization.

5   INFLATION, EXTERNAL DEBT, AND IMF-TYPE STABILIZATION IN BRAZIL, 1983–5

The kinds of adjustment problem that result from heavy public-sector debt accumulation emerged with particular clarity in Brazil's experience in the first half of the 1980s. By the early 1980s, accumulating trade deficits and surging international interest rates had sharply increased the nation's external interest bill. In 1981 the authorities engineered a deliberate recession to diminish import demand, contain inflationary pressures and augment the country's exportable surplus, to generate funds to service the external debt and limit its accumulation. In late 1982, however, in the wake of Mexico's international payments crisis, Brazil's government found it could neither meet its scheduled debt service nor maintain sufficient short-term credit lines, and had to request rescheduling agreements from official and commercial-bank creditors.

In March 1983 Brazil began a three-year IMF Extended Fund Facility, in conjunction with which the IMF, other official entities, and commercial banks provided substantial finance during 1983 and 1984. Before starting the program, in February 1983, the authorities devalued the *cruzeiro* from 292 to 380 per US dollar (a 23 per cent devaluation). Thereafter, they continued devaluing according to the inflation rate, under the "crawling-peg" policy that had prevailed for most of the time since August 1968. Meanwhile, tightened fiscal and monetary policies deepened the recession: real GDP fell 3.1 per cent during 1983. The devaluation and the recession dramatically reversed the external accounts: the merchandise-trade surplus rose from $778 million in 1982 to $6.5 billion in 1983 and $13 billion in 1984; the current-account deficit fell from $16.3 billion (7.1 per cent of GDP) in 1982 to $6.8 billion (4.1 per cent of GDP) in 1983, then reached a $42 million surplus in 1984.

At the same time, however, inflation intensified, and the government's overall borrowing requirement became increasingly difficult to control. The monetary base and money supply rose at rates well above the IMF-program projections, and domestic financial markets underwent severe turbulence. Brazil found it difficult to meet the quarterly IMF-program performance targets, and had to renegotiate the program repeatedly. Partly because government expenditures came under pressure from electoral politics, Brazil missed the fiscal performance targets for the last quarter of 1984 by a wide margin. In March 1985, when a new civilian government replaced the discredited military regime that had held power since 1964, the IMF program was definitively ended.

The program failed to stifle inflation because of the combined effects of devaluation and heavy external and internal debt service, aggravated and magnified by Brazil's extensive indexation mechanisms, including indexation of government obligations and private savings accounts, wage indexation, and the crawling-peg exchange rate. The crawling-peg exchange rate helped sustain inflation-feedback pressure; it set the incentive for the trade surplus, which was itself inflationary.[9] Some of the government's domestic obligations even carried dollar clauses. In domestic-currency terms, the country's external debt and a large part of its internal debt therefore rose directly with the March 1983 devaluation. The inflation rate rose in the wake of the devaluation to a 150 per cent year-over-year annual rate, compared with the 90 per cent rate projected under the March 1983 program.

It is doubtful whether indexation of government debt was the essence of the problem, for even if the internal debt were not adjusted for inflation nominal interest rates would have risen to compensate for anticipated inflation instead: the interest bill might have turned out even higher (see the discussion in Chapter 8). The essential problem was that real devaluation and high real interest rates increased the already substantial public-sector external and internal debt service, quite apart from whatever efforts the authorities made to contain non-financial expenditures and increase revenues. This lifted the public-sector deficit above the IMF program performance target, and so threw Brazil out of compliance by mid-1983.

The Brazilian authorities and the IMF staff disagreed in mid-1983 about how to set new performance targets. The Brazilian authorities argued that, since the inflation rate could not be accurately forecast, the nominal financial charges were unpredictable and in any event too large to be covered through net expenditure reductions. They advocated expressing the public-deficit performance condition net of the inflation adjustment of index-linked government obligations; inflation adjustment, they argued, was part of the principal, not the interest bill. When the renegotiated program resumed in September 1983, the IMF permitted the fiscal performance target to be a ceiling on the so-called "operational," or "real-basis," deficit—the public-sector deficit less that part of financial charges that compensated *ex post* for inflation—rather than the full public-sector deficit (see Chapter 3). This was "fairer" for the Brazilian authorities, in the sense that it made it less likely that uncontrollable public expenditure resulting from uncontrollable inflation adjustment would drive the deficit above the program target. At the same time, however, it implicitly accepted the reality that the program would deal gradually at best with the inflationary pressure arising from the external adjustment, precisely because the crawling-peg devaluation made the inflation-feedback mechanism so robust.

The fundamental problem was that the macroeconomy was so structured that achievement of the external-accounts performance targets would make it extremely difficult to meet the monetary and public-sector-deficit targets. The foreign-exchange influx resulting from improved trade performance increased the monetary base, which was inflationary. Devaluation and indexation helped channel this inflationary pressure into higher financial charges, for the government as well as for the private sector. This was inherently difficult to offset through policy. When the monetary authorities sold government obligations on the open market to offset the money-supply increase, they forced up real interest rates, raising the public sector's financing bill even after taking account of inflation. Apart from the issue of Brazil's maintaining compliance, even if the IMF program now used the "operational deficit" rather than the full deficit as the performance target, the full deficit still had to be financed, and it remained a source of inflationary pressure.

At the end of 1983 Brazil fell out of compliance with the revised program, this time because the external financing it had received during the year proved insufficient: international reserves diminished and Brazil briefly incurred interest arrears to its commercial-bank creditors. By early 1984, however, the recession and the devaluation had increased the trade surplus, enabling Brazil rapidly to eliminate the interest arrears and to accumulate reserves. During 1984 the external accounts performed better than most observers had projected, and the government secured a concerted agreement with the commercial banks involving new credit and rescheduling of amortization. At the same time, inflation settled in at a plateau exceeding 200 per cent per year.

For 1984 the "operational" public-sector borrowing requirement fell to 1.8 per cent of GDP, so that Brazil met this performance criterion through most of the year. The "inflation-adjustment portion" of the deficit rose, however, to about 18 per cent of GDP. Once again, this borrowing requirement posed a dilemma for the authorities. If the government sought central-bank financing, it forced an increase in the monetary base, hence higher inflation rates and higher interest rates; if it sought financing from private sources, it bid up real interest rates, against itself as well as against the private sector. The result during 1984, as during 1983, was an inconsistent policy, with wide swings in interest rates.

Toward the end of 1984, as Brazil's military government prepared to transfer power to a new civilian government and sought to secure the (indirect) election of its favored candidate, it increased its expenditures. Efforts to hold to the IMF performance targets took a lower priority. The candidate the outgoing government favored was defeated, and the government that took office in March 1985, which was built largely on political groupings opposed to the IMF approach, chose not to resume the program. External pressure to have an IMF program had subsided by then: although inflation was still high, Brazil had accumulated sufficient international reserves and its trade surplus covered external interest payments. Moreover, export-led growth was under way: real GDP grew 5.6 and 8.3 per cent in 1984 and 1985, largely recouping the recession losses.

For inflation, the essential point about the program remains that, while it was able to reverse the external performance through recession and devaluation, it was unable to prevent devaluation and the improvement in the trade accounts from locking the economy into an unacceptably high inflation rate. Although real GDP recovered through export growth, the high trade surplus meant the economy was transferring a significant quantity of resources overseas, leaving fewer resources available for capital formation.

The character of Brazil's problem may be understood by simplifying reality somewhat. Imagine that the IMF program amounted to two policy actions, (i) devaluation and (ii) cuts in programmable public expenditure, intended to achieve two performance targets, (i) higher reserve inflows and (ii) a lower public deficit. Devaluation would produce reserve accumulation, while expenditure cuts would reduce the deficit. At the same time, however, the devaluation would increase the public-sector deficit by increasing the domestic-currency equivalent of the external-debt service. The trouble is that, in reality, the inflationary effects of reserve accumulation and stabilizing effects of the lower deficit were therefore difficult to forecast. If the authorities could precisely predict the inflationary effect of the devaluation and the ensuing effect on public-sector debt service, they could program budget cuts to offset them. As a practical matter, government expenditure and revenue programs simply could not change rapidly to offset the unpredictable volatility of the financial flows.

Curiously, deep cuts in programmable government expenditures or heavy tax increases from the outset might not have improved matters appreciably. Sharp fiscal austerity would have diminished aggregate demand, hence reduced inflationary pressure; it would also, however, have reduced imports. The improved external accounts would thus have led to larger international-reserve accumulation—and, consequently, additional inflationary pressure. The monetary authority could sterilize unanticipated reserve increases resulting from the devaluation, but this would increase real interest rates, and increase the public deficit.

In sum, the complex macroeconomic hydraulics of heavily indebted, inflationary economies may cause them to operate in ways that are difficult to manage. Economic performance could veer from performance targets despite vigorous adjustment efforts. In simpler economies with less inflation experience, where the public sector is not so heavily indebted and in which interest rates are less sensitive to inflation, devaluation combined with programmable expenditure cuts might improve both the public-sector deficit and the external accounts. Where public-sector indebtedness is high, however, and where nominal interest rates are sensitive to inflationary expectations and real interest rates are sensitive to tight monetary policy, the authorities may have genuine difficulty complying with both public-deficit and reserve-accumulation performance targets.

6   ON RAISING DOMESTIC INTEREST RATES TO FORESTALL CAPITAL FLIGHT

Nations undertaking IMF-type programs are characteristically advised to maintain high domestic interest rates to forestall "capital flight." As the experience of Argentina and Brazil in the 1980s suggests, however, this policy approach presents significant perils (see Chapter 9). Interest rates high enough to forestall capital flight must be competitive with external interest rates, taking account not only of anticipated devaluation but also of "country risk," which may well be substantial for an economy with an external-debt burden.

Problems arise if the economy has no genuine way to pay the interest bill that results from high interest rates. If, for example, domestic commercial banks offer higher deposit rates and thereby attract significant financial inflows, they must lend the resources in ways that earn sufficient interest to pay for the deposits. Banks may be unable to find lending projects reliably capable of providing such yields. Commercial banks that took on high-interest deposits might then (i) decapitalize themselves or (ii) require inflationary financing to pay their interest obligations. The resulting inflation would drive down the corresponding real interest rates, and sooner or later force devaluation—which would then require still higher nominal interest rates to forestall capital flight.

In all likelihood, the public sector would borrow the funds induced to remain within the nation. First, it might need to borrow, particularly if its external-debt service bill increased and access to external credit diminished. Second, ironically, it would be the economy's most reliable borrower, precisely because of its power to borrow and to inflate. Private borrowers, in contrast, would tend to be "rationed" because high interest rates themselves make their obligations riskier. As recent Argentine and Brazilian experience (described in Chapter 9) shows, however, a public sector that pays high interest charges is in danger of slipping into "distress," in which the interest bill is so large that it can be covered only through further borrowing, leading then to further debt accumulation and intensifying pressure on domestic interest rates.

If it is dangerous for a nation to forestall capital flight by offering interest rates it cannot afford, one may ask, what is the alternative? The broad answer is that, depending on a nation's circumstances, some capital flight—even a very large volume of capital flight—may be preferable to engaging in desperation financing. It may be "less bad" that a government incur external interest arrears or inflate for a time to cover a deficit, rather than slip into a distress cycle that may conclude in hyperinflation. It may even be in a nation's longer-term interest that its citizens "follow the market" to maintain their real wealth stocks through overseas placements at high world interest rates, rather than place their resources within the nation at exorbitant, unpayable interest rates.

7 CONCLUSION

IMF-type stabilization programs work less reliably in nations that have long inflationary experience: because the amount of money their citizens are willing to hold is so small, and because their expectations are so volatile, rapid balance-of-payments improvement tends to induce inflationary pressure. In the best of circumstances, an IMF-type program must perform a finely calibrated adjustment in an inflationary economy. Policy-makers must somehow apply domestic deflationary pressure to offset the inflationary pressure that results from improving the external accounts, in circumstances in which feedback processes are likely to be powerful. External debt complicates the problem. Devaluation, which otherwise serves to generate higher balance-of-payments surpluses, directly increases the domestic-currency equivalent of external-debt service, widening the public deficit. To the extent an economy's saving flow is taken up in external-debt service, fewer resources are available for capital formation, which adds aggregate-supply pressures to the other sources of inflationary pressure. Finally, the danger remains that a government whose external interest bill is rising but whose access to external finance is diminishing will find itself having to take on expensive domestic debt or to inflate.

Had it not been for the IMF and its support for stabilization efforts, the debt crisis would have turned out worse for all concerned. Developing nations' access to external finance would have been even more restricted, and commercial banks would probably have had to write down their asset portfolios more rapidly. The problem is that the IMF programs did not, indeed could not, address the underlying problem, which was that the crisis constituted a sudden, perverse reversal of financial flows between developed and developing nations. As long as this problem remained unsolved, genuine, permanent stabilization was bound to remain elusive: indebted developing nations were being called upon to maintain debt service at the same time they were being decapitalized.

8 Indexation and Dollarization

1 INTRODUCTION: DEFINITIONS AND DISTINCTIONS

"Index-linking," strictly defined, is the use of purchasing power as a unit of account. Since a "price index" is the money price of a basket containing all goods and services in proportion to their relative importance in total output, in principle any value "linked" to the index remains constant in terms of such baskets. "Dollarization" may be defined as the use of the US dollar as a unit of account in an economy that has its own money unit.[1] The dollar's domestic-money value is the current exchange rate—usually the free-market rate if this differs from the "official" rate. The domestic-money value of anything whose value is given in dollars therefore rises whenever the domestic currency depreciates against the dollar. In what follows, save where specifically noted, the public is assumed to expect the currency to depreciate at a rate roughly equal to the inflation rate, so that the dollar amounts practically to a purchasing-power unit.

Inflation has often induced spontaneous dollarization, since dollars are readily available in the form of bills and overseas assets as stores of value. Indexation, in contrast, has appeared only where governments have issued index-linked obligations, partly because "baskets of goods and services" are not convenient stores of value.

Indexation and dollarization have both advantages and drawbacks. Societies that have them often wish they did not, but some have discovered that doing away with them creates more problems than it solves. For example, in February 1986 Brazil's government tried to end financial indexation as part of its Cruzado Plan, having concluded that indexation sustains inflation "inertia." By early 1987, however, when inflation revived it found it had little choice but to restore it. In mid-1985, Peru ended an experiment with dollarization in its banking system dating from 1978, and consequently lost an important, if expensive, source of savings resources.

Indexation and dollarization are means of coping with price-level uncertainty. Where the money unit's future purchasing-power value is highly uncertain, contracting parties find it convenient to specify

126

future payments directly in purchasing power. There are powerful arguments that indexation and dollarization can help stabilization programs. Nevertheless, there are also solid grounds for the view that indexation and dollarization make inflation-feedback mechanisms more robust. That is, any inflationary shock tends to raise the price level more, and a price-level rise in any given period generates more inflationary pressure over subsequent periods, where indexation and dollarization are present.

An argument has sometimes been made that indexation relieves distortions created by inflation, enabling an economy to carry on much as though it had no inflation. Index-linked savings accounts, for example, maintain their purchasing power, regardless of the inflation rate. This chapter argues that indexation and dollarization relieve some distortions, but introduce and aggravate others. Brazil's disillusion arose from the view that the aggravated distortions mattered more than the alleviated distortions. Inevitably, with indexation in place, people perceived the distortions indexation aggravated more keenly than those it alleviated. Once indexation ended, and unaccustomed distortions appeared, the society concluded that these were worse, and so it restored indexation.

This chapter makes two interrelated arguments. First, indexation changes the nature of the inflation-feedback mechanism. Whether the mechanism becomes more robust depends on the economy's particular structure and circumstances; all the same, for various reasons, it probably does become more robust in most instances. Second, indexation changes the way that price-level uncertainty affects an economy. Indexation cannot remove the effects of price-level uncertainty: it relieves some of the consequences of uncertainty, but worsens others. Financial index-linking, for example, shifts the burden of price-level risk from lenders to borrowers.

Two distinctions are essential for further discussion. The first contrasts *ex post* and *ex ante* indexation. *Ex post* indexation is indexation as defined above: in principle, the periodic increases in money values of *ex post* index-linked financial assets are determined *directly after* price-index increases are recorded. In practice, for example, Brazil has adjusted "index-linked" assets with lags, and with different kinds of averages of previous price-index increases; occasionally it "purged" the index. Its principle, however, has been to adjust for inflation that actually occurred. In contrast, the future money values of *ex ante* index-linked financial assets are set *before* price-index increases are recorded, on the basis of the authorities' inflation projections.[2] Only *ex post* indexation qualifies as indexation—and hence as subject matter for this chapter—according to the definition above.

The second distinction differentiates indexation of (i) financial assets and other contracts, (ii) costs and prices, and (iii) accounting values, since each of these has a different economic significance. By definition, a price that is (genuinely) index-linked is fixed in purchasing-power units. Index-linking a price typically raises three issues: (i) Is it best to fix the price at all or to leave it to market forces?; (ii) If the price is to be fixed, is it best to fix it in money or purchasing-power units?; and (iii) Given the unit of account in which the price is fixed, how often and under what circumstances should it be adjusted? In contrast, no price fixing is involved *per se* when an asset or other contracted future payment is index-linked. Purchasing power is being used as the unit of account, but the value contracted could be determined freely or in any other way. Finally, accounting indexation involves the rules and conventions by which enterprises' profits and net worth are *measured*. Without directly affecting any transaction, it may nevertheless have powerful implications for economic behavior.

This chapter considers financial indexation, indexation of wages and prices, and accounting indexation in turn. It first reviews arguments for and against financial indexation and dollarization. It digresses to the question of why financial indexation has almost never appeared spontaneously, and then considers various arguments that availability of index-linked bonds can make macroeconomic policy more efficient. The chapter then turns to the issues raised generally by price indexation, and specifically by wage indexation (and escalation) and "crawling-peg" exchange rates. It then briefly introduces the issues associated with the role of indexation in taxation and in inflation accounting. The chapter concludes with comments on the "purging" of inflation indices and on the problems associated with ending indexation.

2   ADVANTAGES AND DRAWBACKS OF FINANCIAL INDEXATION AND DOLLARIZATION

The macroeconomic advantage of index-linked assets is that they maintain the incentive to save, despite price-level uncertainty. Where index-linked assets are not available, price-level uncertainty discourages saving. This is because money-denominated assets must offer yields high enough to compensate would-be savers not only for inflation they *expect*, but also for at least some of the inflation they *fear*. If money-asset yields are inadequate, financial savings stocks diminish: people consume more, or hold savings in real goods, foreign exchange, and other forms unavailable to domestic borrowers. The problem is that potential borrowers may be unwilling or unable to pay rates high enough to compensate for savers' expectations and fears. Either way, the financial transactions volume would diminish: the supply of savings would be deficient if rates are low; the demand for savings would be deficient if rates are high. Freely adjusting interest rates might move to some intermediate market-clearing value, but the volume of saving would be lower, all other things being equal, the higher is the degree of price-level uncertainty.

A purchasing-power unit of account enables savers and borrowers to agree on real rates of return that future inflation cannot affect. Price-level uncertainty would not then affect the incentive to save. A purchasing-power unit of account cannot neutralize price-level uncertainty entirely, however. It can only change the precise ways in which price-level uncertainty affects the economy. With inflation-proofed assets available, price-level uncertainty may make people less willing to hold money. Moreover, as index-linked assets grow in money terms with inflation, they create pressure for money-supply growth. Inflation adjustment on government obligations, for example, may increase the public sector's overall borrowing requirement. With the consequences of price-level uncertainty changed rather than eliminated, it is by no means clear that having index-linked financial assets actually improves macroeconomic performance. Financial indexation amounts to having two units of account, money and purchasing power, whose "exchange rate" is—by design—fluctuating and uncertain. This makes things better in some ways, but worse in others.

In theory, availability of index-linked financial assets need not make an economy's inflation-feedback mechanism more robust than it would otherwise be, but there are at least four reasons why it may in reality. First, if index-linked financial assets are available as an alternative, money holding becomes more sensitive to increases in price-level uncertainty. True, even with index-linked assets unavailable, rising price-level uncertainty would induce people to hold less wealth in money-denominated assets, but the alternatives—including real goods, real estate, and foreign exchange—would be variously illiquid, risky, perishable, and perhaps illegal.[3] Index-linked assets have none of these drawbacks. In this way, the availability of index-linked assets may contribute to a self-feeding "bear market" in money, effectively "greasing the skids" under the monetary unit.[4] It is impossible to say on theoretical grounds whether rising price-level uncertainty would be more inflationary with index-linked financial assets available. The availability of index-linked financial assets makes the inflation-feedback mechanism more robust on balance if and only if it increases the sensitivity of money demand to price-level uncertainty relatively more than it decreases the sensitivity of saving to price-level uncertainty.[5]

Second, any *unanticipated* price-level increase leaves index-linked financial-asset stocks larger after they earn adjustment and interest than they would have been if they were money-denominated. Aggregate real wealth and hence aggregate demand pressure will accordingly turn out higher than they otherwise would. This reasoning suggests that an unanticipated price-level increase should have a larger inflationary impact in an economy that has accumulated a large stock of index-linked assets than it would in an economy that has only recently introduced financial index-linking. For example, the larger accumulated stock of index-linked financial assets made Brazil's inflation-feedback mechanism more robust in the 1980s than it had been in the mid-1960s, when index-linking was first introduced. Indeed, as Brazil learned in 1983, the presence of a large stock of index-linked or—worse—dollar-denominated assets reduces the effectiveness of an unanticipated devaluation, since they keep the devaluation from reducing real wealth.[6]

Third, unanticipated inflation means that contracted index-linked payments must be larger than they would otherwise have been. To the extent the monetary authority "validates" contracted payments, it may permit larger money-supply growth than it otherwise would have. In particular, unanticipated inflation implies that the government's overall borrowing requirement will be larger, the larger is its outstanding stock of index-linked relative to money-denominated obligations.

Fourth, to the extent financial assets are index-linked rather than money-denominated, any unanticipated price-level surge increases overall income and shifts distribution of income and wealth in favor of financial-asset holders. If financial-asset holders' propensity to spend is relatively higher, aggregate-demand pressure would be relatively stronger. Since people with higher incomes presumably hold more fixed-return assets, unanticipated inflation would provide such people more income if their fixed-return assets are index-linked than if they are not. In general, larger proportions of higher incomes are saved. This suggests that an incipient inflation should induce a larger quantity of stabilizing saving if the fixed-return assets are index-linked. There are grounds for skepticism on this point, however. Even if they save *proportionally* more of their higher income, their higher income may nevertheless induce them to spend more than they otherwise would have. It is possible, moreover, that price-level uncertainty induces people to save *more* when their asset holdings are unprotected against inflation, for fear that their accumulated savings stocks would otherwise fall short of their saving objectives.

If inflation turns out lower than anticipated, of course, money-denominated instruments would have paid higher money interest rates than the *ex-post* returns on index-linked assets. Stabilization would occur more easily if financial instruments and contracts generally are index-linked rather than money-denominated, since asset stocks and borrowing requirements would turn out smaller. The monetary authority should come under less pressure to permit money growth. That is, it is best for an economy to have index-linked financial assets when inflation is likely to turn out lower than people had anticipated.

Co-existence in an economy of purchasing-power and monetary units implies that at least some economic entities assume open—i.e., unhedged, hence risky—balance-sheet positions, with one kind of unit on the asset side and the other on the liability side. Price-level uncertainty means that this increases the riskiness of entities so structured. The political pressure to have the government or the monetary authority assume such risk by backing purchasing-power obligations with the power to inflate is inevitably high. The government apart, many economic entities cannot easily choose their balance-sheet position. Firms may be told by commercial banks, for example, that they must accept dollar-denominated working-capital finance, perhaps because the banks accept dollar deposits and require dollar assets to hedge their balance sheets. Rather than do without credit, firms might reluctantly accept dollar-denominated finance. Unless they can contrive to have dollar-denominated cash, receivables, or inventories (e.g., by being exporters), they will have exposed balance-sheet positions (like importers who have domestic-currency receivables and foreign-exchange payables and have done no forward-market hedging). In theory, such firms could hedge the risk, but only if they could find another entity willing to undertake the risk at a reasonable price.

Uncertainty associated with balance-sheet exposure is one of the fundamental problems arising from financial index-linking and dollarization. It is an aspect of the inflation-feedback problem, through the danger that the balance-sheet exposure will be passed, explicitly or implicitly, to the government or the banking system.

3   ON THE VIRTUAL NON-EXISTENCE OF PRIVATE INDEX-LINKED OBLIGATIONS

Private firms have almost never issued index-linked obligations. This is intriguing: one would think firms could reduce finance costs by protecting creditors from price-level uncertainty. Some nations' legal and tax regimes effectively discriminate against private index-linked obligations, for a variety of reasons. In 1965, however, Brazil's "Capital Markets Law" removed all impediments to private financial indexation; nevertheless, private financial markets simply declined to use it. Two broad hypotheses might explain the absence of private index-linked obligations: (i) demand for index-linked debentures is more limited than conventional wisdom suggests, and (ii) the willingness to sell index-linked debentures is limited.[7]

If the supply of private index-linked obligations is large relative to demand for them, nominal assets would sell at a premium price (hence a lower yield). To minimize finance costs firms would then issue nominal debentures. According to one ingenious argument, demand for index-linked debentures might be limited because people perceive the risky, prospective real rates of return on corporate stock and nominal fixed-yield assets to be "negatively correlated." (This is simply the conventional wisdom that inflation is good for the stock market.) They might prefer to form hedged portfolios with stock and nominal fixed-yield assets; nominal debentures would accordingly be in demand.[8] One problem with this argument is that a premium in the price of one kind of debenture compared with the other should only be temporary: firms would issue the premium (i.e., low-yield) debenture and redeem outstanding issues of the other. As the relative supply outstanding of the premium debenture increased, the premium would disappear.

Indeed, the fundamental theory of financial-asset valuation, the "Modigliani–Miller" theorem, implies that firms gain nothing by obtaining index-linked rather than nominal finance. The theorem states that, in the absence of differential tax treatment, firms cannot reduce their finance costs by changing their mix of bond and stock issues.[9] On similar reasoning, it should also be true that no firm can change its overall finance cost by issuing index-linked rather than nominal debentures. Indeed, on this reasoning, it would seem that firms should ultimately be indifferent between taking on nominal or index-linked obligations.

A more convincing explanation of why firms prefer not to issue index-linked debentures is that managers universally believe they make prospective *real* profits or cash flows unacceptably riskier. The perceived riskiness of a firm's real net income depends, in complex ways, on the relative proportions of the firm's operating inflows and outflows, the risks attaching to each, and their correlations with the prospective outflows on index-linked or nominal debentures—all as viewed by the firm's management.[10] That is, as noted earlier, a firm that issues index-linked obligations not backed by index-linked assets is assuming a speculative position.

The non-existence of primary index-linked assets and income flows may accordingly be the underlying reason why firms do not issue index-linked debentures. Cash and receivables are nominal assets. (Index-linked receivables would be other firms' index-linked obligations.) Inventories and real capital assets may, in the aggregate, maintain real value, but relative-price dispersion makes it risky to regard any particular firm's inventories and capital as adequate backing for index-linked obligations: roughly fifty per cent of all prices, perhaps more, will fail to maintain pace with the price index over any given period.[11] An individual who undertook a index-linked obligation would be backing it with future real income—again, a risky proposition. The primary index-linked assets a firm could hold, it would seem, are government obligations, if any exist. Governments can credibly issue index-linked obligations, because they back them with their capacity to inflate.

One partial counter-example to the general rule that private entities prefer not to issue index-linked obligations has been housing finance. People have been willing to accept index-linked mortgage finance when they had no other option, and several Latin American nations— notably, Colombia and Chile, where annual inflation rates have remained between 10 and 30 per cent—have successfully developed index-linked mortgage credit systems. Brazil's experience illustrates some of the inherent difficulties, however.[12] The military government instituted a mixed public–private "Housing Finance System" in August 1964, hoping to promote more widespread home ownership. The system began using indexation in 1966, both for savings deposits—which received a state guarantee—and for mortgage balances. In 1966, the government established a new social security fund with index-linked contributor accounts, and applied the fund's resources in the housing-finance system. Index-linked mortgage balances were a problem for wage earners, however, because wages were fixed for one-year periods and, at least then, did not maintain pace with inflation. Beginning in 1966, the solution was to adjust monthly mortgage payments annually according to wages, leaving outstanding mortgage balances to adjust periodically several times a year with inflation. Monthly payments were applied first to interest, then amortization; if interest due exceeded the monthly payment, the difference was capitalized into the mortgage.

This solution was clearly imperfect. The possibilities that mortgage balances could grow in real, not only nominal, terms, and that the mortgage might not be fully paid at its term, discouraged potential borrowers. The system also created a problem for intermediaries, since deposit balances were index-linked. Although asset and liability stocks were both index-linked, real cash inflows from mortgage payments lagged behind when inflation was higher; cash-flow problems tended to develop to the extent inflation turned out high. The authorities made some detailed changes in the mortgage-payments adjustment system, but never quite resolved its inherent problems. The system grew well enough into the mid-1970s, although the government found it necessary to stimulate mortgage credit through tax incentives. The funds available to the system grew rapidly over the late 1960s and early 1970s: stocks of passbook savings, housing bonds, and social-security funds exceeded 8 per cent of GDP by 1973. Once inflation rates worsened in the early 1980s, however, the system—particularly its private intermediaries—encountered increasing difficulties. Cash-flow pressure and default problems intensified, and the system as a whole tended to become increasingly deficitary and illiquid.

4   INDEX-LINKED GOVERNMENT BONDS AND THE EFFECTIVENESS OF MACROECONOMIC POLICY

Several analysts have suggested that governments—even those of industrialized nations with mild inflation—could manage macroeconomic policy more effectively by issuing index-linked obligations. There are at least three basic arguments. First, where price-level uncertainty is high, governments could sell index-linked bonds at lower real interest rates than conventional nominal bonds. Second, to the extent their obligations are index-linked, governments effectively return part of the inflation tax to the public. This should leave them less inclined to inflate. Third, open-market operations would affect real economic activity more directly if outstanding government bonds are index-linked.

Where inflation is long-standing, public confidence in the authorities' determination and ability to stabilize understandably weakens. Even if the authorities enact what they consider effective stabilizing measures, the public's inflation anticipations may nonetheless remain worse than the authorities believe warranted. If the government must still issue new obligations to repay maturing obligations or to fund a deficit, financial markets would demand high nominal interest rates. To the extent inflation actually does fall, the government would pay high *ex post* real interest, which might then jeopardize stabilization. If government bonds cannot be index-linked, the authorities may have to choose between issuing bonds at exorbitant nominal interest rates (which advertise financial markets' skepticism) or issuing money. Alternatively, financial markets should be willing to buy index-linked bonds at reasonable real interest rates, since the yield would be independent of price-level uncertainty. This would place less pressure on the government's future real interest bill.

Brazil's experience in the latter half of the 1960s supports the soundness of this reasoning (see Baer-Beckerman 1980). The military regime that took power in March 1964 issued index-linked bonds beginning in 1965 as part of its gradualist stabilization program (see Chapter 6). (The index-linked bonds carried an exchange-rate clause because Brazilian savers feared massive devaluation.) Since the authorities reduced the public sector deficit and raised repressed public-enterprise prices gradually, inflation declined slowly. Inflationary uncertainty would therefore have made it prohibitively costly to finance the continuing deficit with conventional bonds. Sales of index-linked bonds enabled the government to reduce reliance on money creation to finance the deficit. It was important that the government's general policy thrust was gradually stabilizing: annual inflation fell from 90–100 per cent in 1964 and 1965 toward 20–30 per cent by the early 1970s. It was also helpful that total internal debt was still relatively low in the wake of the 1963–4 inflation, when there had been no index-linking. In 1968, the stock of index-linked financial assets, including index-linked savings accounts and Treasury bonds, constituted just under 7 per cent of GDP; conventional money-denominated assets, including narrowly-defined money, amounted to 18.3 per cent.[13]

In the early 1970s, Milton Friedman cited Brazil's experiment when he advocated that the United States government issue index-linked bonds.[14] By ensuring that the government returned part of the inflation tax to the public, he argued, such bonds would diminish the government's incentive to use inflationary finance. To the extent its outstanding debt is index-linked, a government could not reduce its real value with a burst of inflation. (This argument effectively assumes, of course, that the government is the sole beneficiary of the inflation tax.) Friedman's argument was similar to the Brazilian government's motive for issuing index-linked debt: the government expected to pay less real interest on it precisely because it was inflation-proof.

Although having its outstanding debt index-linked removes some of government's benefit from inflation, it would not dissuade a government entirely from using inflationary finance. Suppose a government may finance itself only by issuing money or index-linked bonds. Suppose it runs a non-interest deficit of zero, but has debt outstanding in the form of index-linked bonds. For simplicity suppose real GDP does not grow. To finance the (real) interest, the government must use a mix of money and bond issues. If it uses only money, inflation results, but the bond stock grows at the same rate as nominal GDP, thereby preserving the debt–GDP ratio. If it issues bonds, on the other hand, the real debt stock grows by the real interest rate, and the debt–GDP ratio increases accordingly. That is, policy-makers still face a trade-off between more inflation or a higher debt–GDP ratio. Whether the debt is nominal or index-linked, the larger the stock and the higher the real interest rate, the more acute the trade-off—that is, the larger is the interest bill to be financed.

Earlier, in 1963, James Tobin had argued that, by dealing in index-linked government bonds, the monetary authorities could make open-market operations "more efficient," enabling them to attain given quantitative policy objectives with smaller policy shifts.[15] His intricate argument had two underlying premises. First, open-market operations influence capital formation, hence economic activity, through market valuation of corporate stock: higher valuation makes it easier for corporations to issue stock. Second, given an economy's asset-holding preferences and anticipations about the future, valuation of corporate stock can be influenced by the quantities of and yields on money, short-term and long-term government debt. This means that, by changing outstanding supplies of government and central-bank obligations, open-market operations could influence capital formation and aggregate demand.[16] Tobin then argued that any monetary-policy move should influence stock valuation more, the more people considered stock a "substitute" for bonds, and the less they considered stock a substitute for money or bills. Since financial markets would consider index-linked government bonds closer substitutes than nominal bonds for stock, and weaker substitutes for money and bills, index-linked bonds would presumably permit more efficient monetary policy.

Tobin's argument is debatable on various grounds. Index-linked bonds might not always be closer substitutes for stock than nominal bonds; at some times and in some places, nominal bonds, even short-term government bills and money, might be closer substitutes than long-term bonds for stock. An intricate argument can be made that even if the public considers index-linked bonds closer substitutes for stock than nominal bonds, monetary policy could still be less effective with index-linked bonds.[17] Perhaps most important, in many economies—particularly developing economies—capital formation might not be significantly influenced by valuation of corporate shares. The role of monetary policy might then be more to influence short-term interest rates and financial conditions, and the usefulness of longer-term bonds—nominal or index-linked—might be quite limited.

Again, Brazil's experience is instructive on these points. In the late 1960s Brazil's Central Bank (which the government had formed from units of the government-owned Bank of Brazil in 1965) attempted to carry out open-market operations using index-linked government obligations. This proved impractical: Brazil's "money markets" maintained a short-term focus, and preferred to deal in short-term conventional nominal instruments. Accordingly, in 1970 the government—which had attained a budget surplus by then—issued nominal Treasury Bills for the Central Bank to use in open-market operations.

By 1973 Brazil's gradualist policies had reduced annual inflation below 30 per cent. Conventional nominal instruments were almost 25 per cent of GDP, while index-linked instruments were more than 16 per cent of GDP. In 1974, however, higher world oil prices and supply pressures resulting from uneven growth patterns in the 1969–73 "miracle" years pushed annual inflation up toward 40 per cent. Holdings of nominal instruments (including narrow money) declined to 20.7 per cent of GDP—undoubtedly affected by the availability of index-linked instruments, which rose to 18 per cent of GDP. Short-term interest rates on nominal assets rose, largely because of the competitive pressure of index-linked assets. A series of money-market crises occurred in 1974, 1975 and 1976, essentially because intermediaries that had funded longer-term asset portfolios with short-term liabilities found they had to renew their liabilities at rising interest rates. The monetary authority had to interrupt the struggle against inflation to permit liquidity expansion.[18] Inflation continued on through the second half of the 1970s within a range of 25 to 40 per cent per year. Real annual GDP growth remained between 3 and 5 per cent, however, because the government secured foreign loans to finance oil imports and an ambitious public-sector investment program.

In 1980 inflation surged again, mainly because of the 1979 world oil-price increases and a sharp devaluation in December 1979. At first the government tried to prevent financial indexation from catalyzing inflation-feedback pressure by limiting it over 1980 to 45 per cent, about half what the inflation rate turned out to be. This approach proved inflationary itself, because it discouraged savings. The authorities resumed full indexation in 1981, when they deliberately threw the economy into recession to deal with the deepening external-debt crisis. With price-level uncertainty rising, index-linked bonds again became desirable, which now helped propagate inflation-feedback pressure by discouraging money demand. The price level accelerated as net exports swung from deficit toward surplus.

Again, the competition of index-linking subjected interest rates on nominal assets to intense pressure. Financial activity gravitated to the "overnight" funds market, since longer periods were subject to deepening uncertainty: financial institutions perfected their practice of funding portfolios of public obligations with funds borrowed "overnight." Fluctuating, but generally rising interest rates, together with a rising overall government-debt stock, in turn intensified the pressure on the public borrowing requirement. The problem was compounded after February 1983, when another sharp devaluation activated the government bonds' exchange-rate clauses and increased the outstanding bond stock at a stroke by a corresponding magnitude.

These elements of Brazil's experience suggest that issuing index-linked government bonds can contribute to the success of a serious "gradualist" stabilization program. As the stock of index-linked debt accumulates, however, the importance of inflation in the overall public deficit increases, and the trade-off between inflation and an increasing debt-GDP burden becomes increasingly acute.[19] To the extent the debt is index-linked, its holders are protected against inflation; but the opposite side of the coin is precisely that the government loses the possibility of using a burst of inflation to reduce the claims on itself. In this perspective, index-linked bonds encapsulate a fundamental dilemma of high inflation: it is fair, even efficient, to protect people from inflation; but to the extent the economy is protected from inflation, inflation will tend to persist.

5 INDEX-LINKING OF PRICES

By definition, an "index-linked" price is adjusted periodically so its ratio to a price index immediately following each adjustment remains constant. If the adjustments are sufficiently frequent, the real price remains roughly fixed. If the interval between adjustments is relatively long, the real price diminishes over each interval with inflation, then "spikes" back up with the new adjustment. All other things being equal, the higher the inflation rate and the longer the interval between adjustments, the lower and the more variable—and hence the more subject to price-level uncertainty—the average real price will be. A price adjusted frequently may be described as genuinely index-linked; less frequent adjustment is better characterized as "escalation."

Suppose the price in question is adjusted sufficiently frequently that its purchasing-power value is roughly fixed. (The criterion of "sufficiently frequently" depends on the inflation rate, of course: the higher it is, the more the real price varies over each interval.) Two questions arise at this level of abstraction. First, does price indexation so defined improve economic efficiency?; and second, does price indexation make the inflation-feedback mechanism more robust? The answers to these questions are, respectively, "sometimes" and "probably."

For economic efficiency, there are at least two essential considerations. First, neo-classical theory holds that efficiency is maximized in any array of markets when prices can adjust flexibly to equilibrate supply and demand. Second, however, steady prices facilitate planning and make it easier to manage enterprises and household budgets. Fixed prices presumably run counter to allocative efficiency, even if they are fixed in purchasing-power terms. In reality, however, the practical alternative to an index-linked price may be a fixed nominal price that is adjusted frequently, perhaps unpredictably and erratically. For example, prices charged by public enterprises are often held ("for political reasons") at low levels, then raised suddenly when they lag too far. In cases like these, it may improve efficiency to fix prices in purchasing-power rather than in money units.

All other things being equal, steady prices are better than fluctuating prices. Index-linked prices are superior in this regard, on the view that what matters is that *real* prices be steady. Inflation is likely to make any fixed nominal price highly variable in real terms, declining with the real value of money except when, from time to time, it jumps upward. It is best that prices rise slowly and steadily rather than occasionally, unpredictably and traumatically.

There are two important caveats, however. First, it obviously matters a great deal whether the real price has been fixed at something near a market-clearing level; if not, indexation perpetuates a significant market distortion. Second, to an enterprise or household what may matter is not whether a particular real *price* is steady, but whether the associated profit or cash flow is steady. A firm or household may find its real profit or cash flow made *more* variable and uncertain when one of its real prices is made more certain through indexation. For example, if a household's bus fares are index-linked every month but its wages are index-linked every six months, high inflation could cause its cash flow to vary considerably over time.[20]

It may seem all too obvious that price indexation strengthens the inflation-feedback mechanism: once the general price level rises, an index-linked price rises automatically, and thus directly and indirectly raises the price level still further. Again, however, it is uncertain whether price indexation worsens the inflation-feedback mechanism. A particular price or price array might rise by more in response to a price-level rise if it were not index-linked. The inflation-feedback mechanism might actually be less robust with some prices index-linked. True, the inflation-feedback mechanism must be more robust with some prices index-linked than it would be if these same prices were fixed in nominal terms. Again, though, it is doubtful that any prices could remain permanently fixed in nominal terms in a context of serious inflation: sooner or later, inevitably, prices supposedly fixed in nominal terms will jump.

6   WAGE INDEXATION

In principle, nominal wages could be adjusted upward as frequently as index-linked financial values. Wages are rarely adjusted so frequently, however; that is, genuine wage "indexation," implying a fixed real wage rate, is unusual. The expression "wage indexation" usually refers, accordingly, to something closer to wage escalation. In most economies, wage rates in "formal" labor markets are characteristically governed by periodically renewed contracts at the national, industry, firm, or individual level. At contract renewal, wages could be dictated by the government or determined through negotiation. (Contracts at levels above the individual level generally set percentage increases for categories of worker, allowing individual workers to benefit from wage increases through promotion.) Between contract renewals, wages may be readjusted in nominal terms according to consumer prices: this would constitute "escalation" or, loosely speaking, "indexation." The longer the period between adjustments and the higher the inflation rate, the more the average real wage over the period will differ from the real wage immediately following adjustment (see Chapter 4).

If wages are set through negotiation, the extent of escalation inevitably influences the negotiated base wage. The more frequent the escalation and the lower the degree of price-level uncertainty, the more certain the real wage will be *ex ante*. In general, workers should be willing to accept a lower real wage in exchange for greater certainty, i.e., more frequent escalation. The situation of managements, however, is somewhat more intricate. Escalated wages may subject firms' cash flows and profits to higher uncertainty, since a price-level surge could increase a firm's nominal wage bill but not its output price.

The questions wage escalation (or indexation) pose are broadly similar to those posed by price indexation in general: does it improve the cause of economic efficiency, and does it make the inflation-feedback mechanism more robust? As with price indexation generally, it is impossible to say generally whether wage escalation improves economic efficiency. A relatively steady real wage is an inherently good thing—subject to the caveat that it may make firms' real cash flows and profits more uncertain.[21] Once fixed, as with any fixed price, the real wage at any moment is unlikely to be the market-clearing real wage—that is, the wage at which supply of and demand for labor are equilibrated.[22] As time passes, the real wage may move farther from or closer to the market-clearing real wage, depending on how the economy evolves. Firms may be inclined to dismiss or to hire workers, depending on how the real wage evolves in relation to other price and market conditions.

Some analysts have made the following argument (or variants of it). Suppose wages are index-linked—approximately speaking, fixed in real terms. If inflation occurs because of money-supply growth with a minimum of relative-price dispersion, real costs and prices will presumably remain unchanged; firms should then wish neither to hire nor to dismiss workers. If inflation occurs because of a "real" shock—e.g., "supply-side shock" like an increase in real production costs, such as an energy-price increase—labor productivity would diminish at the same time; since real wages cannot fall if they are index-linked, firms would incline to dismiss workers. That is, wage escalation assures steady real wages, at the cost of making it more difficult for the economy to adjust to unfavorable real "shocks." Without escalation, inflation would reduce the real wage toward—if not below—the point at which firms would maintain the current employment level.

Where wages are escalated, whether through labor contracts or government regulation, the inflation-feedback mechanism is assuredly more *automatic*; whether it is more robust depends on how wage increases would have been managed had they not been escalated. A labor union might demand a large nominal wage increase in response to price-level uncertainty, where it might have been willing to accept a lower but more certain increase in expected real wages with escalation. Where management can persuade labor to restrain wage demands without escalation, the inflation-feedback mechanism would be less robust; otherwise, escalation may actually turn out less inflationary.

All other things being equal, increases in nominal prime cost reduce aggregate supply[23] and increase firms' (nominal) credit requirements. Assuming that wage earners have relatively lower propensities to save, wage increases tend generally to increase aggregate demand. All other things being equal, larger wage increases are, *per se*—quite apart from the issue of whether they are justified and appropriate—always more inflationary than smaller wage increases. The answer to the question of whether wage escalation is "inflationary" depends on whether the alternative wage-setting method would have produced smaller wage increases. With escalation, inflation increases nominal wages, and this in turn generates fresh inflationary pressure.[24] Without escalation, however, inflation also induces wage increases; it is unclear whether these would be higher than they would have been with escalation.

Either way, the important empirical issue is whether the wage–price cycle would tend to converge or explode, e.g., whether a 10 per cent rise in the wage level leads to, say, an 11 per cent or a 9 per cent rise in the price level before the next wage increase. The answer depends in part, of course, on how other all other policies and economic behavior are assumed to operate.

7 CRAWLING-PEG EXCHANGE-RATE POLICIES AND DOLLARIZATION

A "crawling-peg" exchange-rate policy entails frequent devaluation to maintain the parity of domestic prices and international prices converted by the exchange rate.[25] Such a policy presumably neutralizes the effect of domestic inflation on the relative prices that influence external economic relationships. If domestic inflation makes devaluation inevitable, the argument goes, better to devalue slowly and frequently rather than in one politically and economically traumatic blow in the context of an external-payments crisis.[26]

Where inflation is significant, there is a strong efficiency argument for a crawling-peg policy, particularly if the alternative is a fixed nominal rate. A crawling-peg exchange rate should minimize the variation in the "real-effective exchange rate," defined as the purchasing-power value of the exchange rate. Business decisions should, in principle, be easier when the real-effective exchange rate is steadied within a narrow band. Again, however, particular firms' real cash and profit flows may or may not be steadier; in general, though, one would suppose that exporters' cash flows are made more steady if the price of the dollars they earn rises at least as fast as their costs.

In general, crawling-peg exchange rates probably make the inflation-feedback mechanism more robust. The alternatives might be more inflationary, however. An unsustainably overvalued fixed exchange rate, for example, would inevitably be devalued, and that might prove more inflationary than steady, crawling-peg devaluation. Any devaluation, crawling-peg devaluation not excepted, is inflationary *in itself*. Again, as with wage indexation, the question is whether the feedback process converges or diverges, i.e., whether a 10 per cent increase in the domestic-currency price of foreign goods and services by itself generates, say, a 9 or an 11 per cent domestic price-level increase. This is an empirical issue, depending, *inter alia*, on the real exchange-rate level the crawling peg maintains. A crawling-peg exchange rate is a fixed real price for foreign goods and services. Inevitably, the more devalued the exchange rate is maintained, the stronger the inflationary effect is bound to be.

If the alternative to crawling-peg devaluation is a freely floating exchange rate, the comparison is somewhat different. A freely floating exchange rate would presumably be more efficient than any alternative policy, since it would adjust to equilibrate supply and demand. The crawling-peg exchange rate would be steadier in real-effective terms, however; a floating exchange rate could be subject to short-term volatility. Many analysts assume that a floating rate would have the same general tendency over time as a rate devaluing according to a crawling peg, but this is not certain. If the exchange rate is "undervalued," for example, in the sense that foreign exchange is in excess supply, a crawling-peg policy would preserve the undervaluation; a floating exchange rate would appreciate and therefore be less inflationary.

In general, anticipated devaluation induces people to shift wealth into foreign exchange. Domestic rates of return are affected by anticipated rates of return on competing foreign-exchange assets. Financial institutions may accept deposits denominated in foreign exchange, or require clients to accept loans denominated in foreign currency. From this perspective, the crawling-peg exchange rate policy has the advantage of maintaining a steady degree of competitive pressure on real domestic interest rates. If devaluation occurs less frequently but more haphazardly, devaluation expectations could vary considerably—from zero in the days or weeks just following a large devaluation to high values heavily influenced by uncertainty in the days leading up to devaluation. Pressure on domestic interest rates would vary accordingly.

The argument for a crawling-peg exchange rate in an inflationary context is essentially an argument for a policy rule to stabilize the real-effective exchange rate. Once again, economic efficiency calls for two things: (i) a flexible, market-clearing price, and (ii) a reasonably steady real price. The first criterion favors a floating exchange rate policy, and favors a crawling-peg policy over a fixed—or jumping— exchange rate. The narrowness and volatility of many developing nations' foreign-exchange markets implies that complete exchange-rate liberalization poses the risk of excessive instability, however, so that the second criterion favors a crawling-peg policy over a floating rate. A crawling-peg policy may therefore be a sensible compromise between a free-floating and a fixed exchange rate. Nevertheless, it is essential to choose an appropriate real-effective exchange rate to preserve through the crawling-peg adjustment. If the exchange rate remains severely undervalued, it becomes a standing source of inflationary pressure; if severely overvalued, it may lead to international-reserve loss. Either way, policy-makers are sure to want to retain the option of adjusting the real-effective exchange rate as conditions warrant.

8 INDEX-LINKING AND TAXATION

Indexation can be applied to various aspects of taxation, including
(i) progressive income-tax brackets, (ii) the computations involving
taxable interest income, and (iii) tax payments due to prevent erosion
through the "collection lag."

(i) By definition, a progressive income-tax schedule applies higher
percentage rates to higher taxable amounts. If tax "brackets" are
expressed in monetary units, rising prices lift incomes into higher
brackets, thus raising the overall tax rate. Such "bracket drift" can
be corrected by index-linking the tax brackets.[27] Indexation of tax
brackets makes sense where there is any inflation at all, if the brackets
would otherwise remain unchanged for many years. One possible
objection is that bracket drift is an "automatic stabilizer": higher
taxation caused by bracket drift reduces aggregate demand and hence
inflationary pressure. There are at least three responses to this
objection. First, if brackets are not index-linked, inflation lifts tax
rates permanently; unless prices actually fell, tax rates would rise even
when the inflation *rate* diminished. Second, as "supply-side" economists have often noted, higher income-tax rates affect production
incentives. Employees, having to pay higher income tax, will try to
pass this increased cost to firms, making wage levels higher than they
would be otherwise.

Third, a tax-based automatic stabilizer could be added to an index-
linked tax schedule, if this were considered desirable. Higher inflation
rates could, for example, trigger higher income-tax rates. This should
induce no bracket drift because tax rates would rise only if inflation
rose, and could fall as inflation diminished. A tax-rate increase might
still reduce aggregate supply in the short term, but should not do so for
the longer term.

(ii) Something like indexation could easily be applied to correct a
problem inflation causes for taxation of interest income (and financial
yields generally). The part of any nominal interest rate that compensates for corrosion of principal through inflation should not be treated
as taxable interest income. In effect, the inflation component simply
needs to be removed from interest income in calculating the taxable
base: if x is the *ex post* inflation rate and n the interest rate, the
proportion (x/n) of the interest income ought to be deductible.

While a number of nations, including the United States beginning in 1986, have index-linked income-tax brackets, less attention has been given to the deductibility of the inflation component of interest. Many income-tax systems permit deductibility of interest *payments*, at least for home mortgages, and perhaps to some degree this compensates for the unfairness inherent in taxing total interest income. (Of course, if the inflation component of interest *receipts* were deductible, consistency would imply that only the real component of interest *payments* should be deductible.)

(iii) Indexation could also help compensate for the collection lag. Taxes are typically paid some time after the "taxable events" that gave rise to them (see Chapter 3). The higher the inflation over this time interval, the lower the government's real revenue. In principle, this problem could be solved directly by index-linking the tax due, so the government receives the full real revenue corresponding to the tax. Where the collection lag is relatively short—under thirty days—true indexation is impractical, because payment is due before the inflation rate can be calculated. The principle could be approximated, however, by applying an estimated daily inflation rate.

Where the collection lag is longer—say, an annual income tax due in April of the following year—indexation of income on a monthly basis may be the only fair basis for the tax calculation where inflation is high. Unfortunately, the calculation can become quite intricate. Suppose 1991 taxes are due on April 15, 1992. The tax due on each paycheck during 1991 ought, in principle, to be index-linked for purposes of calculating the tax balance due on April 15. Each 1991 paycheck would have to be reflated by a different percentage—a larger percentage for January 1991 paychecks, a smaller percentage for December 1991 paychecks. In practice, the tax authorities might apply a general average index to all amounts withheld during 1991 (although this would penalize or reward people according to the particular pattern of their paychecks over a given year).

Tax-withholding practices introduce further intricacies. If taxes due are index-linked, amounts withheld also ought to be index-linked. Thus, when the tax balance due is computed, before subtracting it from the total tax, the amount withheld ought to be reflated to the current price level. The possibilities for manipulation are considerable, however: by announcing a high indexation rate for withheld taxes, the authorities reduce the tax balance due on April 15; *vice versa* if they announce a low rate of indexation.[28] Some nations with high inflation rates—e.g., Brazil—moved, in some desperation, to quarterly and even monthly tax declarations to avoid the problems caused by indexation over longer time periods.

There is a strong case for index-linking tax payments in arrears, where inflation is significant. At a minimum, sensible tax administration requires that taxes in arrears carry interest equal to the risk-free interest rate in the local financial market, to discourage people from earning interest on accumulated tax arrears. Indexation would be appropriate in any economy where index-linked financial assets are generally available.

9   INFLATION AND ACCOUNTING CONVENTIONS

The objective of inflation accounting is to prevent inflation from distorting reporting of income, costs, profits, assets, liabilities, and capitalization, to ensure that they closely approximate the true economic magnitudes. For example, consider the familiar depreciation problem. Under conventional accounting methods, fixed assets are depreciated on the basis of their original purchase value—"historic cost." As a result, the depreciation reserve will be insufficient for replacement when the asset depreciates completely, because inflation will have lifted the asset's current money price above the historic cost. Having depreciated insufficiently, the firm will have overstated its profit flows, which may have led in turn to excessive dividend and tax payments. (Baer and Simonsen (1965) described this "profit-illusion" problem.)

Ideally, firms should revalue fixed assets in each balance sheet according to current replacement value and depreciate accordingly. This would maintain a depreciation fund sufficient to finance replacement. Keeping track of replacement costs (and documenting them for the tax authorities) is difficult in practice. Besides, firms might not want to replace all their fixed assets with similar assets. A more practical solution, then, would be to permit firms to index-link fixed-asset values. This should ensure maintenance of a roughly adequate depreciation reserve and prevent significant over-reporting of profits, dividends, and taxes.[29]

Apart from the depreciation problem, it is essential to compare real values when comparing balance sheets at two different dates. Where taxation depends on comparison of balance-sheet values at two different dates, for example, indexation is appropriate. For example, it is important to track the real value of working capital (short-term assets less short-term liabilities): Brazilian tax regulations permit some deduction from profits to reconstitute real working capital. More generally, "inflation accounting" is essential to take account of any inflation, even at the mild rates of the advanced industrial economies.[30]

Inflation accounting should improve economic efficiency, on the view that anything that improves information quality helps economic efficiency. Hard-pressed tax authorities tend to believe inflation accounting reduces measured profits, hence reduces tax revenues. Nevertheless, it should be anti-inflationary in practice: to the extent it prevents over-statement of profits, it forestalls excessive dividend and tax payments, which firms are likely to attempt to meet by reducing saving and by making demands on the credit system.

10 OBSERVATIONS ON "PURGING" AND ON PHASING OUT A PURCHASING-POWER UNIT OF ACCOUNT

Policy-makers have occasionally "purged" or "edited" inflation-adjustment indices. In the mid-1970s, for example, Brazil's authorities occasionally purged "accidental" price increases from the adjustment index, to prevent their contributing to inflation-feedback pressure. They used two arguments to justify the practice. The first was that indexation should reflect only price-level increases resulting from excess money supply, not from diminished aggregate supply. Thus, the argument went, if a crop failure raises grain prices, the index used for financial indexation should not incorporate the resulting price-level rise: the crop failure made goods more scarce, and the price rise reflects the change in real conditions. One reply to this argument was that a crop failure ought to induce a relative-price shift, not a price-level increase. In any case, there is no *a priori* reason why indexation should not reflect reduced aggregate supply as well as excess money supply. (A government could, if it wished, issue obligations explicitly linked to the money supply rather than to a price index.)

The second argument was that, if a "real shock" in a given market raises real prices, some expenditure reduction might occur in response. The expenditure weights of the index would then be inappropriate for the current period: purging would be justified on the grounds that expenditure on the commodity in question is really a smaller proportion of total expenditure than the index weights reflect. (In principle, price-index weights could be adjusted to conform with changing expenditure patterns, but in practice the technical survey problems are too formidable.)

A better approach than purging supply-related price increases might be to defer incorporating such price increases in the index. Thus, suppose the price index rises over a January–March quarter by 10 per cent, of which, the authorities judge, 4 percentage points resulted from supply shocks. The authorities could decide then to set the January–March adjustment at 7 per cent, and add a percentage point to each of the year's remaining three quarterly adjustments. On the whole, however, precisely because doing so is inevitably arbitrary, the authorities are probably best off not meddling with an index. If indexation is in use, it is best to preserve public confidence in the procedure.

Suppose a nation resolves to end an experiment with indexation or dollarization. The first question is whether to end it gradually or from one day to the next. Ending it at a stroke means converting index-linked assets to monetary-unit assets at one moment: all previously index-linked government bonds, savings accounts, debentures, henceforth pay a fixed nominal interest rate. Unless the inflation rate—more precisely, inflationary uncertainty—has fallen very low at the moment chosen, such an approach is likely to produce some financial disarray as wealth-holders reshuffle their portfolios. Unless the expected inflation rate and associated uncertainty fall sharply—say, through a simultaneous price freeze—they will insist on sharply higher nominal interest rates or move their wealth into the stock market, commodities or foreign exchange. Particular financial enterprises whose funding had depended on their offering inflation protection may either suffer heavy withdrawals or have to raise interest rates sharply.

Alternatively, the authorities could proceed gradually. They could maintain outstanding index-linking contracts, but issue no new government index-linked obligations, and perhaps gradually repurchase those outstanding. Index-linked assets should appreciate in value as they become increasingly scarce—except in the event that de-indexation so succeeds in reducing price-level uncertainty that index-linked assets lose their appeal.

In the February 1986 "Cruzado Plan," Brazil combined "once-and-for-all" de-indexation with a price freeze, the aim being simultaneously to end indexation and to make it unnecessary. The authorities allowed indexation to continue—in somewhat diluted form—only for savings accounts in the Housing Finance System, which might otherwise have suffered excessive withdrawals. When the stock market reopened after a brief holiday, it rose sharply, mainly because wealth-holders sought stocks as inflation hedges. The dependence of financial institutions, including commercial banks, on holdings of index-linked government obligations proved more important than the authorities had realized before the Cruzado Plan. The price freeze failed well before the end of 1986. Nominal interest rates spiralled up dramatically between November 1986 and January 1987, and public demand for restoration of indexation—as a means of coping with price-level uncertainty—became irresistible.

Complete elimination of financial indexation may be neither necessary nor desirable. It may be advisable to discourage indexation of shorter-term assets, but not for longer-term assets. Price-level uncertainty matters more for longer-term assets, while shorter-term assets compete more closely with money. A gradualist de-indexation strategy could include longer intervals between indexation adjustments, obliging people to hold assets for longer periods in order to benefit from indexation.[31] Passbook savings accounts might be adjusted on a single date each year, providing price-level adjustment only for minimum money balances between adjustments.[32] The point of this approach would be to reserve price-level adjustment for savings stocks held for longer terms, and to remunerate short-term savings in such a way that they more closely resemble money—so that index-linked savings instruments do not compete with money in short-term portfolios.

One de-indexation proposal suggests a transition period of several weeks, during which *all* financial assets—*including* money—would be index-linked. Thereafter, the purchasing-power unit would become a conventional nominal monetary unit (see Arida and Lara-Resende 1985). This would resolve the "two units of account" problem directly: all financial assets would be denominated in purchasing power during the transition period. That is, de-indexation would take place by first converting nominal to index-linked assets, then converting all index-linked into nominal assets, rather than directly converting index-linked into nominal assets. Prices could be index-linked—i.e., fixed in real terms—during the transition period. One problem of the proposal is its sophistication: people would probably not understand a dramatic program of de-indexation and price stability that transitionally increased the scope of indexation, making it impractical politically.[33]

11 CONCLUSION

Financial indexation changes the way in which price-level uncertainty affects financial contracts. It cannot make price-level uncertainty irrelevant, however. Price-level uncertainty makes any conventional money-denominated contract risky for both parties: the receiving party fears high inflation, the paying party fears low inflation. An index-linked contract may worsen the risk for the paying party, whose assets and income flows may not be guaranteed to maintain their purchasing-power; it should mitigate the risk for the receiving party, except to the extent the paying party is likelier to default. This probably explains why private economic entities prefer not to issue index-linked obligations. Governments can issue index-linked obligations, but this is because they ultimately back them with the capacity to inflate.

The various forms of indexation and dollarization affect the functioning of a real economy in many ways. Beyond the theoretical points, however, the issues are essentially empirical. Whether indexation makes an economy more efficient, or more inflationary, depends on particular circumstances and on the alternatives to indexation. In examining experience, it is important to remember that it is impossible to know how the economy in question might have behaved had it not used indexation. Brazil has had severe inflation with indexation; its inflation might have been worse without indexation. Accordingly, to understand how economies behave with and without indexation, economic analysis needs not only to examine actual experience but also to simulate well-specified economic models representing the alternatives. This is formidably difficult. To represent the difference that financial indexation makes, dynamic simulation models must incorporate the effects of people's price-level uncertainty on asset-holding patterns, with and without indexation, and then—somehow—represent the dynamic effects of inflation outcomes on people's price-level uncertainty.

9 Recent "Heterodox" Stabilization Experience: Argentina, Israel and Brazil, 1985–9[1]

1 INTRODUCTION: "HETERODOX" STABILIZATION PROGRAMS

Where inflation has been chronic and severe, sharply restrictive monetary and fiscal policies taken alone—"slamming on the brakes"—are likely to engender widespread bankruptcy, recession and unemployment, for several reasons. Firms tend to purchase labor, finance, and other inputs on contract: the inflation expectations implicit in contracts outstanding when a shock occurs will exceed actual inflation following the shock, leaving firms' real costs high relative to real output prices. Furthermore, monetary stringency may leave aggregate means of payment insufficient to validate outstanding contracts. Firms may respond to such a shock by cutting production, staff, wages, or input purchases. In addition, higher taxes and reduced government expenditures have direct and multiplier effects on economic activity.

Worse, an economy with lengthy inflation experience is likely to have powerful inflation-feedback, or "inertial" mechanisms. Thus, fiscal and monetary stringency notwithstanding, inflationary momentum is likely to persist. Firms that possess monopoly power and sell in markets characterized by inelastic demand, or retain access to as much credit as they need even after the credit supply is reduced, are likely to raise output prices to cover costs governed by "old" contracts. Even after tightening policy, a monetary authority may find itself under intense pressure to allow liquidity creation to forestall widespread bankruptcy.

If the stabilization effort includes devaluation, there will be additional inflationary pressure. Devaluation directly increases tradeable goods' prices, and places indirect pressure on prices generally. In addition, it encourages sale of foreign exchange to the central bank, and so creates additional expansionary pressure on the money supply. If the monetary authority attempts "to sterilize" the money expansion, the stock of public-sector debt outstanding increases, increasing interest rates and deepening the tendency to recession. Experience of devaluation induces expectations of and uncertainty regarding further devaluation, adding to the pressure to raise interest rates.

External and domestic public-sector indebtedness has become the core of the stabilization problem for many inflationary economies, notably Argentina and Brazil. Devaluation and higher interest rates increase real public debt service, increasing the public-sector borrowing requirement (PSBR), thereby complicating the stabilization effort. Argentina's quasi-fiscal mechanism was a case in point: Argentina's central bank created money to pay interest on commercial-bank reserves (i.e., central-bank debt to commercial banks), at rates linked to deposit rates. In October 1987 the deposit rates were liberalized: in determining them, financial markets took account of expectations and uncertainty regarding not only inflation, but devaluation as well. Debt and money creation came therefore to be linked to inflationary expectations and uncertainty in a feedback loop.

Inflationary expectations, price-level uncertainty and the relative-price dispersion produced by inflation figure in the processes that propagate inflation forward through time. Inflationary expectations and uncertainty make people unwilling to hold assets denominated in the currency unit generally and money in particular. A diminished disposition to hold money reduces a stabilization program's margin for error. Suppose, for example, that the foreign-exchange inflow is US$50 million rather than US$40 million as originally programmed in the first month of a stabilization program: the excess would clearly be more damaging if the initial monetary base were US$100 million rather than US$1 billion. Relative-price dispersion combined with "downward price stickiness"—in part the consequence of expectations that inflation will recur sooner or later—also induces inflationary pressure: if a price array is out of equilibrium, but prices cannot fall, there will be powerful pressure to create money, hence allow all nominal prices to rise at different rates, to restore equilibrium.

The argument for, combining "orthodox" fiscal and monetary stringency with "unorthodox" contract revision and controls on prices, wages, and other costs is that the "unorthodox" aspects of such "heterodox" programs components relieve inflation feedback, thereby making the orthodox policies more effective and less damaging. Granted, *ex post* contract revision is troubling from the legal standpoint, and freezing prices and costs suspends the price system (although severe inflation was probably already causing substantial price-system malfunctioning). Assuming the public believes prices will remain frozen, however, price-level uncertainty diminishes for the anticipated duration of the freeze. Firms need not raise prices preemptively, and inflation expectations and uncertainty should be minimized.

In addition, the lower inflation rate *per se* should help improve the fiscal accounts, partly because it reduces the decline in real tax receipts resulting from the collection lag (the "Olivera–Tanzi effect"), and also because lower price-level uncertainty should reduce real interest rates on public-sector debt. An additional benefit is that, with other prices in the economy frozen, public-enterprise prices and the price of foreign exchange rate hold their real values. This should buttress the fiscal contraction, relieving the government's borrowing need and so relieving inflationary and interest-rate pressure, in what one would hope would be a virtuous circle. Revision of old contracts incorporating high inflation expectations should mitigate the economy's tendency to slip into stabilization recession.

To the extent they reduce inflationary expectations and uncertainty, and so encourage people to hold money, price controls also permit— arguably, require—less restrictive, even moderately expansionary, monetary policy. This in turn permits lower real interest rates, mitigating the pressure on the public interest bill and moderating recession. This remains one of the more controversial claims regarding heterodox stabilization: conventional wisdom still holds that successful stabilization requires high real interest rates to discourage credit use, defend the exchange rate, and encourage domestic saving.

An obvious danger is that supposedly "heterodox" programs come to rely entirely on the "unorthodox" elements. Politicians often suppose that freezing prices is all it takes to overcome inflation. If relative-price dispersion has been severe, however, prices will be frozen in an arbitrary, hence untenable array. This, in combination with downward price stickiness, implies that the price array is under pressure to melt, if not explode. Moreover, if the sources of monetary expansion remain in place, freezing prices is obviously futile.

Since 1985, Argentina, Israel and Brazil have undertaken several heterodox stabilization efforts. Argentina's "Austral Plan" came first, in the middle of June 1985, followed several weeks later by Israel's July 1985 program. Brazil's "Cruzado Plan" began at the end of February 1986. The 1985 Argentine and Israeli plans combined orthodox and unorthodox policies, and so were "heterodox." The Cruzado Plan itself was unorthodox, since it incorporated no significant fiscal or monetary tightening; arguably, however, the December 1985 tax reform and various monetary reform measures taken early in February 1986 constituted its "orthodox" components.

The 1985 Argentine and 1986 Brazilian programs simply failed, unfortunately. Inflation returned to high levels well within a year. Emergency attempts during 1986 and 1987 to place the programs back on track—more accurately, perhaps, to stave off hyperinflation—also failed. Argentina's August 1988 "Plan Primavera" ("Spring Plan")—also an emergency policy package—not only fell short of its relatively modest ambitions, but broke down in early 1989 in a spiral of public-sector debt and traumatic hyperinflation. Brazil's January 1989 "Plano do Verão" ("Summer Plan"), which had been prepared for a longer time but undertaken unenthusiastically by a discredited departing government, also collapsed within months in spiralling public debt and hyperinflation. Argentina's July 1989 "Bunge y Born" program, an improvised heterodox program by a newly-elected government, also collapsed by the end of 1989 in much the same way as the Primavera Plan. Israel's July 1985 stabilization program managed a precarious but encouraging success, however.

Viewed in retrospect, the Argentine and Brazilian experiments incorporated important errors not inherent in the heterodox approach, and their failure does not definitively imply that heterodox policy could not have worked. The unorthodox elements of Israel's stabilization program appear to have contributed to its success.

2 ARGENTINA, 1985–9

Argentina's monthly inflation averaged about 9 per cent, with a standard deviation of about 7 percentage points, from 1971 through 1988. Argentina's macroeconomy has performed disappointingly for several decades, particularly in view of the nation's generous endowment of human and capital resources. Over the 1980s, real per capita GDP declined at an annual average rate of 0.4 per cent; real capital formation slipped from higher than 20 to below 10 per cent of GDP over the decade. This happened in spite of a substantial accumulation of external debt over the late 1970s—although, of course, partly because of the rising burden of debt service.

Argentina's first brush with hyperinflation came in the mid-1970s: consumer prices quintupled between March 1975 and March 1976. A military regime took power in that month, and, while it succeeded in forestalling hyperinflation, inflation persisted at monthly rates ranging between 5 and 13 per cent. In 1977 the Government announced liberalizing economic and financial reforms. It reversed the previous Government's banking "centralization," under which deposits were subject to 100 per cent reserve requirements and commercial banks provided loans on the basis of Central Bank "rediscount" credit. It liberalized interest rates. To increase banks' lending capacity, it reduced reserve requirements directly to 45 per cent in 1977, then— to forestall inflationary pressure—gradually to 10 per cent by late 1979. To relieve the pressure on banks to charge high lending rates to cover interest on deposits, the Central Bank began paying interest on reserves held against savings and time deposits, a policy that would later have troubling consequences. In addition, the Central Bank retained its deposit insurance, covering banking-system deposits for a monthly fee of 3 per 10 000.

The public and private sectors borrowed heavily in the late 1970s, both overseas and in domestic financial markets. Domestic interest rates rose to high real levels, even as banking activity expanded. The military government, which was engaged in a violent struggle against domestic political opposition and making preparations for external conflict, carried out no serious reform of public administration. With external credit available at relatively low rates, the Government found it easier to borrow to cover its deficit than to improve tax collection. To limit inflation and encourage capital imports, the Government set a policy of pre-announced devaluation, implicitly supported by the high domestic interest rates and external borrowing—that produced sharp real-effective appreciation. This set the price incentive favoring a trade deficit, which transferred the financial inflow to Argentina.

High interest rates and mounting indebtedness thrust many private firms into "distress." A wave of bank crises beginning in March 1980 closed 70 banking institutions by mid-1982, and forced the monetary authority to issue heavily, not only to maintain the system's liquidity but also to pay insured deposits. Inflation worsened steadily: monthly consumer-price increases averaged 5.4, 7.1, and 9.9 per cent in 1980, 1981, and 1982. A cycle of corrective devaluations beginning in early 1981, which reduced the real effective value of the *peso* by half between 1980 and 1982, intensified pressure on prices, on the public accounts, and on private firms with external debt; it also stimulated capital flight.

Public expenditure surged with the April–June 1982 conflict with Great Britain. The onset of the "debt crisis" in August 1982 closed Argentina's access to "voluntary" foreign credit. The Central Bank effectively assumed the service on most private external debt during 1982: foreign creditors would no longer voluntarily refinance it, and devaluation made the debt service exorbitantly costly. In July 1982 the authorities required domestic commercial banks to reschedule private-sector debt for sixty-month terms at a monthly interest rate of 4 per cent. They imposed controls on deposit rates, then permitted inflation to run sufficiently high—consumer prices rose an average of 15 per cent per month in 1983—to dilute the debt in real terms. The main policy to hold inflation within bounds was higher bank reserve requirements, which functioned as a means by which the Central Bank borrowed from the public through the intermediation of private banks. The Central Bank still paid interest on the reserves, however.

When constitutional government resumed in December 1983 under President Raul Alfonsin, it inherited massive external debt, recession, and inflation. During 1984 the new Government tried to revive real economic activity by stimulating demand. Meanwhile it confronted foreign commercial-bank creditors over interest payments due. The economy failed to revive over 1984 and early 1985, but prices accelerated sharply, and hyperinflation threatened: consumer prices rose 18.8 per cent per month during 1984 and 25.4 per cent over the first five months of 1985. The Alfonsin Government's first economic ministerial team resigned early in 1985, and the new team made price stability its highest priority.

The "Austral Plan", which the president announced in a televised address to the nation on June 14, 1985, comprised (i) a wage and price freeze; (ii) introduction of a new currency unit, the *austral*, equal to 10 000 *pesos*; (iii) devaluation from 0.60 to a fixed exchange rate of 0.80 *australes* per US dollar; (iv) sharp increases in public-enterprise prices; and (v) a promise that the Central Bank would henceforth create no money to provide credit to the Treasury. The Plan also incorporated an ingenious conversion table under which the old *peso* devalued every day against the new *austral* at a 14 per cent monthly rate. In this way, *austral* values of contracts signed before but coming due after the Plan would reflect the lower inflation, effectively purging the expectations embedded in the contracts.

In the months immediately following the Austral Plan, the authorities largely kept to the letter of their promise that the Central Bank would create no money to finance the Treasury—although it did provide the Treasury some credit for purchases of foreign exchange from the Central Bank. (These transactions entailed no direct money creation, and so complied with the Austral Plan's promise; nevertheless, if the Treasury had not secured credit from the Central Bank for its foreign-exchange purchases, it would have absorbed money from the economy.) The Central Bank did, however, provide credit flows to financial institutions, including such public-sector entities as the national housing and development banks and banks owned by provincial governments. It also provided resources to failing banks, either through deposit insurance or through "rediscount" credit, in order to meet withdrawal demands. Some money creation resulted from the external accounts, since the devaluation increased the trade surplus in the second half of 1985. Meanwhile, however, because the price freeze reduced inflationary anticipations, money demand increased. Narrow money holdings rose from 2.5 per cent of GDP in the second quarter of 1985 to 5.8 per cent by the second quarter of 1986; broad money holdings rose over the same period from 10.8 to 17.4 per cent of GDP. (Since the frozen prices were lower than they would have been had they been free, however, the measured real money stock was surely higher than it would have been had prices been free.)

Reimposition of interest-rate controls in 1982 had stimulated "informal" financial operations, including "money desks" and interfirm credit operations. Higher money demand increased the rates in late 1985, and the authorities had little choice but to permit relatively high controlled rates. This created a peculiar problem for the Austral Plan. The public sector still had domestic debt outstanding, and the higher interest rates affected its deficit. Moreover, as real interest flows were capitalized into interest-bearing deposits, total deposits grew. Similarly, as Central Bank interest on commercial banks' reserve holdings was capitalized into bank reserves, the monetary base grew. (The conversion table had especially helped the Treasury control its interest due.)

The Austral Plan went through several phases after June 1985. Although prices were generally supposed to remain frozen through March 1986, monthly inflation rates remained between 2.5 and 3.5 per cent from July 1985 through March 1986. Real wages fell in the wake of the June 1985 devaluation and public-sector price adjustments. Real GDP fell 5.6 per cent in the third quarter of 1985 (it was 8.7 per cent lower than in the third quarter of 1984), but then surged (partly seasonally) by 13.8 per cent in the fourth quarter. A (partly seasonal) decline of 5.6 per cent in the first quarter of 1986 left it 0.7 per cent higher than in the first quarter of 1985. The overall public-sector deficit was below 3 per cent of GDP in the second half of 1985, compared with about 12 per cent in the first half of 1985, through a favorable Olivera–Tanzi effect, higher public-enterprise prices, lower nominal interest rates and the fixed exchange rate. The balance of payments improved to the extent the current account went into surplus in the third and fourth quarters. (Although merchandise exports have exceeded imports since the 1981 devaluations, external interest due has generally exceeded the trade surplus through the 1980s, keeping the current account generally in deficit.) The new policy approach enabled Argentina to secure external support in the form of a new-money and restructuring agreement with commercial banks and government creditors, backed with an IMF program.

With the recovery, the trade balance diminished and the current account returned to deficit. Money-supply growth drifted upward, and early in 1986 the Government's indicative guidelines permitted real wages to rise. Prices came under intensifying pressure, largely because the price array had been frozen at a particular moment, and was becoming increasingly distant from market conditions. In April 1986, the authorities relaxed the freeze, and the Plan entered what they described as a "flexibilization" phase. They devalued the *austral*, and instituted a crawling-peg exchange-rate policy. As prices drifted up, the overall public-sector deficit weakened, and Argentina missed its IMF program targets. Inflationary pressures revived: wage increases and public-sector price readjustments lifted monthly inflation rates from 4.4 per cent in the second quarter to 7.6 per cent in the third quarter. These readjustments reactivated the economy's inflation-feedback processes. In September 1986, the Government concluded that inflationary pressures had become severe and renewed price controls, tightened monetary policy, and made more assertive wage-control efforts. Economic activity levelled off, but inflation fell back to 5.4 per cent a month.

Inflationary pressures intensified during 1987, however, partly because of "corrective" relative-price adjustments. In late February the Government announced a broad policy package including higher public-sector prices and tighter expenditure controls. The Government sought new accords with foreign creditors: it negotiated a new IMF stand-by agreement, reached agreement with Paris Club creditors, and concluded a rescheduling and new-money agreement with commercial banks. Inflation worsened as the year progressed, exceeding 10 per cent in July and August. Meanwhile, declining export prices—a worsening of a secular decline that had gone on since the early 1980s—suddenly reduced the trade surplus. The public-sector deficit, pressured by accelerating prices, exceeded 6 per cent of GDP in the second quarter of 1987, above the 3.9 per cent target to which the Government had committed itself under the IMF program. Implementation of the IMF program was therefore delayed.

Despite increases then considered inflationary, real wages fell sharply through the first half of the year. Campaigning for legislative and gubernatorial elections held in mid-September left the Government unable to take vigorous stabilization measures. Expenditure drifted upward, and the Central Bank increased credit flows to public banks that provided term financing for housing and investment finance. Largely because of the disappointing macroeconomic performance, the Government suffered an election setback.

With the election past, the economic team resumed its stabilization struggle: its October 1987 "little Austral" economic package combined stiff devaluation, higher public-enterprise prices, and renewed commitment to expenditure reduction. It also incorporated full liberalization of interest rates. The Central Bank remunerated reserves held against interest-bearing deposits at floating rates, according to the freely determined deposit rates. The devaluation had an immediate inflationary impact, and the Central Bank attempted to sterilize by raising reserve requirements. Since early 1985, the Central Bank had required that banks hold an increasing proportion of reserves in the form of "inaccessible deposits," interest-bearing accounts at the Central Bank to which the banks had no access even when their own deposits declined. The Central Bank had adopted this approach for several reasons, the most important of which was that floating-rate interest payments on bank reserves were themselves a source of monetary-base creation. By capitalizing them into the inaccessible deposits, the Central Bank sterilized the interest payments. The problem was that Central Bank debt to the commercial banks grew through the interest capitalization. The interest bill deepened the Central Bank's own borrowing requirement, particularly since it received limited income in cash from its own asset holdings, which comprised Treasury obligations and credit to banks.

The October 1987 measures permitted resumption of the IMF program, but severe inflationary pressure re-emerged in early 1988: monthly inflation rates averaged 11.4 per cent and 17 per cent in the first and second quarters. In July consumer prices rose 25.6 per cent.

As a result the IMF program faltered; in the absence of a new external financing program, the Government stopped paying interest to commercial banks. The Central Bank used inaccessible deposits in attempts to control money-supply growth. Monetary growth received further impetus from external developments. Summer drought conditions elsewhere in the world raised grain-export prices and improved the terms of trade, hence increased the trade surplus. The public-sector deficit remained high. The Treasury had issued inflation-adjusted bonds in 1987 and early 1988, and it directed the Central Bank to amortize bond issues as they matured.

By mid-1988, hyperinflation threatened again. Hence, in early August 1988 the authorities revived their heterodox strategy through the "Plan Primavera". They devalued the *austral*, which had appreciated more than 10 per cent in real-effective terms since the beginning of the year, from 10.77 to 12 per dollar; instituted a pre-announced 4 per cent monthly crawling-peg devaluation; and introduced a multiple exchange-rate system, through which the Central Bank would earn an operating profit by purchasing export proceeds at an official rate and selling foreign exchange for imports at a parallel-market rate. Monetary policy would be calibrated to set domestic interest rates so as to hold the parallel rate about 20–25 per cent above the official rate. This profit, which the authorities expected to run on the order of 1.5 per cent of GDP, would exceed the increase in the Central Bank's interest bill. The predictable real-effective appreciation of the *austral* seemed appropriate in view of the mid-1988 terms-of-trade gain. The authorities also adjusted public-enterprise prices sharply upward, and instituted a system of price increases under which different public enterprises' prices would rise each month so as to maintain their real revenues.

Prices were almost 30 per cent higher in August than in July, but the increases occurred almost entirely with the initial shock. The private sector had raised some prices in anticipation of a new freeze. Price deceleration through August was buttressed by informal accords with industrialists to limit price increases and with labor unions to moderate wage demands. (Industrialists went along in the hope that moderate inflation could prevent a Peronist victory in the presidential elections scheduled for May 1989; the Peronist labor unions cooperated as well, partly to avoid charges of obstruction.) Again, the price deceleration was expected to raise tax revenues through the Olivera–Tanzi effect. The 4 per cent monthly devaluation was intended to help limit inflationary pressure, and to encourage imports to help the Central

Bank sell foreign exchange and realize its profit. The authorities limited their ambitions to maintaining single-digit monthly inflation for six to nine months. This, they hoped, would set a context within which deeper reforms would be possible, which would permit deeper reductions in the inflation rate.

Monthly inflation remained just below 10 per cent from September through January. The financial markets required high interest rates to sustain the parallel exchange rate at its targeted value, however. The combined Treasury and Central Bank deficit therefore remained high, and the Central Bank's scheme to sell foreign exchange at a profit fell short: high interest rates available on time deposits induced would-be importers to place their funds at interest rather than purchase foreign exchange for imports. Meanwhile, the deeper reforms of the public sector needed more time; the proximity of elections made them politically difficult. The tax reform the Congress approved in December 1988 contained many compromises, and although it incorporated a number of efficiency improvements, it came too late and its effect was too limited to offset the mounting pressure of the interest bill on the public deficit.

Through November, December and January the Central Bank limited money creation and supported the exchange rate by requiring commercial banks to form new interest-bearing inaccessible deposits against the banks' time deposits. This tight monetary policy pressured interest rates sharply upward. Capitalization of interest into time deposits—whose terms tended now to be only seven days—meant that broad liquidity tended to grow at the monthly deposit rates. These rates averaged 9.6 per cent in November and 11.9 per cent in December, while consumer prices rose 5.7 and 6.8 per cent respectively. The foreign exchange attracted by these high rates increased the Central Bank's dollar holdings. Nevertheless, since the rates exceeded the devaluation rate, the stock of *austral*-denominated assets grew faster than (the *austral* equivalent of) the dollar stock, and the *austral* came under pressure in the parallel market. In January the Central Bank sold dollars to relieve this pressure. Once it became generally clear that the Central Bank was selling dollars, however, devaluation expectations developed, and people began to withdraw *australes* to buy dollars. Banks offered higher interest rates to hold the deposits, but this increased the Central Bank's interest bill and created new liquidity. As pressure intensified on the parallel rate, efforts to raise interest rates became futile and the stabilization effort became unsustainable.

Early in February 1989 the authorities devalued sharply, effectively concluding the program. Over subsequent weeks, a devaluation-inflation cycle developed. Uncertainties created by the campaign for the May 1989 presidential election added to the crisis. Commercial banks faced increasing withdrawal demand, and as their illiquidity situation became increasingly acute the Central Bank had to (i) release bank reserves, (ii) release inaccessible deposits, (iii) provide rediscount credit, (iv) limit withdrawals, and finally (v) permit reserve deficiencies, and even (vi) permit overdrafts by commercial banks on their reserve checking accounts. Consumer prices rose 33.4 per cent in April, 78.5 per cent in May, and 114.5 per cent in June. The authorities revised exchange-rate policy several times, briefly attempting a floating exchange rate before returning to a crawling peg. In early May they raised export taxes, in an attempt to reduce the growing deficit. By May, however, Argentina was evidently in hyperinflation.

The opposition Peronist candidate won the May election. The Government agreed to turn over power on July 8, 1989, before the constitutionally scheduled date of December 1989. The new President, Carlos Menem, indicated that his Government would adopt orthodox stabilization and liberalizing structural policies, including privatization and subsidy reduction, although this was not the traditional Peronist policy platform. Menem formed his economic team from the executive staff of the Argentine multinational grain-trading firm Bunge y Born. The day after taking office, the new authorities announced another heterodox stabilization program, the "BB Plan." The initial measures were devaluation from A$303 to a fixed exchange rate of A$655, intended to encourage exporters to surrender foreign exchange (and so to increase export-tax revenue; the objective of this devaluation was thus partly fiscal). Monetary policy would henceforth be run to prevent any gap from emerging between the parallel and official exchange rates. There were also massive increases in such public-enterprise prices as fuel charges, electricity rates, telephone rates (and so in associated taxes). Partly because private firms had anticipated a new freeze, prices were about three times higher in July than in June.

The new Government's short-term strategy was to secure agreements to freeze the economy's key prices and work on deeper reform measures; this would establish sufficient credibility so that the Central Bank could cover its interest bill by borrowing in domestic markets at steadily diminishing rates, at least until the deeper reforms reduced the overall public borrowing requirement to zero. Later in July, about 400 of the nation's largest enterprises agreed to freeze their output prices for as long as the Government froze the exchange rate and the public-sector prices. Meanwhile, the authorities submitted three important pieces of legislation to the Congress, (i) an Economic Emergency Law to provide the Government authority to suspend or cut subsidies and expenditure programs; (ii) a Public Sector Reform Law to provide the legal basis for a vigorous program to reorganize, close, and privatize public enterprises—including the national telecommunications monopoly, the railways, and the national airline; and (iii) further tax reform, intended to close loopholes and to extend the base of the value-added tax.

Until the Government achieved a non-interest surplus sufficient to cover the Treasury and Central Bank interest bill, however, monetary policy would carry the stabilization burden. Hyperinflation had so reduced money demand that the money creation resulting from devaluation and surrender of export proceeds were significant proportions of the existing stock. The narrow money supply averaged only 2.6 per cent and the broad money supply only 11.7 per cent of annual GDP in the second quarter of 1989, compared with 4.3 and 19.2 per cent of GDP in the first quarter. Since the trade surplus was running at 5 per cent of GDP, it was generating monthly pressure to create money amounting to 5/12 of a per cent of annual GDP, a significant flow measured against the small money stock. The price freeze would increase money demand somewhat, but not enough to carry all, or even a significant part of, the money creation. The Central Bank would still have to pay interest on about US$2.5 billion in bank reserves and inaccessible deposits, at rates linked to the rates on seven-day bank time deposits. The new authorities promised that the Central Bank would manage liquidity growth through open-market sales of Central Bank bills, not further inaccessible deposits.

From mid-July to mid-October, this approach appeared to work. Monthly time-deposit rates fell from 15 to 4 per cent, reducing the floating interest rates the Central Bank paid on inaccessible deposits and bills. The Central Bank increased the stock of Central Bank bills outstanding from near zero to almost US$3 billion (annual GDP was running at about US$70 billion) within ten weeks. No significant gap appeared between the parallel and (fixed) official exchange rates, and monthly inflation rates remained under ten per cent. The Central Bank bills were purchased almost entirely by private commercial banks: although not obliged to do so, they bought them because their yields were higher and safer than the alternatives—particularly lending to the private sector. The banks funded these purchases through time deposits, which recovered on the promise of the fixed exchange rate and nominal interest rates an order of magnitude higher than overseas rates. Meanwhile, by September the vigorous emergency measures brought the Treasury's non-interest budget into surplus. The Congress passed the economic reform legislation in August and September with relatively few changes. In September 1989 the Government and the IMF staff agreed on a stand-by program built around continuation of the BB Plan into 1990; an initial US$220 million disbursement was made in November following IMF Board approval.

In mid-October, however, once the monthly bank-deposit rates fell to 4 per cent, the parallel exchange rate depreciated. The Central Bank quickly forced interest rates up, but the parallel-market gap persisted. Financial markets probably perceived that interest rates were too low to compete with dollar assets, but with the Treasury and Central Bank debt now having swollen to around US$7 billion, the interest bill would soar if interest rates rose high enough to compete: each percentage point of monthly interest amounted to US$70 million, on the order of one per cent of monthly GDP. In early December, with monthly interest rates nearing 20 per cent and the parallel exchange premium approaching 35 per cent, the authorities devalued from A$655 to A$1000, effectively ending the BB Plan. When this failed to calm the markets—as evidenced by immediate re-emergence of a similar parallel-market premium and high interest rates—the economic team resigned. The new authorities immediately floated the exchange rate and announced the complete liberalization of all prices. Over the remainder of December the exchange rate depreciated rapidly, and in spite—or, again, because—of rising interest rates the economy slipped into a new hyperinflationary spiral: the price level roughly doubled over the month.

The Primavera and BB Plans were both temporary stabilization programs intended to buy time for deeper economic reforms. They worked by anchoring the price level with the exchange rate, and anchoring the exchange rate by paying high interest rates. The problem with this approach was that the interest rates required to stabilize the exchange rate were so high that the public sector's own interest bill substantially exceeded its primary (non-interest) surplus. The public sector could pay interest only by running a huge, arguably infeasible non-interest surplus or by borrowing further. As *austral*-denominated assets became increasingly abundant relative to dollar-denominated assets, the *austral* came under pressure to depreciate. In effect, Argentina's public sector had slipped into debt "distress."

3   ISRAEL, 1985–7

Israel's heterodox stabilization effort, which began in July 1985, succeeded in relieving severe inflation. Consumer prices rose at monthly average rates of 9.3 and 15.2 per cent in 1983 and 1984, and 10 per cent over the first six months of 1985; after the July 1985 shock, monthly rates of increase remained steadily between 1 and 2 per cent through 1989.

Israel's long-standing indexation and dollarization practices, covering financial assets and wages, had made its inflation-feedback mechanism particularly robust. The inflation contributed to chronic balance-of-payments difficulties, which forced increasingly frequent devaluation; devaluation and public-sector price increases caused the inflation rate to ratchet upward through the early 1980s. Like other nations undergoing severe inflation, money holding diminished with inflation, imparting a stronger inflationary bias to the economy: the narrow money supply fell as a proportion of GDP from 3.8 per cent in 1981 to 1.7 per cent in 1984. Dollar accounts became increasingly important, which made devaluation more inflationary, hence less influential for export and import decisions.

Israel has taken on substantial amounts of debt at home and abroad, and debt service has always been an important problem. In December 1987 Israel's external debt totalled about US$26 billion, of which public and publicly guaranteed debt totalled US$16.8 billion, compared with a GDP of about US$35 billion: external debt service has run on the order of 6 per cent of GDP. Unlike most Latin American nations in the 1980s, however, Israel maintained its ability to borrow (partly on the implicit basis of Israel's foreign support), and there was no process of concerted negotiations with foreign banks. During the 1960s, Israel's government budget had been roughly balanced, but the 1967 and 1973 conflicts generated heavy defense expenditures, and these pushed the public deficit well above 10 per cent of GDP by the early 1980s. Tax collection remained high by world standards, but in the mid-1980s it slipped below 50 per cent of GDP, partly through the Olivera–Tanzi effect. At several points in the early 1980s the authorities experimented unsuccessfully with expansionary policies, hoping to increase aggregate-supply growth and tax revenues, and so slowly reverse inflationary pressure; this approach was difficult, however, in an economy so extensively index-linked and dollarized. A financial crisis in mid-1983—in the course of which the Government provided special guarantees to bank equities—

stimulated inflationary expectations and sharply increased the public sector's domestic debt.

By September 1984, when the Labor–Likud National Unity coalition government was formed, the public sector's domestic debt exceeded GDP and its external debt had risen to roughly half of GDP. For several months the coalition found itself unable to get a grip on the economy. It applied several policy programs, including significant expenditure cuts; these moderated inflation somewhat (and set the stage for subsequent expenditure cuts), but still left it unacceptably high. Many stabilization proposals involved rigidly fixing the exchange rate, even substituting the dollar entirely for the domestic currency.

On July 1, 1985, the Government announced an ambitious heterodox stabilization program. The initial measures were a devaluation of approximately 25 per cent (and unification of the exchange rates for exports and imports); a program of public expenditure cuts, mainly in defense, intended to reduce the deficit by 6 percentage points of GDP—enough to slow and reverse the build-up of domestic debt; and a price freeze covering 90 per cent by weight of the consumer price index. (About 25 per cent of the index was normally subject to controls.) The Government convened national wage negotiations, promising to maintain a fixed exchange rate if wage increases could be restrained.

In mid-July, the Histadrut Labor Federation, representing 90 per cent of Israel's labor force, and the Manufacturers Association, acting as bargaining agent for the largest industrial firms, agreed to set an initial wage increase equal to only half the 28 per cent June–July price increase implied by the July 1 measures. They agreed also to suspend the usual quarterly cost-of-living increase until October 1, and to adjust the system governing the cost-of-living increases. The (central) Bank of Israel tightened monetary policy, which rapidly drove annualized real interest rates above 100 per cent. The monetary authorities prohibited conversion of domestic currency into dollar deposits, and set a minimum term of one year for dollar deposits. For the first time they made domestic public-sector bond issues tradeable, hoping this could provide a basis for open-market operations.

The United States provided a $1.5 billion grant to shore up international reserves, to be paid in two tranches in 1985 and 1986. International reserves totalled about US$2.4 billion on June 30, compared with US$3.8 billion one year earlier and US$3 billion on March 31. The exchange rate played a central role in the stabilization strategy. Given the economy's relatively small size and open character, the authorities used the exchange rate quite deliberately "to anchor" the price level. The US support bolstered international reserves sufficiently to make the fixed exchange rate credible.

Israel's inflation rate has run since July 1985 at about 15 to 20 per cent a year—still high, but much lower than the double-digit monthly rates that prevailed during 1984. Monetization has recovered: in 1985, 1986, 1987, and 1988 the narrow money supply averaged, respectively, 2.1, 3.8, 4.8, and 5.4 per cent of GDP. Real industrial growth remained positive in the wake of the July 1985 announcement, reaching 2.7 per cent a year in 1985 and 3.7 per cent in 1986. During 1986 the falling dollar, lower world oil prices, and the United States' assistance combined to keep the external accounts reasonably firm despite the fixed exchange rate. Even after taking account of the United States' grant, the external accounts improved: the current account reached surpluses of US$1.1 and US$1.6 billion in 1985 and 1986, compared with deficits of US$1.9 and US$1.3 billion in 1983 and 1984. The merchandise-trade deficit fell from US$3.1 billion in 1983 to US$1.9 billion in 1986; imports increased, but exports increased more. The Government was even able to take advantage of the stabilization to begin deeper reforms, including some tax liberalization, financial-market liberalization, and cuts in government expenditure. During 1987 economic activity and the external accounts remained satisfactory, while the annual inflation rate fell to about 16 per cent.

From July 1985 through December 1986 the international-reserve position improved by an amount roughly equal to the United States grant—implying that the Government used the grant, appropriately, as a safety net for the exchange rate. (One wonders whether external support of comparable magnitude could have improved the prospects for stabilization efforts elsewhere.) Attempts to have exchange rates serve as both the relative price for internationally traded goods and the price-level anchor have, of course, brought many stabilization programs to grief, when external pressures forced devaluation which in turn destabilized domestic prices. The Israeli authorities were well aware that they were using the exchange rate for dual purposes, and that this kept their program precarious long after July 1985. Between July 1985 and August 1986, they kept the *sheqel* fixed against the dollar. The dollar fell against other convertible currencies over this period, and so the *sheqel* fell against a large proportion of Israel's trading partners. This helped the external accounts, but contributed to inflationary pressure. In August 1986, the authorities therefore pegged the *sheqel* to a five-currency basket in proportion to Israel's trade weights.

The public-sector deficit fell sharply, from between 10 and 15 per cent of GDP before 1985 to between 2 and 4 per cent of GDP thereafter. Government consumption fell from 38.6 per cent of GDP in 1984 and more than 40 per cent of GDP in the first half of 1985 to roughly 34 per cent of GDP over the twelve months following the start of the program, and to around 31 per cent of GDP in the second half of 1986. Tax collection recovered from about 45 to about 50 per cent of GDP, and expenditure—particularly subsidy—cuts accounted for the remainder of the improvement. A favorable Olivera–Tanzi effect improved tax revenue; in any case, the wage restraint and the greater certainty of the economic context created by the price freeze simplified budget programming. As fiscal policy tightened, monetary policy eased, allowing interest rates and bank credit to ease.

Real GDP fell 6.5 per cent in the third quarter of 1985 and remained unchanged in the fourth quarter, but then rose 3.4 per cent in the first quarter of 1986: it grew 3.3 per cent in 1986 compared with 1985. Real wages drifted upward toward the end of 1985 and remained high through 1986: the average real-wage index (1985 = 100) rose from 85.8 in the third quarter of 1985 to 101.7 in the first half of 1986 and to 105.7 in the second half of 1986. The authorities reduced wage-related taxes to offset the effects of rising wages on business profits. The wage recovery and lower inflation rates contributed to the consumption resurgence that began toward the end of 1985. Private consumption reached 62.4 per cent of GDP in 1986, compared with 54.4 and 58.5 per cent respectively in 1984 and 1985. At the beginning of 1986, financial institutions and retailers revived consumer-credit facilities—a sign that businessmen were convinced that stability would hold. During 1986 the authorities worried that consumption expansion could generate heavier exchange-rate and inflationary pressure than they could manage, and after the middle of 1986 the Bank of Israel tried to control demand by tightening monetary policy. Despite the pressure of consumption demand, inflation remained relatively well in hand, partly because imports rose over the twelve months following the start of the program.

In retrospect, the exchange rate worked in such a way that the external accounts vented some of the inflationary pressure, without permitting serious balance-of-payments deterioration. Again, the fact that the exchange rate was fixed against the depreciating dollar over the first year of the program enabled policy-makers to have it both ways: the exchange rate was visibly stable with respect to the dollar but depreciating against other currencies. The decision in mid-1986 to fix the exchange rate against a currency basket made it work more to stabilize domestic prices, less to stabilize the external accounts. As the year ended, however, policy-makers became increasingly concerned about the external accounts, particularly as the United States' special assistance flows concluded.

In January 1987 the authorities devalued the currency 10 per cent against the currency basket. This percentage was what was presumably necessary to make exports as profitable in real terms as they had been on average over 1986. Once again, the authorities headed off the inflationary pressure of the devaluation by securing a new agreement with the labor unions and private industry: labor waived part of the cost-of-living wage increases in return for promises of price restraint by large firms. Thereafter the exchange rate was fixed in terms of the currency basket. The authorities also revised the 1987–8 budget then in preparation, extending a number of expenditure ceilings and generally reinforcing the tight fiscal stance. This policy thrust was generally successful, in that it prevented inflation from rising substantially over the year and prevented the balance of payments from deteriorating excessively. Consumer prices rose only 1.3 per cent per month during 1987, compared with 1.5 per cent during 1986. The 1987 merchandise trade deficit was US$3.8 billion, however, a considerable increase from the US$1.9 billion deficit in 1986: imports rose to US$12.9 billion from US$9.6 billion, while exports rose to US$9.1 billion from US$7.7 billion.

Following this "mid-course adjustment," policy-makers directed more attention to longer-term structural reforms. In April 1987 they reduced the corporate tax scale and cut marginal individual tax rates. They also undertook some financial-market reforms, liberalizing requirements that banks hold government bonds against deposits, reducing a tax-system bias that favored holding government rather than private obligations, and deregulating securities issues. The Bank of Israel took further steps to create a genuine open market.

Real GDP grew 7.1 per cent in 1987. In the first part of 1988, however, GDP growth reversed sharply: the growth rates for 1988 and 1989 slipped below 2 per cent, so that per capita growth became negative. Private consumption and capital formation levelled off toward the end of 1987 and remained stagnant through at least 1989. During 1987 government consumption rose from about 30 to about 35 per cent of GDP, although it remained below the percentages prevailing before 1985. The recovery of wages and taxes, combined with a relatively high exchange-rate value, may have discouraged investment: in 1988 and 1989 wages were 19 per cent higher, and the real effective exchange rate 10 per cent more appreciated, than in 1985. The violent uprising in the occupied territories undoubtedly discouraged investment further, of course. Nevertheless, consumer prices rose only 1.3 and 1.6 per cent a month during 1988 and 1989, even though the Bank of Israel loosened policy to encourage private borrowing. The balance of payments remained under control: the recession limited merchandise imports, and the merchandise trade deficit went from US$3.8 billion in 1987 to US$3 and then US$1.8 billion in 1988 and 1989.

While it is always possible that an external-accounts crisis could force devaluation and restart the inflationary spiral, Israel's struggle to stabilize its inflation and its external accounts appears to have been largely successful. In any case its policy-makers are clearly in a better position to cope with a crisis, having earned "credibility" with their public and having forged stronger policy instruments. The authorities are still using the exchange rate to manage both the domestic price level and the trade accounts; the inflation rate is still too high; and the downturn in GDP growth has been disappointing. Nevertheless, Israel's experience indicates that capable, pragmatic policy-makers can use heterodox policy methods to reduce triple-digit inflation down to low double-digit inflation, once government, business, and labor all agree to forgo some purchasing power.

4 BRAZIL, 1985–9

Brazil's President announced the "Cruzado Plan" in a televised speech on February 27, 1986. Monthly inflation rates were threatening to exceed 25 per cent a month, a higher monthly rate than the country had ever experienced. The inflationary surge resulted from a combination of pressures. Like Argentina, Brazil had had an inflation problem for decades, which worsened sharply following the debt crisis: consumer prices rose at a monthly average rate of 6 per cent in 1981 and 1982, then 8.9, 9.9, and 10.7 per cent respectively in 1983, 1984, and 1985. As a result of sharp real devaluation in February 1983 and recession, merchandise exports were 23 per cent higher in 1984 than in 1983 and 34 per cent higher in 1984 than in 1982, while merchandise imports fell from US$22.1 billion in 1981 to US$13.9 billion in 1984. Between 1982 and 1984 the balance of payments' current-account deficit fell from 5 per cent of GDP to nearly zero. With real GDP growth rates of 5.7 and 8.4 per cent in 1984 and 1985, the economy recovered its output levels from the 1981–3 recession. By early 1986, with the merchandise trade surplus running at 4–5 per cent of GDP, there was a strong argument that the exchange rate—which was devaluing in a crawling peg according to the domestic price level and was therefore roughly fixed in real-effective terms—had become undervalued. Since drought conditions in the second half of 1985 had raised domestic agricultural prices faster than industrial prices, the exchange rate had become particularly favorable to industrial exporters.

At the same time there was a persisting public deficit. Debate about the significance of this deficit has been clouded by the striking difference between the measures of the deficit on nominal and on real ("operational") bases: in 1985 the overall PSBR was 28.1 per cent on a nominal basis but 4.3 per cent on a real basis (roughly half these figures corresponded to the central government, the remainder to state enterprises, part of whose borrowing was to cover capital formation, and state and municipal governments). The difference was the inflationary erosion of the principal of the public sector's voluminous domestic debt, most of which was short-term, inflation adjusted, or linked to short-term interest rates. The outstanding stock of marketable Treasury obligations, which constituted the bulk of the debt, was running between 30 and 40 per cent of GDP. When capitalized into the domestic debt, indexation and high interest rates more than maintained its value.

The high interest and inflation adjustment paid on external and domestic debt made short-term fiscal adjustment simultaneously more necessary and more difficult. In the short term, real and nominal interest due were heavily subject to current developments in inflation rates, local interest rates, and the exchange rate. Interest rates—even index-linked rates, which included various lags and corrections—were influenced by price-level uncertainty: they tended, accordingly, to be high in *ex ante* terms and therefore to exert heavy pressure on the public deficit. By the early 1980s, Brazil's financial institutions had developed the practice of funding portfolios of public obligations with "overnight" deposits. Yields on public obligations came to be set in floating terms, i.e., the overnight rate plus a spread.

By the early 1980s there was broad consensus that Brazil's non-financial public-sector had become oversized: public-sector employment continued to grow, despite efforts to contain it; the government had become involved in a wider range of economic activities than it could effectively manage; and there were many costly subsidy and tax-incentive programs. Despite increases in employment, the demands of a rapidly industrializing society were overwhelming the quality of government services. Tax revenues had been slipping since the late 1970s as a proportion of GDP.

The Government had particular political motives for taming inflation quickly and relatively painlessly. It was a transitional regime, which was taking the nation from two decades of military rule to reconstituted democracy. The President, José Sarney, who had been elected Vice President by an electoral college in January 1985, assumed the presidency in March 1985 upon the illness and subsequent demise of the popular president-elect. Important gubernatorial and legislative elections were scheduled for November 1986—the new Congress would sit as a constitutional convention—and the governing parties feared they would be blamed for any stabilization recession or runaway inflation.

Like Argentina's Austral Plan eight months earlier, the Cruzado Plan centered around a price freeze and a fixed exchange rate with a new currency unit. There was also a conversion table from the old *cruzeiro* to the new *cruzado* for contracted payments. There was no initial devaluation, however. On the other hand, the Cruzado Plan largely suspended Brazil's elaborate financial indexation system, which was widely regarded as a fundamental inflation-feedback channel. Financial indexation would henceforth remain only in attenuated form for the housing-finance savings institutions, which had come to rely heavily on it. A crucial difference from the 1985 Argentine and Israeli programs was that Brazil's Government began the Cruzado Plan with a general wage increase of 8 per cent. The economists who designed the Cruzado Plan had originally proposed that each worker's wage (w) be set to that value which, when deflated by the frozen March 1 price level (p), would leave it equal to the average of the deflated wage rates for the previous six months:

$$w_{Mar}/p_{Mar} = \frac{[(w_{Feb}/p_{Feb}) + (w_{Jan}/p_{Jan}) + (w_{Dec}/p_{Dec}) + (w_{Nov}/p_{Nov}) + (w_{Oct}/p_{Oct}) + (w_{Sep}/p_{Sep})]}{}.[6]$$

The problem was that this formula implied that workers whose wage had been adjusted within the past month or two would receive lower money wages. The Government added the 8 per cent increase so that no money wage would fall. It also instituted a "trigger mechanism," promising inflation adjustment for negotiated labor contracts once the official consumer-price index had accumulated 20 per cent from the outset of the Plan.

Many observers noted critically that the Cruzado Plan itself incorporated no significant fiscal or monetary measures. The economists who had drawn up the Plan had two broad responses. First, the Government had carried out an ambitious tax reform in December 1985. Moreover, in the weeks preceding the Plan there had been several monetary and credit reforms. The most important was the termination of the Banco do Brasil's "movement account" (since 1965, when the government had formed the Central Bank from various units of the Banco do Brasil, the huge state-owned commercial bank had retained—and used—this open credit line with the Central Bank). Henceforth, the Banco do Brasil would be subject like other commercial banks to reserve requirements and have no privileged money-creation capacity. Second, although the initial wage increase heavily affected public-sector accounts, the price freeze itself would have stabilizing fiscal and monetary consequences. Price deceleration would have a favorable Olivera–Tanzi effect; termination of financial indexation would help contain public-sector debt-service expenditure; and the fixed exchange rate would help control the domestic-currency equivalent of external debt service. Moreover, Argentina's experience persuaded Government economists that demand for money would rise, so that monetary stringency would prove unnecessarily contractionary.

The judgment that money demand would rise sharply induced the authorities to permit rapid money-supply growth. The narrow money supply grew 80 per cent in March 1986 and 19 per cent in April 1986—mainly through expanded lending by the Banco do Brasil. With prices frozen, the measured increase in the willingness to hold money was equal to the money-supply growth. (With inflation repressed, of course, it was doubtful that money demand really had increased as much as the money-supply increase.) In any case, the monetary expansion maintained expansive liquidity conditions and kept interest rates relatively low. The low interest rates discouraged saving, contributed to pressure against the exchange rate, and contributed to the productive economy's overheating, however helpful they were for the public deficit.

Nevertheless, the Cruzado Plan seemed dramatically successful at first. Popular euphoria characterized the Plan's first weeks: the President and Finance Minister Dilson Funaro enjoyed unaccustomed political popularity, and citizens enthusiastically monitored shop prices and reported price-freeze violations to the authorities. Measured consumer prices actually fell slightly in March 1986, then rose at rates between 1 and 2 per cent through October 1986. Economic activity continued to grow: GDP rose 8.3 per cent for the year as a whole, paced by 12 per cent industrial growth. According to the São Paulo Federation of Industry, real average wages in São Paulo industry were 9 per cent higher in October 1986 than in February 1986, total employment was 6.3 per cent higher, and capacity utilization was up from 78.7 to 83.4 per cent. With economic conditions seemingly much improved, the governing parties secured their election victory in November 1986.

Within weeks of the Plan's beginning, however, it became clear that overheated aggregate demand was placing excessive pressure on productive capacity. Overall capital formation had been only about 16 per cent in 1983, 1984, and 1985, compared with more than 20 per cent in the 1970s and early 1980s. Public capital formation had fallen after 1981 as part of austerity efforts in the face of the external-debt crisis, while private-sector capital formation had been discouraged by the general uncertainty, price controls, and the high cost of investable funds. The Cruzado Plan boom followed almost two years of vigorous recovery. As a result, shortages developed in many sectors, particularly where the price freeze happened to catch prices at low relative values. Various pharmaceutical products became difficult to find, and meat and milk all but disappeared from markets as producers withheld output. Payment of illegal premiums over official published prices became increasingly widespread through the middle of 1986. For example, purchasers could reduce the three-to-five-months' waiting list to which new automobiles were subject by paying such premiums to dealers.

As early as June 1986, the Finance Minister proposed "readjusting" the frozen prices, but this was now politically difficult. The Government made a half-hearted stabilization attempt in July 1986, raising various taxes and instituting forced-saving schemes. Meanwhile, however, with the exchange rate fixed, heavy domestic demand was reversing the external accounts. Once exporters concluded that devaluation was inevitable, they postponed exports. The trade surplus plummeted from $12 billion a year to deficit in the fourth quarter—normally, Brazil's strongest trade season—of 1986.

One week after its victory in the November elections, the Government devalued substantially and instituted special taxes on luxury items. These measures—called the "Cruzado Plan II"—directly raised prices. The Government hoped the price-level increase would be a once-and-for-all corrective, but the increase activated financial-market uncertainty and inflation-feedback processes. In late November and December short-term rates rose dramatically, responding to tightened monetary policy, surging inflation anticipations and the reduction in disposable income resulting from the tax increases. Part of the financial markets' problem was that it was impossible to distinguish real and nominal interest-rate increases: people inclined to save more in response to higher real interest rates were dissuaded to the degree they thought higher interest rates reflected only higher inflation expectations. By December 1986 monthly inflation had returned to double digits: with 20 per cent accumulated from February, the "trigger mechanism" began to increase wages. The balance-of-payments deterioration caused international-reserve loss, and in February 1987 Brazil was forced to suspend interest payments to overseas commercial-bank creditors.

In retrospect, the initial 8 per cent real wage increase and the large money-supply increase were the Cruzado Plan's fatal flaws. Curiously, in the confusion of early March 1986 it was not clearly understood that real wages had risen. The Government vaguely justified the increase as compensation for the fifteen days of inflation between the middle of February and the beginning of March, since price indices were measured on the basis of monthly averages. This was incorrect, though: the increase at the month's end left wages roughly 8 per cent higher in real terms than they had been on average *at the ends* of the preceding six months. The real wage increase accordingly amounted to a substantial inflationary shock. Since public-sector workers received higher wages like everyone else, the increase must be set against whatever other good the Cruzado Plan did for the public-sector accounts. Moreover, private-sector wage increases continued in the euphoric months following the declaration of the Cruzado Plan. The wage increases boosted aggregate demand and set off further rounds of wage increases, as firms hired and even competed for workers to produce for the growing demand.

Because Brazil's "heterodox" shock was accompanied by a wage increase—an inflationary shock—heterodox stabilization in general should not be judged unworkable on the basis of this particular experience. In addition to the rapid money-supply growth, the trade surplus was running on the order of 5 per cent of GDP. Although the fixed exchange rate appreciated in real effective terms and the trade surplus fell after March 1986, they were a source of inflationary pressure at the Plan's outset. Furthermore, the public deficit was influenced by the fact that the freeze caught many state-enterprise prices—notably, electricity prices—at relatively low levels. In any case, the Government had made an insufficient effort to make the public sector more efficient, and influential public opinion continued to perceive the deficit as a key problem; this meant that the Government's failure to address it was a problem.

Prices accelerated through the first half of 1987 in the wake of the Cruzado Plan's failure. Consumer prices rose 15 per cent per month in the first quarter and more than 20 per cent in the second quarter. The economic ministers who had designed the Plan resigned. A series of devaluations induced a dramatic recovery in the trade surplus by mid-1987, but contributed to resurgent inflationary pressure. Short-term interest rates fluctuated at high real levels. A record number of bankruptcies occurred, mainly affecting the many new businesses that were created in the euphoria of the Cruzado Plan.

In June 1987, the new ministerial team attempted another heterodox shock. This policy package came to be known as the "Bresser Plan" (after the Finance Minister who conceived it, Luiz Carlos Bresser Pereira). The Bresser Plan was an improvised emergency plan, and its ambitions were plainly modest. The freeze was limited to three months, and the stated objective was relief from high inflation rather than the "zero inflation" promised by the Cruzado Plan. The new minister planned a deeper stabilization program within a few months. Government expenditure cuts were announced, making this policy package somewhat more genuinely heterodox. Although the trade balance was clearly recovering, the Government felt that the international-reserve position was still inadequate, and was determined to take no chances. Accordingly, it carried out a "maxi-devaluation" of about 10 per cent.

In retrospect, this was probably an error like the Cruzado Plan's wage increase—an inflationary shock in conjunction with a price freeze. Consumer prices rose only 3 per cent in July and 6.5 per cent in August, but the monetary base—fuelled mainly by international-reserve accumulation accompanying record $1.4-billion monthly trade surpluses—grew 28 and 25 per cent. Rising international-reserve levels caused the money supply to grow sharply through the remainder of the year. Inflation inevitably returned to double-digit monthly levels once the Bresser Plan's price-freeze phase expired in September and pressure developed to adjust relative prices. During September and October the President decided against tax increases and approved some public-sector wage increases in excess of what the Finance Minister had publicly indicated would be consistent with price stability, precipitating the minister's resignation.

A new economic team took office at the end of 1987. It indicated that it would return to orthodox methods, particularly fiscal restraint. The new Finance Minister, Mailson da Nobrega, characterized the new policy stance as "rice and beans," implying a basic, orthodox approach with no experimentation. He indicated that Brazil would take a more accommodating stance in negotiations with external creditors. Bresser Pereira had actively sought new negotiations with external creditors, but, partly because international reserves were still low, had maintained the suspension of interest payments to commercial banks. By mid-1988, the new team secured rescheduling and new-money agreements to enable Brazil to normalize its amortization schedules and pay down its interest arrears. Since the agreements with the IMF and commercial banks required a substantial trade surplus to pay the interest bill, the crawling-peg exchange rate remained in place. Domestic interest rates remained high and the public sector's domestic debt continued to accumulate. The 1988 trade surplus exceeded US$19 billion, roughly 5.4 per cent of GDP.

The new team proposed postponing part of the indexation for public-sector wages, and struggled, with some success, to reduce various other categories of public expenditure: the January-June 1988 "operational" public deficit was just over one per cent of GDP (compared with 1.8 per cent for January–June 1987). The Government decided against drastically cutting its public investment program, however. The Congress elected in November 1986 refused to approve the Government's attempts to limit public-sector wages; the President, who was then seeking a one-year extension of his term of office to March 1990, avoided confronting the Congress. By early 1988 financial indexation was virtually restored, with government bonds henceforth linked to the average monthly overnight interest rate; open-market operations would be run so as to keep the overnight interest rate on the order of the inflation rate. Consumer prices rose 18 per cent per month in March, April, and May; over the remainder of the year inflation drifted higher, reaching 28 per cent in November and December.

On January 15, 1989, five months after Argentina's "Spring Plan," the Government announced yet another heterodox shock, the "Summer Plan". It included a devaluation of approximately 17 per cent, this time with another change of currency unit: one new *cruzado* was equal to 1,000 *cruzados* (and also to one dollar); the exchange rate was thereafter to be fixed. Prices and wages were frozen, and deep fiscal adjustment was promised. The economic team had expressed deep skepticism regarding heterodox approaches during 1988, but it now presented the program as the last hope of avoiding hyperinflation. It called on the Congress to support the program with legislation to permit deeper measures to reduce public expenditure.

The monetary base grew rapidly at first under the pressure of strong external accounts and heavy devaluation. The monetary authority sought to sterilize the monetary growth, forcing interest rates up in the process. The authorities believed that low interest rates had contributed to the failure of the Cruzado Plan, and accordingly decided to maintain high real rates. The nominal overnight interest rate persisted at around 20 per cent per month. (It had exceeded 30 per cent in December, but that was then the monthly inflation rate.) The increasing real public-sector interest bill deepened the public deficit, however. Total Treasury debt in the form of bonds and bills, which amounted to about US$73.6 billion (excluding Central Bank holdings) in December 1988 just before the Summer Plan was announced, rose to US$121.6 billion by the end of 1989. Unadjusted for inflation, the interest on this debt exceeded 20 per cent of 1989 GDP, double what it had been in 1987. The debt was index-linked or linked to overnight market interest rates; as in Argentina, since it was held by financial institutions in portfolios funded by very short-term deposits, the interest capitalized into it produced nearly direct liquidity creation.

Consumer prices rose sharply in January and February as expected, on account of the initial price rises. The 5.9 and 8.1 per-cent inflation rates in March and April, however, were clearly disappointing. The inflation resulted partly from a record trade surplus, but the Government could not afford to purchase the proceeds, and began incurring external interest arrears beginning in April 1988. With the early campaigning for the November 1989 presidential elections already under way and the Government discredited by public opinion, the Congress distanced itself from the Summer Plan. During the second half of 1989 monthly inflation ranged between 35 and 50 per cent. The ministerial team openly gave up after September, saying that a new stabilization effort would have to await the government that took office in March 1990.

5   CONCLUDING OBSERVATIONS

A skeptical observer might conclude that Argentina's and Brazil's experiences indicate the futility of heterodox approaches, while Israel's success resulted from external support combined with orthodox monetary and fiscal rigor that would have sufficed without the program's unorthodox elements. The present argument is that the Argentine and Brazilian programs incorporated errors and shortcomings that were not essential aspects of heterodox stabilization, while the unorthodox aspects contributed, perhaps decisively, to the success of Israel's program.

A basic—if seemingly obvious—lesson from the Brazilian experience is that inflationary shocks should not accompany stabilization programs. Policy-makers may be under pressure to sustain wages and incomes, or to shore up the external accounts, but wage increases and devaluation work against inflation stabilization. Brazil's external trade was heavily in surplus at the moment of the Cruzado Plan, and a case might be made that the new currency unit ought to have been *revalued* somewhat—although no conceivable revaluation could, by itself, have offset the inflationary effects of the wage increases. On the other hand, the initial devaluation reduced the Bresser Plan's chances of success. Apart from its monetary consequences, since devaluation directly increases any price linked to external prices, devaluation is logically difficult to combine with a general price freeze.

Israeli policy-makers deliberately used the exchange rate as the price-level anchor after 1985, largely because they had no other. If exchange-rate policy is used to manage the price level, however, it may be unavailable to manage the external accounts. Israel had critically important advantages compared with Argentina and Brazil, in that it was under less pressure regarding its external debt and the United States grant made its fixed exchange rate more credible.

Without adequate international reserves, a monetary authority can defend its exchange rate and so anchor its price level only through high interest rates. Argentina's and Brazil's experiences clearly indicate the dangers of this approach. If the private sector must pay high interest rates, particularly if it is heavily indebted, it may be decapitalized; recession is more likely. If the public sector must pay high interest rates, it must either (i) run a highly contractionary non-interest surplus or (ii) increase its domestic indebtedness, either in the form of money or in the form of interest-bearing debt.

Heavy public domestic debt and high interest rates together complicated the more recent Argentine and Brazilian stabilization efforts. In Argentina's August 1988 and July 1989 plans and Brazil's January 1989 plans, the authorities tried to stabilize the exchange rate and the price level through high interest rates. Since the public sector was the economy's principal debtor, higher interest rates worsened the public-sector deficit. Fearing that money financing would be destabilizing, the authorities placed more debt to finance the deficit. Public-sector "distress"—a cycle of swelling interest bills financed by additional debt—resulted. Once the debt exceeded what the private sector could be persuaded to hold, only an inflationary explosion or outright default could reduce it.

While money demand increases after a stabilizing shock, the Argentine and Brazilian experiences suggest that a monetary authority must create liquidity circumspectly. With prices frozen, higher money demand is in some degree a measurement increase. The Argentine authorities may have allowed higher money demand to raise real interest rates excessively over the second part of 1985. The Brazilian authorities made the opposite error, allowing the money supply to increase too rapidly in the months following the Cruzado Plan. In the wake of a stabilizing shock, a monetary authority would be best advised to carry out active policy, targeting financial rates on a day-to-day basis to gauge the public's willingness to absorb increased liquidity issues, and holding money stocks just below it. Similarly, policy-makers should not rely excessively on a price freeze to improve public-sector finances through a favorable Olivera–Tanzi effect. Unless inflation has fallen from exceedingly high levels or the collection lag is uncommonly long, the Olivera–Tanzi improvement is small in magnitude and easily reversible.

In sum, Argentina's and Brazil's heterodox programs failed, largely for reasons that were not inherent in heterodox stabilization. Israel's July 1985 program was as successful as could reasonably be expected. The evidence is insufficient to assert definitively that the heterodox elements made the difference for Israel, but a strong case can be made that the inflation rate could not have fallen so far without the labor-business accords and the stabilized exchange rate.

In any case, public opinion and political leaders must clearly understand that freezing prices does not constitute sustainable stabilization. At best, a price freeze produces artificial, temporary stabilization, a truce rather than genuine peace. Used realistically, its purpose should be to interrupt the inflation-feedback process long enough to set a context for deeper stabilization measures.

10 Toward a Theory of Self-Perpetuating Inflation

Inflation is one possible manifestation of a macroeconomic inconsistency in which a society's economic entities collectively exercise more claims on goods and services than the quantity available. Since goods and services are scarce relative to exercised claims, their prices are bid up. In a "non-inflationary" resolution of this inconsistency, the disequilibrium would be temporary: once prices rose, money values of claims and available goods and services would settle into equilibrium. In an inflationary process, however, the value of exercised claims grows as fast as, or faster than, the value of the goods and services. It follows, then, that to understand an inflationary process is to understand how economic entities—considered individually or as definable entities—maintain or increase their claims even after a presumably equilibrating price-level rise.[1]

In evolving arrangements to live with inflation, societies like Argentina and Brazil have developed robust devices to keep purchasing power growing along with inflation. These include mechanisms that sustain or increase prices, incomes, contract values, and credit and money stocks. These societies have refined and strengthened these devices through the experience of inflation, particularly after the debt crisis began in 1982 and the rest of the world became a competitor for, rather than a supplier of, purchasing power. Lenders of financial resources have learned, for example, to insist either that they be paid interest rates high enough to compensate for *possible* as well as for *expected* inflation, or else that their contracts be denominated in purchasing power. They have learned to lend for the short term, so that they constantly revise interest rates against changing expectations. Suppliers of labor services have learned to make similar demands regarding their contracts. People who borrow financial resources or hire labor have learned that they can commit themselves to pay relatively high real interest rates or high contracted wages as long as everyone else does so, precisely because a widespread need to validate existing contracts compels monetary authorities to increase the money supply as necessary.

People in a position to set their selling prices have learned to lead inflation, setting high prices to the extent they have monopoly power or face inelastic demand. People whose prices are set by the authorities have learned effective political arguments to support claims for higher prices or subsidies—for example, they have learned to argue that on such-and-such a date in the recent past the real price was at such-and-such a real level, and that it would be appropriate for the real price to return to that level. Where the price in question is the exchange rate received by exporters, for example, foreign financial institutions—whose interest is that the nation maintain a high external resource transfer—are likely to be the exporters' allies in advocating a high foreign-exchange price. Where the price in question is the wage rate, labor typically finds few sympathizers in foreign financial institutions, but stronger supporters among domestic "wage-goods" business interests.

Conventional macroeconomic policy is less effective in societies where people have developed and refined powerful mechanisms to maintain their purchasing power and force credit and money creation. Indeed, people have learned to defend themselves against conventional monetary and fiscal policy as against inflation. Thus, a central bank that runs tight monetary policy and drives up interest rates may find that the high interest rates deter few borrowers and lenders—ironically, because borrowers and lenders alike expect the monetary authority ultimately to create sufficient means of payment to validate their contracts at any interest rate. In effect, expected inflation rises along with the nominal interest rates, leaving real interest rates almost unaffected.

To the frustration of advocates of fiscal soundness, societies with lengthy experience of inflation and stabilization often have powerful means to resist fiscal tightening. Public-sector workers often secure contracts that protect their employment, or make dismissal extremely costly, and maintain their wage levels. Partly through increased evasion, tax revenues tend to decline as a proportion of GDP when inflation rises. Inflation and recession inevitably stiffen political resistance to tax-rate increases. (The disposition to pay taxes may have been diminished in some nations by the perception that public expenditure is likely to go to bureaucrats, corrupt contractors, or external-debt service rather than, say, essential public services or infrastructure investment.) Social-security programs are under political pressure to maintain real income levels; public-enterprise prices come under political pressures to lag behind the inflation rate. In many nations, years of high interest rates and heavy debt accumulation have made public-sector interest bills exorbitant.

Against such pressures, governments and finance ministers often have narrow scope to cut public expenditure. Legislatures and ministers often find large parts of their budgets effectively committed under contracts or entitlements. Legislatures inevitably find it difficult to program within a global expenditure total.[2] A finance minister's easiest possibilities for cuts may be (i) to delay payments to suppliers—who may be able to secure credit from their commercial banks on the basis of the government's promise eventually to pay; (ii) to reduce the quality of public services; and (iii) to cut maintenance and capital-formation expenditure—an approach that is possible for short time periods, but which eventually leads to infrastructure deterioration, with inevitable negative consequences for productivity.

This book has argued that, in order to succeed permanently with a limited amount of damage to production systems and capital formation, stabilization strategies need to be attentive to inflation-feedback processes and to the purchasing-power maintenance mechanisms that underlie them. Where inflation rates have been successfully reduced, the stabilization policies have amounted to a significant reduction in the growth rate of purchasing-power claims—whether through agreement among labor, industry, and government (e.g., Israel); fiscal discipline with wage limitations and dismissals (Bolivia); or public-sector budgeting by dictatorship (Chile). In contrast, the determination with which people maintain income claims helps explain the disappointing results of some recent heterodox programs. Frozen prices and wages ultimately cannot work if total claims on goods and services continue to exceed total goods and services available. Even before the inevitable day they are freed, prices and wages are likely to rise, reflecting the underlying reality of excessive claims. No "policy" can work unless economic entities' claims, or exercise of claims, can be made consistent with the overall availability of goods and services.

The seven unsuccessful Argentine and Brazilian stabilization attempts between 1985 and 1989 (June 1985, October 1987, August 1988, and July 1989 in Argentina; February 1986, June 1987, and January 1989 in Brazil) were explicitly intended to subdue their nations' respective inertial-inflation processes. In both nations, the cycle of freezing and freeing prices has become a problem in itself—a source of business uncertainty, a standing demonstration of policy impotence, and a source of deepening cynicism. Among other things, when businessmen sense another "shock" coming, they raise prices pre-emptively. Societies are visibly weary not only of inflation but of repeated ambitious policy packages.

Nevertheless, it would be unfortunate if the Argentine and Brazilian failures discredited the inertial-inflation concept and the importance of dealing with it in stabilization programs. The price freezes and de-indexation, in themselves, undoubtedly made inflation-feedback processes less robust. To understand what went wrong, two points are essential. First, the freezes could not stop the inflation-feedback processes, particularly since they left relative-price arrays frozen in disequilibrium.[3] Reliance on the price freeze evaded the issue of how purchasing-power would henceforth be reconciled with available aggregate supply. In particular, it evaded the issue of who—wage earners, exporters, importers, holders of public debt—would give up purchasing power. Successful stabilization required a second, more difficult and comprehensive phase of policies to deal with this issue. Second, powerful inflationary shocks accompanied all of the programs as they were implemented. Devaluation figured in all the programs except the Cruzado Plan. The Cruzado Plan incorporated substantial wage increases that set off a "wage bubble," which generated shortages, excess aggregate demand, and repressed inflation, and finally hastened the resurgence of inflation.

The Cruzado Plan wage increases bring the role of purchasing-power allocation in inflationary processes to the fore. The Cruzado Plan might have worked better had real wages not risen at the outset— if they could have been set at their average real value over the preceding six months. As explained in Chapter 9, this would have required money wages that had recently been adjusted to decline. The Government considered this politically unacceptable, and so instead it increased real wages by 8 per cent. That is, income could not explicitly be taken from people whose wages had recently risen. On the other hand, it would have been unfair, and probably politically impossible to allow them alone to keep their higher real wages (i.e., by freezing everyone's money wages). The generalized 8 per cent wage increase was inflationary, however. As this episode suggests, part of the sustaining force of an inflation is the general consensus that no one in a civilized industrial economy ever ought to suffer a money-income loss.

Israel's experience suggests that inflationary pressure can be reduced where people can be persuaded to moderate real-income claims all together. The heterodox stabilization program that began in July 1985 has worked long enough to describe it as reasonably successful. The national labor federation agreed to forgo cost-of-living adjustments; private manufacturers agreed to price restraint; and the government reduced expenditure. Against this accord, the Bank of Israel stabilized the exchange rate. Even with all this, the special emergency stabilization support provided by the United States undoubtedly made an essential difference, permitting the authorities to accumulate sufficient foreign exchange to make the exchange rate credible. Moreover, although it does have substantial external obligations, Israel has not had to struggle with a cartel of external creditors pressuring it for large resource transfers.

It is uncertain how applicable Israel's experience is to nations like Argentina and Brazil. Israel is a small nation, with a unified labor confederation and a single industrial bargaining entity. The government that carried out the stabilization program was a broad political coalition. The labor confederation owns and manages many enterprises, and accordingly comprehends a management viewpoint. Neither Argentina nor Brazil are likely to receive external support of the relative dimension Israel secured. External debt apart, an important part of the underlying problem for nations like Argentina, Brazil and Peru is that their governments are administratively weak. Years of military rule have affected the legitimacy that these governments command within their own societies. Transitional regimes like the one that governed Brazil from 1985 to 1990 or newly re-democratized governments like Argentina's find themselves having to deal all at once with claims by impatient foreign creditors, domestic financial markets, civil servants, labor unions, and others, none prepared to accept any responsibility for the state of affairs, let alone offer sacrifices.

Unfortunately, such governments cannot fully establish authority nor set a framework within which a society can discipline itself if they cannot control the inflation they inherited. That is, they must somehow control inflation without quite being able to do so, in order to acquire sufficient time and legitimacy to set the conditions necessary for full stabilization. This perspective helps explain why the Argentine and Brazilian governments attempted heterodox stabilization programs within a year and a half of receiving power from military regimes. People caught up in the peculiar euphoria of the time did not perceive that the price, wage and exchange-rate freezes were not stabilization policies *per se*; rather, they were more like *pre*-stabilization policies, measures whose true purpose was to create an economic environment in which genuine stabilizing measures could take hold. They constituted truces, not genuine peace, in the inflationary struggle.

The challenge for medium-term stabilization policy is to devise rules that hold aggregate claims broadly within the means defined by the aggregate supply of goods and services, and then to set institutional relationships through which shorter-term macroeconomic policy can adjust aggregate claims more precisely, within a shorter-term context. In broadest terms, the rules must (i) rely on, not work against, market mechanisms, to the extent possible—not because market mechanisms are necessarily "good," but because they are powerful and self-activating; and must (ii) constrain the non-market and semi-market components of the economy—essentially, the public sector and the banking system—to a reasonable degree of austerity.

In recent years at least two alternative, or complementary, stabilization approaches have been proposed: (i) "supply-side" approaches and (ii) social accords. At various times strong claims have been made for these approaches in Argentina, Brazil and Peru, and they have acquired a bad reputation because attempts to apply them were mismanaged. This chapter concludes with some comments on their relationship with the "inertial" approach. The premise of supply-side inflation stabilization is that, if inflation results from relative abundance of money and scarcity of goods and services, it might be more effective, less painful and at all events more constructive to increase production rather than make money more scarce. A supply-side stabilization program would set incentives to productive resource use, through better incentives to employment, reduced taxation of productive activity, expansion of credit facilities for productive purposes, and so on. The idea of social accords, of course, is to agree explicitly on how to share purchasing-power claims.

Nothing in the "inertial" analysis contradicts these approaches. Encouraging efficient output and employment is desirable on the face of it, as long as the means chosen are sustainable. It is essential, for example, that the production incentives be set by relieving, not creating, price distortions, and that the price system be made more, not less, effective in the process. Subsidies and tax breaks provided should be self-financing, i.e., covered by the ultimate tax yield of the increased economic activity. They should also be clearly regulated, transparent entries in a national budget, and should not operate through direct price manipulation. Nevertheless, supply-side approaches cannot significantly relieve a high inflation sustained by inertial processes, stubborn anticipations, and automatic money-creation mechanisms. If well-designed, they could make the economy function better and more productively while appropriate measures are taken to deal with inertial inflation. Peru's experience after 1985 illustrates the dangers of a supply-side approach, however: first, to induce increases in output, the authorities distorted the price system severely; and second, the increases in real output and income generated import pressures that depleted Peru's international reserves even though Peru suspended the bulk of its external debt service. Peru slipped into hyperinflation and severe recession by 1988.

"Social accords" are unquestionably consistent with this book's argument that the rules regarding purchasing-power allocation need to be addressed, explicitly or implicitly, to ensure stabilization. From time to time, Argentine, Brazilian and Peruvian officials have proposed such pacts with varying degrees of seriousness, but never made significant progress. As Brazil's Cruzado Plan broke down toward the end of 1986, and several times thereafter, the Labor Minister attempted unsuccessfully to piece together a social pact. Peru's Labor Minister attempted to negotiate a "social accord" with labor and industry representatives in the early 1980s; the attempt failed, partly because labor insisted on job stability and on rehiring of workers who had lost jobs in earlier years, partly because private industrialists were suspicious of the approach.

Nevertheless, the Israeli experiences in July 1985 and January 1987, when labor and business representatives reached agreements with the government, suggests that progress is possible if the participants are predisposed to make them work. Where some groups believe their chances are better with inflation than with social accord, however, agreement may be impossible. Some groups may need some inflationary experience to learn that their chances are probably worse over the long run. Even then, bad experience may only drive some people to conclude that they need to be tougher and more insistent at the next bargaining round. External claimants may, of course, be the most important potential participants in the social consensus; again, in Israel's case, the external sector provided an important, perhaps crucial, concession in the form of the United States grant.

Without explicit or implicit social consensus regarding purchasing-power allocation, no economy can overcome inflation permanently. To be sure, economies unable to achieve implicit social understandings are unlikely to succeed with explicit understandings. Social consensus must somehow be built, and maintained; this is the true underpinning of price stability. A temporary, if precarious, stabilization program may make it possible to reach a consensus on a more permanent understanding regarding income allocation.

Inflation is likely to remain a serious problem in many economies for years to come. Gradually, as experience accumulates, as techniques of policy control improve, as political sophistication deepens, as governments gradually deepen and extend their administrative capacity, and as external-debt management becomes more realistic, inflation should gradually diminish in intensity. This will probably happen more slowly than people hope, and this could slow economic development. Societies will be called upon to remain realistic and patient, and above all to continue longer-term programs of public-sector restructuring.

Notes

1 The Inflation Enigma

1. Several generations of Brazilian economists have written extensively about self-perpetuating inflation. Rangel 1963 treated the self-perpetuating character of inflation. Simonsen 1970 discussed the "inflation-feedback" idea. Bresser and Nakano 1984 and Lopes 1986 discussed the "inertial-inflation" concept.
2. See Galbraith 1975, pp. 44–7.
3. The school of economic thought now called "neo-classical" dates back to the mid-nineteenth century. It encompasses the theories of such writers as John Stuart Mill, W. Stanley Jevons, Alfred Marshall, and Leon Walras. These neo-classical economists considered their work to be the elaboration of "classical" economics, as elucidated, principally, by David Hume, Adam Smith, Thomas Malthus, James Mill, and David Ricardo. As Keynes noted in the single footnote in Chapter 1 of his *General Theory*, however, this was not really so. The essence of neo-classical theory is the view that the relative values of goods and services derive from their relative "scarcities"—i.e., relative "supply and demand." After rejecting the "mercantilist" theory that gold and silver embody value, the classical economists had substituted a "labor" theory of value, according to which the relative values of goods derive from their labor content. Karl Marx took his labor theory of value from the classical writers (it was Marx who first called them "classical"). With the decline of Marxian economic thought, neo-classical analysis appears now to have become the universal paradigm of economic analysis.

2 Why Inflation is "A Bad Thing"

1. An extensive literature has appeared since the 1970s on the subject of "the welfare costs of inflation." Okun 1971 and Jaffee and Kleiman 1977 provide valuable broad discussions of the issue. Stanley Fischer has made particularly important contributions; see the papers collected in *Indexing, Inflation and Economic Policy* (MIT Press, 1986).
2. Statistical analysis of data published by the IMF for these nine economies suggests that, in general, (i) year-over-year inflation rates, and (ii) the ratios of narrow and broad money supply to GDP are negatively correlated over time. Correlation coefficients for ten- to fifteen-year time series ending in the mid-1980s are negative and statistically significant in most instances, except for Colombia, Venezuela, and Peru's broad money supply. The Peruvian exception may be explained by the fact that over much of the period its broad monetary aggregate included dollar-denominated deposit accounts; dollar denomination roughly preserved their purchasing-power value (see Chapter 8). Money-holding behavior

is subject to many different influences, but the data seem broadly consistent with the point that people prefer to hold less money when the real cost of holding it—in particular, the inflationary erosion of purchasing power—is higher.

3. See Keynes 1936, Chapters 13, 14, 15, and 17.

4. If the money interest rate is n, an asset worth one *peso* at the start of a period will be worth $(1+n)$ *pesos* at the end. Suppose one *peso* buys one basket of goods at the start of the period. If the inflation rate over the period is x, $(1+x)$ *pesos* buy one basket of goods at the end of the period. It follows that $(1+n)$ *pesos* buy $(1+n)/(1+x)$ baskets of goods at the end of the period. In terms of baskets of goods, then, the rate of return is

$$r = \{[(1+n)/(1+x)]-1\}/1 = (n-x)/(1+x)$$

Note that if money itself has a nominal interest rate n of zero, its real rate of return is

$$-x/(1+x)$$

Here n, x and r are expressed as decimals; use 100 instead of 1 in the formula to use percentages for n and x.

5. A simple example can make the point. Suppose that (i) lenders must pay a 20-per-cent tax on interest earnings when received; (ii) interest is received when the financial instrument matures; and (iii) the real interest rate is to be 20 per cent over the period in question. If no inflation is anticipated, the nominal interest rate would be 20 per cent. The anticipated real tax rate would be 20 per cent of 20 per cent, or 4 per cent of the principal. Now, however, suppose inflation of 25 per cent is anticipated over the period. The nominal interest rate would have to be 50 per cent in order for the real interest rate to be $[(100 \text{ times } (.50-.25)/(1+0.25)]$, or 20 per cent. In this case the same tax would be 20 per cent of 50 per cent, or 10 per cent of the principal. Since the tax is paid at maturity, it would lose 20 per cent of its value (a 25 per-cent inflation causes a 20 per cent purchasing-power loss for any money value). The resulting 8 per cent, however, would be 40 per cent of the real interest rate; the anticipated tax rate would thus be double what it would be in the absence of inflation.

If the tax is paid at the moment the interest is paid and received, i.e., when the financial instrument matures, the real after-tax interest received (r') becomes

$$r' = [(n-x)/(1+x)]-[n \, t/(1+x)]$$

The first term here is the real interest rate paid by the borrower, and the second term is therefore what the lender fails to receive out of what the borrower pays. The second term divided by the first gives the effective real tax rate on the interest income—i.e., the proportion of the real interest rate paid in tax:

$$t/[1-(x/n)]$$

Since higher inflation causes lenders to pay higher percentage taxes on the same real interest, higher anticipated inflation may induce them to seek higher before-tax real interest rates.

The supposition that the tax is paid when the financial instrument matures affects the precise formulas, though not the general point that the effective real tax rate rises with the inflation rate. If there is any inflation, however, the effective real tax rate will be lower, the farther into the future the tax is paid. Taxes on financial returns that are paid some time after the interest is paid must be deflated by a longer inflation accumulation. (Tanzi 1984 discusses the intricacies of the relationships among inflation, interest rates and taxation.)

6. Friedman 1977 incorporates a now "classic" discussion of price-level uncertainty. Also, see Holland 1984.

7. In a "Dutch" auction, a lot of goods is to be sold; bidding opens at a top price and proceeds downward until a price is reached at which the entire lot is sold.

8. More precisely, the government's proceeds from the sale of the bonds will be smaller in the second case, even though the government will be indebted to the same degree.

   Some economists have suggested that under certain special conditions the general principle stated here might not apply. The public's subjective probability distribution of the future inflation rate might be characterized by negative or positive covariance with the probability distributions for yields on other assets. Such covariance may produce counter-intuitive outcomes. For example, suppose the public perceives the real rates of return (i.e., the yields in purchasing-power terms) on bonds and equities to be negatively correlated. That is, while both are uncertain, the public figures that if one yield turns out higher than expected, the other will tend to turn out lower than expected. In this instance, an increase in the perceived uncertainty attaching to the bond yield might lead to a higher bond price. This would happen to the degree the risk-averse public maintains a high demand for bonds to form "hedged" portfolios in bonds and equities—mixed portfolios whose yield is perceived to be less risky on the view that if one asset performs poorly the other will perform well (see Fischer 1975).

9. Cukierman and Wachtel 1979 and 1982 treat this subject.

10. The literature on the subject of "relative-price dispersion" includes Glejser 1965, Vining and Elwertowski 1976, Parks 1981, Bordo 1980, Blejer 1981, Hercowitz 1981, Blejer and Leiderman 1982, Silva and Kadota 1982, Blanchard 1983, Cukierman and Leiderman 1984, and Sellekaerts and Sellekaerts 1984.

11. On this point, see Patinkin 1965.

12. In an unpublished study of the behavior of the 36 components of the Peruvian consumer price index for the period January 1973–May 1980, this writer calculated a relative-price dispersion index. This index was defined as the weighted average of the absolute values of the monthly percentage changes in the 36 relative-price indices; the weighting was according to the relative importance of the 36 components in the index. Consumer prices rose an average of 2.77 per cent per month over this period. The average monthly value of the index—that is, the average monthly variation in relative consumer prices—was 2.64 per cent over the period.

13. Robert Lucas has crafted ingenious analytical models that turn, in part, on people's inability to distinguish concurrent changes in particular prices and in prices generally. See Lucas 1981.

14. Silva and Kadota 1982 provides empirical evidence on this point for Brazil. The unpublished study of Peruvian consumer prices by this writer previously cited found that 62.9 per cent of the 36 price categories weighted by relative importance in the index lagged behind the price index each month. In each quarter an average of 57.5 per cent by weight of the prices in the index lagged behind the overall consumer-price increase. The weighted percentage of price increases that lagged behind the price index was below 50 per cent only in 5 of the 28 quarters in the period.

15. Notable contributions include Cagan 1956, Sargent 1982 and Dornbusch 1987.

3 Inflation Feedback

1. Economists generally accept this section's subject matter as "standard," and so readers acquainted with basic monetary theory may prefer to skip it.

2. Non-monetary banking-system liabilities would include (apart from such things as banks' outstanding bills for office supplies) commercial banks' less liquid financial liabilities, as well as any non-monetary central-bank obligations.

3. Galbraith 1975 provides a highly readable summary history of monetary institutions and their development. Hammond 1956 is the most thorough treatment of the early development of banking institutions in the United States.

4. Central banks developed the practice of lending to commercial banks by "rediscounting" the commercial banks' discounted promissory notes. A commercial bank that lent money by "discounting" a three-month, £1000 promissory note for £980 might have it "rediscounted" by the central bank for £990. Upon redemption, the central bank and the commercial bank would thus share the £20 in earnings. The rediscounted note constituted collateral for the central bank; central banks accordingly took care to rediscount the most secure merchant obligations. Most central banks permit commercial banks to use rediscount credit rarely, under restrictive conditions, and then only for temporary liquidity problems—that is, heavy deposit withdrawals judged to be unrelated to the particular bank's fundamental soundness. A few central banks use routine rediscount lending as an active policy instrument, however.

5. The seminal description of a banking system's structure and the central bank's role was provided by Bagehot 1873. The work of Irving Fisher early in this century—particularly Fisher 1911—refined economists' understanding still further.

6. An open-market sale has a more powerful contractionary effect on the money supply if the central bank is paid with a check drawn on a commercial bank. The central bank debits the check against the commercial bank's reserve account. The commercial bank might then have to reduce demand deposits proportionally to maintain compliance with the minimum reserve ratio. For example, suppose the minimum reserve ratio is

20 per cent. If a bank is operating at this ratio, and its reserve account at the central bank falls by one *peso*, it must reduce demand deposits by five *pesos* to maintain the 5:1 deposit–reserve ratio.

7. See Friedman 1956 for the seminal statement of monetarist principles. The contributions to Meiselman 1970 are classic examples of monetarist analysis.

8. Cagan 1956, a seminal monetarist analysis of hyperinflation, drew analysts' attention to the effect of expected inflation on money demand. "Rational-expectations" analysts of the 1970s drew analysts' attention to the importance of expectations generally.

9. Prebisch 1981 provides a clear exposition of structuralist tenets. The contributions by Campos, Felix, Grunwald, and Hirschman in Hirschman 1961 indicate the state of the monetarist–structuralist debate at that time. Taylor 1979 provides a structuralist perspective of more recent vintage.

10. Increased excess demand for all other things may also include increased demand for or decreased supply of financial assets. It is therefore possible for inflation to occur with *excess supply* of goods and services, as long as there is excess demand for financial assets (or excess supply of borrowed funds).

11. Mundell 1970 discusses this point. Using the symbols defined in the discussion of the banking system's structure, the central bank's balance-sheet identity is given by

$$A + F + H = B + V$$

(i.e., foreign and domestic assets sum to the central bank's monetary base plus net worth). The inflation rate resulting from a central bank acquiring assets of $\triangle A/Y$, $\triangle F/Y$, and $\triangle H/Y$, and earning profits of $\triangle V/Y$, where Y represents nominal GDP, may be calculated as follows. In flow terms (excluding "valuation changes" such as revaluation of international reserves resulting from exchange-rate changes and capital gains on government obligations),

$$\triangle A + \triangle F + \triangle H = \triangle B + \triangle V$$

Since $\triangle M = \text{m} \triangle B$,

$$\triangle M = m (\triangle A + \triangle F + \triangle H - \triangle V)$$

or

$$\triangle M/Y = m (\triangle A + \triangle F + \triangle H - \triangle V)/Y$$

Let g_p, g_y, g_M and gv represent, respectively, the growth rates of prices, real GDP, the money supply, and velocity of circulation. (Since "v" is equal to Y/M, $1/v$ equals the "monetization rate," or demand for money as a proportion of GDP, M/Y; g_v is the negative of the growth rate of monetization.) Since

$$g_M = g_p + g_y - g_v$$

and

$$\triangle M/Y = (M/Y) g_M,$$

the inflation rate is given by

$$g_p = g_y - g_v + m\,v\,[\triangle A + \triangle F + \triangle H - \triangle V]/Y$$

12. A "rational" expectation is not necessarily a correct expectation. It is a "reasoned" expectation, given available information and theory. Theoreticians have constructed intricate analytical models in which they have embedded the analytical models and information of people forming rational expectations. Convincing answers to the question of whether it is fair to presume that people form expectations "rationally" remain elusive, however. See the contributions to Lucas and Sargent 1981.

13. The Survey Research Center of the University of Michigan has done work of this kind for the United States. For example, see Katona and Strumpel 1978.

14. Or, perhaps more truthfully stated, to infer the expectations that would explain people's observed behavior.

15. Researchers have concentrated more on price-level expectations than on uncertainty, in part because most statistical techniques cannot convincingly distinguish them.

16. In effect, Cagan and others argued that their analyses indicated that such a "bubble" cannot continue indefinitely unless money is created.

17. Suppose GDP grows at a real annual rate of g, and that the annual inflation rate is x. Suppose there is a "collection lag" of n days, i.e., that tax revenues based on prices and incomes at any given moment are received by the government n days later. Let t' be the proportion of GDP that tax receipts would be if they were collected with no lag or if there were no inflation. The government will actually receive tax receipts amounting to the proportion t of GDP:

$$t = t'/[(1+x)\,(1+g)]^{(n/365)}$$

The nominal "base" tax rate t' can be approximated from the observed tax-revenue rate by

$$t' = t\,[(1+x)\,(1+g)]^{(n/365)}$$

18. Sargent and Wallace 1981 describe this problem.

19. This became a particularly important problem in Argentina, where high reserve requirements were used to fight inflation throughout the 1980s but high interest rates were paid on the reserves. See Chapter 9.

20. Brazil's central bank issued Central Bank Bills in 1986 and 1987, and used them to carry out open-market operations. Argentina's central bank issued short-term interest-bearing securities in the late 1980s.

21. One implication of this approach has been that, whenever the authorities tried to tighten monetary policy by raising bank reserve requirements, the central bank would have to create money to pay interest on the additional reserves. In the late 1980s the Argentine central bank increasingly found it necessary to capitalize interest payments due the commercial banks, and to

make the resulting liabilities "inaccessible"—that is, unavailable to the banks as a basis for credit expansion. (See Chapter 9.)

22. Let Z represent the public sector's non-interest deficit, D the public sector's average outstanding domestic debt during the period in question, $\triangle D$ the change over the period in this debt stock over the period, n the nominal interest rate on the government's debt, and x the inflation rate over the period. Assume for simplicity that there is no external debt. The nominal deficit and its financing are given by

$$Z + n\,D = \triangle D$$

To calculate the "real-basis" deficit and its financing, subtract the inflation adjustment of the outstanding debt and interest from both sides:

$$Z + [(n-x)/(1+x)]\,D = \triangle D - [x\,(1+n)/(1+x)]\,D$$

23. The basic indicator of the public sector's domestic borrowing pressure is the ratio of the *stock* of domestic public-sector debt to GDP. Suppose for the moment (i) that the non-interest borrowing requirement is zero and that (ii) the interest on the debt is all accrued, i.e., capitalized into the outstanding debt. The debt–GDP ratio would increase, decrease, or remain the same according to whether the *real* interest rate on the debt exceeded, fell short of or equalled *real* GDP growth. Another way of seeing the point is as follows: suppose inflation suddenly and definitively ceased and all outstanding debt were immediately refinanced at interest rates reflecting expected inflation of zero. The full PSBR would immediately equal the real-basis PSBR. That is, the real-basis PSBR measures the pressure to increase the public sector's domestic debt relative to the economy's size, and hence the extent to which the public-sector borrowing requirement is likely to result in some combination of *higher* real interest rates, *higher* external debt, and *higher* inflationary pressure.

24. The Scots philosopher David Hume described this principle in 1752; accordingly, it has come to be known as the "Hume specie-flow mechanism."

25. Central banks may be able to limit exporters' ability to sell their foreign-exchange proceeds in parallel markets by forcing them to register merchandise transactions. Exporters can evade the central bank's controls in some measure by "under-invoicing" their exports—that is, registering a sales invoice with the central bank with a lower unit price than the price actually paid the exporter by the foreign purchaser.

26. The literature is too voluminous to review here. Santomero and Seater 1978 remains one of the best summaries of the literature, most of which dates from the 1950s through the mid-1970s.

27. Thus, for example, one line of reasoning was that the wage rate is the bulk of prime cost, and, following basic price theory, price is determined by prime cost. Another argument was the following: labor income is the wage rate (w) multiplied by the number of people working (n), and total income is the price level (p) multiplied by the volume of real economic activity (y); if business sets prices so that labor income is a roughly constant share of total income, wn/py is a constant. Let g represent "growth of"; then

$$g_w + g_n = g_p + g_y,$$

or, rearranging,

$$g_p = g_w - g_{y/n},$$

that is, the price level tends to rise at a rate equal to wage-rate growth, less labor-productivity growth. Over short time-intervals for which labor productivity changes little, the inflation rate ought then to be closely related to wage-rate growth.

28. Because the Chicago school is particularly associated with "monetarism," its critique of the Phillips curve came to be associated with monetarism, although they are not the same thing. The critique was first enunciated in Milton Friedman's 1968 address to the American Economics Association when he was inaugurated as its president, then developed in a series of influential papers by such writers as Robert Lucas.

29. Bresser Pereira and Nakano (1987) have distinguished "accelerating," "decelerating" and "inertial" factors affecting the price level over the career of an inflation. In the absence of accelerating and decelerating influences, an inflation would be propagated forward by the inertial influences; inflationary or deflationary shocks would then cause prices to accelerate or decelerate. This taxonomy differs subtly but significantly from this chapter's approach. Here, a price-level rise is at once a stabilizing event and an inflationary shock giving rise to inflationary pressure in subsequent periods. Although the Bresser–Nakano taxonomy is appealing, it has some of the troubling arbitrariness of the distinction between demand-pull and cost-push inflation: one observer (e.g., a worker) might describe a round of wage increases as "inertial," while another (e.g., a businessman) might call it an "accelerating" shock. This chapter would simply call it an inflationary shock—the price level will rise faster than it would have if the event had not occurred—without attempting the distinction. Moreover, the same price-level increase can generate different amounts of subsequent inflationary pressure, depending on the circumstances. Thus, for example, a price-level increase might have a larger subsequent inflationary effect, the larger the increase in price-level uncertainty that accompanies it.

4 Inflation Feedback and Competition for Purchasing Power

1. Suppose a wage contract specifies a money wage rate of w to be paid over a one-year period. If the (decimal) inflation rate over the year is x, the real value of the wage at the very end of the year—the end-year value of the wage at start-of-the-year prices—will be $w/(1 + x)$. The real wage accordingly varies from a high of w to a low of $w/(1 + x)$. The (geometric) average of w and $w/(1 + x)$ is the approximate average real wage over the year,

$$v = w (1 + x)^{-1/2}$$

Suppose the wage contract period is h years. Over the contract period the real wage falls from w to

$$w/[(1 + x)^h]$$

and the approximate (geometric) average real wage becomes

$$v = w/[(1 + x)^{h/2}]$$

Given values of w and x, a shorter contract period h implies a higher average real wage and a narrower range of variation. Given some expected inflation rate, these formulas can be solved for the nominal wage w corresponding to any desired average real wage v.

2. A firm facing *inelastic* demand can raise earnings by raising its price, but reduces its earnings if it lowers its price; an entity facing *elastic* demand can raise earnings by lowering its price, but reduces its earnings by raising its price.

3. See Minsky 1982. Since Minsky's book appeared, there have been several other instances in which the Federal Reserve allowed monetary expansion in the wake of crises, notably the 1984 failure of the Continental Illinois Bank and the October 1987 stock-market collapse.

5 Inflation and Financial Systems

1. The "neo-liberal" school of economic thought, which has come to dominate the economics profession, may be described as the reaffirmation of neo-classical economics for policy-making. Its essential principle is that economic growth requires markets to function freely and efficiently, that prices be set either by markets (or, at worst, by authorities intent on equilibrating supply and demand), and that public sectors should limit their demand for resources to the minimum strictly necessary for government functions. McKinnon 1973 and Shaw 1973 are seminal expositions of the neo-liberal approach to financial development.

2. The argument that a free financial market can deal tolerably well with changes in expected inflation is as follows. Assume that, with perfect price-level stability, the supply and demand schedules for loans would yield an equilibrium rate of return r and an associated quantity of loan transactions q. Suppose anticipations change suddenly: inflation of x is now expected. Suppose the inflation is "ideal"—neutral and perfectly certain to occur. The higher expected inflation should shift both the supply and demand schedules leftward, in such a way that the new schedules both lie precisely $(1 + r) x$ vertically above the schedules for which expected inflation is zero. That is, anyone willing to receive or pay r when $x = 0$ should be willing to receive or pay a money interest rate of $n = r + x (1 + r)$ for any value of x, for the same quantity transacted. This formula is the solution of the Fisher formula for n in terms of r and x. The new equilibrium interest rate accordingly lies at the new schedules' intersection, exactly $x (1 + r)$ vertically above the previous intersection, at the same quantity transacted.

3. A subtle problem arises for installment loans. Since the monetary unit depreciates over the course of the repayment schedule, each *peso* of interest and principal paid in earlier installments is worth more in real terms than each *peso* of interest and principal paid in later installments. A higher money interest rate shifts the time profile of real repayments, weighting it more heavily toward dates closer to the present. That is, a higher money

interest rate shortens the "duration"—the average time interval from the start of the loan to the installment payments, with each interval weighted by the present discounted value of the payments. All other things being equal, the shorter duration makes borrowing less attractive, and so reduces loan demand and pressures the real interest rate downward. Installment repayment schedules could be readjusted to counteract this effect, although they rarely are.

4. For example, a person wishing to borrow $1000 to "borrow" $2000 leaves $1000 on interest-free deposit in a "compensating balance" and pays interest on the whole. In some places the practice is illegal, although it is obviously difficult to control.

5. If people have "money illusion"—that is, if they care only about how much money, not purchasing power, they expect to pay or receive—this too could explain non-positive real interest rates. As noted in Chapter 2, however, this book assumes that no one has any "money illusion."

6. This is known as the "Tobin–Mundell effect," described in Tobin 1961 and Mundell 1963.

7. A given inflation expectation combined with a given degree of price-level uncertainty may be considered to affect asset-holding decisions in quantitatively the same way as a higher expectation with no price-level uncertainty. That higher expectation would then be the "certainty-equivalent" expectation.

8. Another way of saying the same thing is to note that accumulation of goods inventories is a kind of investment project, quite as capable as any other investment project of yielding a real loss.

9. In the 1970s, Brazilian financial intermediaries financed portfolios of longer-term private and public obligations by "selling" them with "repurchase letters"—promises to repurchase the assets in question at a pre-arranged price after a short time period. In such operations, the longer-term obligations were collateral; the repurchase letter, which was often marketable, was the true financial instrument. An intermediary that financed portfolios with repurchase letters was subject to the risk of interest-rate increases, since it had to roll over its financing constantly. At several moments during the 1970s (particularly late 1975) there were "open-market crises," which obliged the monetary authority to ease off tight monetary policies in order to provide sufficient liquidity to the financial markets.

10. Discussions with Ricardo Lago have helped the writer clarify this point.

6   The Dilemmas of Inflation-Stabilization Policy

1. Introduction of a new currency unit facilitates such contract revision. Suppose expected inflation was x' per cent after the shock program, but old contracts incorporated inflation expectations of x per cent. For purposes of settling old contracts, the old currency could depreciate daily against the new currency at a rate of $[(1 + x)/(1 + x')] - 1$.

2. George Jackson Eder, who headed the IMF mission that helped design the program, described this experience in a lengthy monograph, Eder 1968.

3. On Bolivia's 1985–6 experience, see Sachs 1986.

4. Mário Henrique Simonsen, who worked with Finance Minister Octávio Gouvéia de Bulhões and Planning Minister Roberto Campos on the Government Economic Action Plan (PAEG), described and analyzed the program in Simonsen 1970.

5. The United States' experience since 1979 demonstrates the power of tight monetary policy to reduce inflation, but also illustrates the damage high interest rates and credit restriction can cause. See Greider 1987 for a critical discussion of Federal Reserve policy. Throughout the 1980s the inflationary consequences of the United States' persisting high Federal budget deficit were largely offset by a persisting deficit in the current account of the balance of payments.

6. Credit starvation is best measured not by the net credit *flow*—disbursement less amortization—to the firm, but by the net credit *transfer*—the flow less interest due. The credit transfer measures what the firm can use to finance its operations.

7. Like any business, it may be reasonable enough for a public sector to obtain short-term financing from a monetary authority through a bill issue, an overdraft credit, or a simple advance to cover a temporary or seasonal cash flow deficit—for example, to meet a payroll several days before tax proceeds arrive to cover it. The inflation danger arises from continuing public borrowing that is not rapidly, or ever, repaid.

8. That is, the borrowing requirement *of* the non-financial public sector, to be distinguished from the non-interest part of the NFPSBR.

9. Fiscal policy affects aggregate demand according to the "multiplier principle" described by Keynes in his *General Theory*. Each one-*peso* addition to government expenditure induces an increase in aggregate demand flow considerably in excess of one *peso*. Any additional *peso* of expenditure increases someone's income by one *peso*; some fraction of this increase will be spent, generating an increase in someone else's income, and so on in a theoretically infinite but mathematically convergent series. For example, if income-earners spend an average of 90 per cent of each additional *peso* of income received, each additional *peso* of government expenditure should lift aggregate demand by

$$\{1 + (9/10) + (9/10)^2 + (9/10)^3 + \ldots\}$$

$$= 1 \text{ } peso \text{ times } \{1 / [1-(9/10)]\} = 10 \text{ } pesos$$

A one-*peso decline* in tax revenue affects aggregate demand less than a one-*peso increase* in expenditure, because taxpayers save some part of their one-*peso* increase in disposable income. The first round of additional expenditure is therefore a fraction of one *peso*, not one *peso*. If income-earners spend nine tenths of each additional *peso* of income on average, each additional *peso* of tax relief should increase aggregate demand by (9/10) times one *peso* times

$$\{1 + (9/10) + (9/10)^2 + (9/10)^3 + \ldots\}$$

$$= (9/10) \text{ } pesos \text{ times } \{1 / [1-(9/10)]\} = 9 \text{ } pesos$$

10. This interpretation of the effects of fiscal policy may help explain an asymmetry in observed effects of tax policy. Conventional macroeconomic

analysis suggests that, if a tax cut is inflationary on balance in a given economy, a tax increase should be stabilizing, and vice versa. Macro-economic models tend to be characterized by such "reversibility": they predict quantitatively equal but opposite consequences from quantitatively equal but opposite policies (e.g., a tax increase and a tax cut). United States experience since the 1960s suggests, however, that tax increases and tax cuts may both be inflationary. Tax cuts and tax increases could both intensify purchasing-power competition: the tax cut enhances the private sector's capacity to engage in the struggle; the tax increase increases the private sector's determination to engage in the struggle.

11. See Scheetz 1986. Peruvian governments often described such price increases as *desembalses*, "overflows," metaphorically, of water over a dam. Taxation and revenue earnings on motor fuel (produced and sold by a state enterprise) came to constitute more than 20 per cent of total public-sector revenue in the early 1980s.

12. Brazil's Cruzado Plan was effective between March and November 1986; high inflation revived thereafter, until the June 1987 "Bresser Plan" price freeze. For the first half of 1987 Brazil's "operational" public-sector borrowing requirement (i.e., excluding the *ex post* inflation component of the public-sector interest bill) surged to about 6 per cent of GDP, compared with 3.7 per cent for 1986 as a whole and only about 1.5 per cent for the first half of 1986. The November 1986 policy package not only caused a sharp price increase, it advertised the government's difficulty with policy management, and over the coming weeks inflationary expectations, nominal interest rates, and even real interest rates rose sharply, as Brazilian financial markets concluded that the approach was doomed, thereby sealing its fate (see Chapter 9).

13. These last are conventionally considered "negative revenues" in the national accounts because they are income transfers rather than expenditure on the final goods and services that constitute the gross domestic product.

14. Note 11 to Chapter 3 provides an analytical structure that can be used to determine the largest NFPSBR consistent with a given inflation rate. Some assumption must be made regarding the extent to which this NFPSBR is financed through money issue; that amount would then be $\triangle F$ in the formula given there.

15. In fact, Brazil's Cruzado Plan freeze applied only to consumer prices. Wholesale prices had to be re-determined through complex re-negotiation processes in each industry during March 1986.

16. Although lower prices encourage demand, it is a fair generalization that selective price controls tend to fall on goods and services in inelastic demand. They therefore limit money income from sales, and so limit profits. If lower prices generated higher profits, the firm or industry would presumably not have to be compelled to reduce its prices.

17. Price controls have been used foolishly or maliciously to destroy firms or industries; the present discussion abstracts from that possibility.

18. As noted in Chapter 3, however, it is at least possible that higher wages could increase workers' disposition to supply labor in certain contexts, and so increase aggregate supply.

19. There is an undeniable possibility, of course, that even if the government limits itself to setting the adjustment for future inflation, the "real" negotiation could implicitly turn on adjusting for the government's inflation anticipation.

7 Inflation Stabilization under External Constraint

1. The IMF lends under various terms and conditions, depending on circumstances. Some lending is relatively short-term, compensating for circumstances that are likely to improve rapidly. The IMF carries out routine liquidity operations with central banks managing their reserve positions. As long as this borrowing is small relative to the nation's IMF "quota" (or capital subscription), such borrowing entails no serious conditionality. The IMF operations considered here are longer-term, however, generally 12–18-month "stand-by" programs, and occasionally three-year "Extended Fund Facility" programs. Such programs are intended to carry out more profound stabilization efforts in nations with severe "imbalances."
2. IMF involvement is likely to be "politically sensitive," of course, to the extent (i) previous IMF programs have imposed severe austerity, (ii) the austerity seems to be associated with the interests of foreign financial institutions, and (iii) previous IMF programs have failed, particularly when they were considered excessively ambitious.
3. In principle, a devaluation could be made sufficiently large "to compensate" the encouragement to imports set by trade liberalization. Alternatively, a nation can secure credit to cover the presumably brief period following trade liberalization between the time that imports increase and the time that exports increase.
4. The increase in net central-bank domestic assets is measured by subtracting the increase in international reserves from the increase in the monetary base.
5. Some programs set a fifth maximum on central-bank acquisition of public-sector obligations, so the entire allowable increase in domestic credit does not go to the public sector at the expense of the private sector.
6. Analysts who argue that devaluation need not be inflationary may be confusing terms in their reasoning: it may be possible to devalue *and* carry out simultaneous offsetting, deflationary policy; but devaluation is inflationary *per se*.
7. If each percentage point of devaluation provokes a percentage point or more of price-level increase, devaluation may fail permanently to affect even price-sensitive exports and imports. Price sensitivity presumably refers to the *real*, rather than the *nominal*, price of foreign exchange: a one percentage point increase in the price of foreign exchange followed by a one-per-cent increase in the price level leaves the real exchange rate unchanged (assuming no change in international prices). In deciding whether to devalue, policy-makers must forecast whether devaluation will affect exports and imports before the price level catches up, or whether they can rapidly counter the devaluation's inflationary shock with a deflationary policy shock.

In reality, of course, policy-makers cannot always restrict themselves to weighing the benefits and costs of devaluation for the economy *per se*. Opinions of managers of external financial institutions obviously matter in themselves. Thus, one of a devaluation's practical benefits may be that it pleases external creditors and so leads to increased external financing. This may outweigh a policy-maker's judgment that devaluation will damage the domestic economy or even fail to reduce the external borrowing requirement.

8. These developments may be understood according to one of the fundamental national-accounts identities: total capital formation over any time interval is effectively "financed" by private and public saving flows together with the external resource deficit. Public saving is the difference between tax revenues and current (non-capital) expenditure, including interest. The external resource deficit is the difference between imports and exports of goods and non-factor services. Import compression and export expansion reduced the resource inflow; higher interest charges reduced public saving; and reductions in expenditure and higher taxation helped reduce private disposable income, hence private saving. All together, these developments served to diminish the resources available for capital formation. At the same time, heightened risk and uncertainty made capital formation less desirable.

9. Brazil could probably have attenuated the inflationary pressure in 1984 if it had introduced a floating exchange rate. The trade surplus might well have induced real-effective appreciation, which would have reduced inflationary pressure. Simultaneously, however, it would have reduced the export incentive. The trade surplus was the primary objective, inflation control the secondary objective, of the IMF program. The dollar sold at a premium in Brazilian parallel exchange markets during 1984, but this does not imply that a floating exchange rate would have depreciated further. The premium resulted mainly from restrictions: certain entities were not permitted to buy foreign exchange from the Central Bank for certain purposes—e.g., for purchases of restricted imports, for profit repatriation, for capital flight, and so on.

8 Indexation and Dollarization

1. Some analysts define dollarization as the use of the dollar as a transactions medium. The definition here is simply the use of the U.S. dollar as a unit of account.

2. *Ex ante* indexation is no more than legal authorization for fixed-yield financial instruments to provide additional yield to compensate for anticipated inflation. This circumvents regulations that otherwise limit nominal yields. It permits more favorable tax treatment for interest income where taxes are limited to the "real" component. Where financial rates are controlled, *ex ante* indexation is a means of justifying the rate. Where financial rates are freely determined and not taxed, *ex ante* indexation is beside the point, since freely determined financial rates would take account of expected inflation (as described in Chapter 2).

In Brazil, *ex ante* indexation was introduced in the mid-1960s. The government stipulated that the 1933 usury law applied to the "real" components of interest rates; the rates could incorporate *ex ante* adjustment announced periodically. More important, that part of the yield that was called *ex ante* indexation was not taxed, on the view that this was part of the asset's real value, not its yield.

3. Unless there are severe penalties, it may make little practical difference that holding foreign exchange is "illegal." It may matter, however, if informally index-linked or dollar-denominated contracts have no legal standing.

4. If it is true that price-level uncertainty rises when prices accelerate, and that this reduces money demand relatively more when index-linked assets are available, symmetry suggests that decelerating prices would reduce price-level uncertainty, and that this would increase money demand by more if index-linked assets are available. If availability of index-linked assets really made money demand more responsive to *declining* price-level uncertainty, declining uncertainty might more rapidly increase money demand and make stabilization easier once some initial price-level deceleration had been achieved. This is unlikely, unfortunately. The fact that index-linked assets make it easier to get out of money when price-level uncertainty worsens does not imply that people return more easily to money when price-level uncertainty diminishes. Moreover, if indexation is perceived as inflationary, continuing availability of index-linked assets may help price-level uncertainty persist. In any case, accelerating prices increase price-level uncertainty more easily than decelerating prices relieve it.

5. Financial indexation should change the sensitivities of saving and money holding only to price-level uncertainty, not to inflation expectations. Suppose price-level uncertainty remains unchanged. A moment's thought should make it clear that an increase in *expected* inflation should affect saving and money holding the same, regardless of whether non-monetary financial assets are index-linked. In either case, if people hold inflation expectations with certainty, people would regard both nominal and real interest rates as certain. Since availability of index-linked financial assets would not change the economy's response to changes in inflation expectations *per se*, behavioral relations in short-term macroeconomic models incorporating inflation expectations but not price-level uncertainty should yield the same results with financial assets denominated in money or in purchasing power.

6. Here it matters whether the purchasing-power unit is the dollar or the basket of goods and services. In most Latin American nations the monetary authority sets or closely manages the exchange rate; unless price controls are very extensive, no authority can "set" the price index. The authorities therefore more easily control the timing of the feedback process if the purchasing-power unit is the dollar, if they are willing—and able, given balance-of-payments conditions—to use exchange-rate policy for this end.

7. More precisely, the two kinds of hypothesis are (i) that the demand schedule for index-linked assets (as a function of their real yield) lies far to the left, and (ii) that the supply schedule lies far to the left. Either way,

the equilibrium demand and supply would be characterized by a high real interest rate and low quantities issued.

8. Suppose people consider the *ex ante* (before market-valuation) expected real rates of return on nominal corporate debentures and capital to be *negatively* correlated random variables. That is, suppose people believe that, whatever happens, inflation tends to be higher (lower) when real rates of return on stock are higher (lower). Risk-averse wealth-holders might then prefer portfolios of stock and nominal debentures to index-linked debentures: real debenture yields would be higher when stock yields were lower, the portfolios would be "hedged," and their expected real yields might exceed that of a comparable holding of index-linked debentures (see Siegel 1974 and Fischer 1975).

9. This is because financial markets value firms' stock and debentures together on the basis of the underlying producing assets. In effect, when a firm issues debentures, financial-market participants recognize that part of the firm's earnings go to service them, and devalue stock accordingly. If earnings on stock and debentures receive different tax treatment, of course, this conclusion changes. The original Modigliani–Miller analysis made the important simplifying assumption, however, that financial markets were convinced that firms would not fail to pay the service on debentures (see Miller and Modigliani 1958).

10. Suppose a firm produces q output units per period with an input of z units per period. Let p represent the *real* unit output price and w the *real* unit input price over the coming period. The firm's *real* cash flow, or net income, over the coming period is given by

$$u = pq - wz$$

The question of whether u is more uncertain if the unit input price is index-linked may be addressed in terms of "mean-variance" analysis. Applying standard statistical formulas for the variance of linear equations, the variance of u is given by

$$\text{var}(u) = q^2 \text{ var}(p) + x^2 \text{ var}(w) - [2\ q\ x\ R\ \text{var}(p)^{0.5}\ \text{var}(w)^{0.5}]$$

where R is the "correlation coefficient" of p and w. To simplify, suppose q equals x (this is a choice of units). If p and w are fixed under nominal contracts and inflation is the only source of their uncertainty, their correlation coefficient would be one; var(u) would therefore be given by

$$q^2 \text{ var}(p) + \text{var}(w) - 2 \text{ var}(p)^{0.5} \text{ var}(w)^{0.5}$$

If p is fixed under a nominal contract and w under an index-linked contract, since var(w) would therefore equal zero, var(u) would be given by

$$q^2 \text{ var}(p)$$

This formula could perfectly well turn out larger than the preceding formula. For example, if var(w) equals var(p), then the preceding formula is smaller; that is, u would be less uncertain *ex ante* if the unit input price is nominal rather than index-linked.

11. Blinder 1977 suggests a way around this problem. Financial intermediaries could be established to hold obligations of firms linked to their own (or their industry's) prices. The intermediaries could then issue index-linked obligations to finance portfolios of obligations linked to different prices. This would enable firms to relieve their price-dispersion risk, and permit private index-linked debentures to be made available to the public.

12. The Brazilian Housing Finance System's early history is discussed in various issues of *Conjuntura Econômica*, and Kampel and Miranda do Valle 1974.

13. See Goldsmith 1986, p. 411.

14. Friedman advocated index-linking in his *Newsweek* column in 1971 and 1973. See Friedman 1971a and 1973.

15. Tobin advanced this argument in a seminal 1963 paper on monetary policy and government-debt management (Tobin 1963).

16. Metzler 1951 elegantly set out this analytical approach to open-market operations.

17. Tobin assumed that availability of index-linked bonds makes demand for stock more sensitive *and* demand for money less sensitive to changes in bond yields. Both assumptions are necessary to be sure that monetary policy would be more efficient with index-linked bonds. It is unlikely, however, that both assumptions would simultaneously hold. If availability of index-linked bonds makes stock holding more sensitive to changes in the real bond yield, it would probably also make money demand more sensitive to changes in the real bond yield. If falling real interest rates have an enhanced expansionary effect through encouraging stock holding where bonds are index-linked, they are likely also to have an enhanced contractionary effect through encouraging money holding. Accordingly, it is uncertain that index-linked bonds would make monetary policy more efficient even if they are closer substitutes for shares than nominal bonds (see Beckerman 1980).

18. Beckerman 1983a discusses these events.

19. In 1985, according to Central Bank figures, the central government's overall deficit was 13.6 per cent of GDP, but inflation adjustment on central-government domestic debt (both the explicit adjustment of index-linked debt and the implicit adjustment of nominal debt) was 11.8 per cent of GDP. In 1986, during which indexation was suspended for ten months, the central government's deficit was 6.7 per cent of GDP; inflation adjustment was still 4.6 per cent of GDP. In 1987, when indexation was restored, the central government's deficit was 17.2 per cent of GDP, of which inflation adjustment was 13.9 per cent of GDP.

20. See the note above discussing the uncertainty attaching to profit and cash flows.

21. Suppose a given wage rate is escalated with n annual adjustments. If w represents the real wage restored each time, and x is the annual inflation rate (in decimal terms), the real wage would vary between w and

$$w (1 + x)^{-(1/n)}$$

The (geometric) average real wage would be

$$v = w (1 + x)^{-(1/2n)}$$

22. Labor contracts characteristically specify only the wage rate, not the quantity of labor services to be hired. (That is, workers can be laid off.) In this regard they differ from contracts that commit the purchaser to some specified quantity of purchases.

23. There is at least one caveat to this point. Higher wages presumably encourage supply of labor services. Economists assume that in general, at least in the short term, higher wages discourage labor demand more than they encourage labor supply, and so conclude that higher wages tend to reduce employment and aggregate supply. Nevertheless, it is at least possible that in some contexts higher wages discourage labor demand less than they encourage labor supply—in which case higher wages would tend to reduce employment and aggregate supply.

24. One way to consider the inflationary consequences of indexation is to assume that "market forces" imply that the average real wage over a given period must equal v^*; if the real wage set by indexation is w^*, then, a simple rearrangement of the first formula above permits solution for the inflation rate x that would reconcile v^* and w^*:

$$x = [(w^*/v^*)^{2n}] - 1.$$

25. If p represents domestic prices, p^* external prices, and e the exchange rate, the parity condition requires the exchange rate to be set so that

$$et\, p^*_t\, /p_t = e_{t-1}\, p^*_{t-}\, /p_{t-1},$$

$$\text{or, } e_t\, /e_{t-1} = (p_t\, /p_{t-1}) \, / \, (p^*_t\, /p^*_{t-1})$$

That is, e must grow at a rate roughly equal to the differential between the growth rates of domestic and external prices to maintain the initial parity relationship.

26. The expression "crawling-peg exchange rate" is used here in a restricted sense, to refer to an exchange rate that is adjusted so as to maintain the purchasing-power parity. The expression is sometimes used in a broader sense, to mean an exchange rate adjusted *frequently* according to any rule, or even to no publicly-stated rule.

27. Thus, if in one year taxable incomes between 20 000 and 21 000 *pesos* paid income tax of 20 per cent, and prices were 10 per cent higher in the subsequent year, then taxable incomes between 22 000 and 23 200 *pesos* in the subsequent year should pay income tax of 20 per cent, since 22 000 and 23 000 *pesos* have the same purchasing power in the later year as incomes of 20 000 and 22 000 *pesos* in the earlier year.

28. The Brazilian authorities sharply increased the income tax due in 1987, for example, by declaring a relatively low rate of indexation for amounts withheld during 1986.

29. It may be best to adjust fixed assets according to a capital-goods price index, rather than the general price index ordinarily used for indexation. Firms should still be permitted to revalue specific assets according to replacement value if it matters enough to them to go to the trouble of maintaining appropriate documentation.

30. With a rising wholesale-price level the use of "first-in, first-out" inventory valuation sets a lower cost of goods sold in the income statement, hence a higher reported profit than the use of "last-in, first-out" inventory valuation. Particularly for high inflation rates the "last-in, first-out" procedure is therefore more appropriate from the point of view of "accounting conservatism"—i.e., to ensure that profit estimates err on the low rather than on the high side.

31. This should have only a limited effect in a context where government bonds can be traded easily in an open market: between adjustments the market would probably adjust the bond value along with the index.

32. Nominal interest could be paid on daily or weekly balances; the *ex post* inflation component of the accumulated nominal interest credited on the adjustable balance could then be subtracted from the annual adjustment.

33. Contrary to what was widely believed at the time, the Arida–Lara Resende proposal was not what was actually carried out as the "Cruzado Plan" in February 1986. The essence of the Arida–Lara Resende proposal was the transitional conversion of nominal assets to index-linked assets; the Cruzado Plan incorporated nothing like this (see Chapter 9).

9 Recent "Heterodox" Stabilization Experiences: Argentina, Israel, Brazil, 1985–9

1. A slightly different version of this chapter was presented as a paper at the conference on "The Economic Crises of Latin America in the 1980s and the Opportunities of the 1990s," at the University of Illinois, September 6–8, 1990. The writer gratefully acknowledges comments by participants at that conference.

10 Toward a Theory of Self-Perpetuating Inflation

1. A recent essay on the subject of corporate takeovers by Andrei Shleifer and Lawrence Summers (1988) introduced a valuable concept that may be applicable in the present approach to inflation. Corporate takeovers, the essay argued, operate to redistribute a corporation's value from "stakeholders" generally to stockholders—defining "stakeholders" as anyone whose welfare is significantly bound up in a corporation, including employees, customers, suppliers, and bondholders. Corporations that become takeover targets, in this view, tend to be those under excessive claims by stakeholders, and one objective of a takeover would be to reduce such claims. In theory, the new owners earn their return to the extent they dilute other stakeholders' claims.

In an inflation, the point would be that the national economy's "stakeholders" possess and are exercising too many claims: the problem of stabilization policy is to find a feasible way to dilute these claims. An even greater challenge, of course, would be to find a way to dilute their claims in some way that the society at large should—or even would—regard as fair and acceptable.

2. The political difficulty of controlling a budget deficit is illustrated by the United States Congress' continuing struggle with its deficit. In December 1985 the Congress passed the Gramm-Rudman-Hollings Law, which required automatic expenditure cuts over a period of five years unless the President and the Congress could agree on a better plan. At this writing, the automatic cuts have never occurred, even though the deficit targets have remained well outside of the targets envisaged, because the Congress has been able to exploit every loophole it could to escape the cuts. See "Talking Chop," in *The Economist*, February 18, p. 26.

3. It might be possible in theory to combine a relative-price realignment with a heterodox shock. The objective would be to restart the price structure, say, from a point at which each price and wage is set to its average real value over the preceding—say—six or twelve months. One approach might be the following. Before temporarily freezing them, all prices and wages could be raised by different amounts averaging—say—50 per cent. Each price would be set so its deflated value, at the 50-per-cent-higher price level, equalled its average real value over the preceding six or twelve months. With luck, the price structure would then be roughly coherent, although if further adjustments were required during the freeze period the authorities could try to combine price increases and cuts to avoid affecting the price level. The money supply and other financial-asset and credit stocks would immediately be inadequate, since the price-level increase would diminish their real value. The monetary authority could then carry out a managed increase in the money supply.

Bibliography

(Chapter number in brackets indicate the chapter of this book for which each reference is most relevant.)

ARIDA, Pérsio (ed.) *Inflação zero: Brasil, Argentina, Israel* (Paz e Terra: Rio de Janeiro, 1986) [chs 6, 9].

ARIDA, Pérsio and LARA-RESENDE, André (1985) "Inertial Inflation and Monetary Reform: Brazil," in Williamson, John (ed.) *Inflation and Indexation: Argentina, Brazil and Israel*, Institute for International Economics, Washington, DC, pp. 27–45 [ch. 8].

AUERNHEIMER, Leonardo (1974) "The Honest Government's Guide to the Revenue from the Creation of Money", *Journal of Political Economy*, May/June, 82, pp. 598–606 [chs 2, 6].

BAER, Werner (1967) "The Inflation Controversy in Latin America: A Survey," *Latin American Research Review*, February, 2, pp. 3–25 [ch. 1].

BAER, Werner (1990) "Social Aspects of Latin American Inflations", working paper [ch. 4].

BAER, Werner and BECKERMAN, Paul (1980) "The Trouble with Index-linking: Reflections on the Recent Brazilian Experience", *World Development*, September, pp. 677–703 [chs 5, 8].

BAER, Werner and BECKERMAN, Paul (1989) "The Decline and Fall of Brazil's Cruzado", *Latin American Research Review*, 24, no. 1, 1989, pp. 35–64 [ch. 9].

BAER, Werner and SIMONSEN, Mário H. (1965) "Profit Illusion and Policy-Making in an Inflationary Economy", *Oxford Economic Papers*, July, pp. 279–90 [ch. 8].

BAGEHOT, Walter (1873) *Lombard Street*, London, [chs 3, 4].

BAILEY, Martin J. (1956) "The Welfare Cost of Inflationary Finance", *Journal of Political Economy*, April, 64, pp. 93–110 [ch. 2].

BALIÑO, Tomás J. T. (1987) "The Argentine Banking Crisis of 1980," IMF Working Paper, November [ch. 9].

BANCO CENTRAL DE LA REPUBLICA ARGENTINA (1987) *Argentine Economic* Memorandum 1987: Economic Policies and Prospects, Buenos Aires [chs 6, 9].

BANK OF ISRAEL (1986) *Annual Report, 1986* [chs 6, 9].

BARRO, Robert J. (1976) "Rational Expectations and the Role of Monetary Policy", *Journal of Monetary Economics*, January, 2, pp. 1–32 [ch. 2].

BECKERMAN, Paul (1978) "Adjustment for Inflation in the Brazilian National Housing Finance System", University of Illinois Urbana-Champaign: Working Paper no. 519 [ch. 8].

BECKERMAN, Paul (1979) "On the Non-Existence of Index-Linked Corporate Debentures", Boston University, Working Paper no. 57, July [ch. 8].

BECKERMAN, Paul (1980) "Index-linked Government Bonds and the Efficiency of Monetary Policy", *Journal of Macroeconomics*, Fall, 2, (4), pp. 307–31 [ch. 8].

BECKERMAN, Paul (1983a) "Index-linked Financial Assets and the Brazilian Inflation-Feedback Mechanism", in Schmukler, Nathan and Edward Marcus (eds) *Inflation through the Ages: Economic, Social, Psychological and Historical Aspects* New York: Columbia University Press, pp. 571–615. Published in Portuguese as *"Indexação financeira e o mecanismo de realimentação inflacionária no Brasil, Pesquisa e Planejamento Económico*, August 1979 [ch. 8].

BECKERMAN, Paul (1983b) "Inflation and Inflation Feedback", in Schmukler, Nathan and Edward Marcus (eds) *Inflation through the Ages: Economic, Social, Psychological and Historical Aspects* New York: Columbia University Press, pp. 17–32 [chs 3, 4].

BECKERMAN, Paul (1988) "Non-Positive Market Clearing Real Interest Rates", *International Review of Applied Economics*, 2 (2) [ch. 5].

BECKERMAN, Paul (1990) "Public-Sector 'Debt Distress' in Argentina's Recent Stabilization Efforts", World Bank Latin America and the Caribbean Region Internal Discussion Paper no. 66, July [ch. 9].

BICKSLER, James and HESS P. (1976) "More on Purchasing Power Risk, Portfolio Analysis, and the Case for Index-Linked Bonds: A Comment", *Journal of Money, Credit and Banking*, May, pp. 264–5 [ch. 8].

BLANCHARD, Olivier (1979) "Wage Indexing Rules and the Behavior of the Economy", *Journal of Political Economy*, August, pp. 789–815 [ch. 8].

BLANCHARD, Olivier (1983) "Price Asynchronization and Price Level Inertia", in Dornbusch, Rudiger and Mário Henrique Simonsen (eds) *Inflation, Debt and Indexation*, Cambridge, Mass.: MIT Press, ch. 1 [ch. 2].

BLÉJER, Mario I. (1981) "The Dispersion of Relative Commodity Prices under Very Rapid Inflation", *Journal of Development Economics*, December, 9, pp. 347–56 [ch. 2].

BLÉJER, Mario I. and LEIDERMAN, Leonardo (1980) "On the Real Effects of Inflation and Relative-Price Variability: Some Empirical Evidence", *Review of Economics and Statistics*, November, pp. 539–44 [ch. 2].

BLÉJER, Mario I. and LEIDERMAN, Leonardo (1982) "Relative-Price Variability in the Open Economy", *European Economic Review*, April, 18, pp. 387–402 [ch. 2].

BLÉJER, Mario I. and LIVIATAN, Nissan (1987) "Fighting Hyperinflation: Stabilization Strategies in Argentina and Israel 1985–86", *IMF Staff Papers*, 34, (3), September, pp. 403–38 [ch. 9].

BLINDER, Alan (1977) "Indexing the Economy through Financial Intermediation", in Brunner, Karl and Allan Meltzer (eds) *Stabilization of the Domestic and International Economy* Amsterdam: North-Holland, pp. 69–105 [ch. 8].

BORDO, Michael D. (1980) "The Effects of Monetary Change on Relative Commodity Prices and the Role of Long-Term Contracts", *Journal of Political Economy*, December pp. 1088–1109 [ch. 2].

BRAGA, Carlos Alberto Primo *et al.* (eds) (1986) *O Plano Cruzado na visão de economistas da USP*, São Paulo Ed. Pioneira: 1986 [ch. 9].

212   *Bibliography*

BRESCIANI-TURRONI, Constantino (1937) *Inflation: A Study of Currency Depreciation in Post-War Germany, 1914–23*, London: Allen and Unwin [ch. 6].

BRESSER PEREIRA, Luiz Carlos (1988), *"Os dóis congelamentos de preços no Brasil"*, Revista de Economia Política, October–December, 8, (4), pp. 48–66. [ch. 9].

BRESSER PEREIRA, Luiz Carlos and NAKANO, Yoshiaki (1984) *Inflação e recessão*, São Paulo: Editora Brasiliense [ch. 1].

BRESSER PEREIRA, Luiz Carlos and NAKANO, Yoshiaki (1987) *The Theory of Inertial Inflation: The Foundation of Economic Reform in Brazil and Argentina*, Boulder, Colorado: Lynn Rienner Publishers [ch. 3].

BRESSER PEREIRA, Luiz Carlos (1990) "Brazil's Inflation and the Cruzado Plan", in Falk, Pamela (ed.) *Inflation: Are We Next: Hyperinflation and Solutions in Argentina, Brazil and Israel*, Boulder, Colorado: Lynn Rienner Publishers [ch. 9].

CAGAN, Phillip (1956) "The Monetary Dynamics of Hyperinflation", in Friedman, Milton (ed.) *Studies in the Quantity Theory of Money*, Chicago, Ill.: University of Chicago Press [ch. 2].

CALVO, Guillermo (1990) "The Perils of Sterilization", IMF Working Paper, March [ch. 9].

CAMPOS, Roberto de Oliveira (1961) "Two Views on Inflation in Latin America", in Hirschman, Albert (ed.) *Latin American Issues* pp. 69–79 [ch. 3].

CANAVESE, Alfredo J. and DI TELLA, Guido (1988) "Inflation Stabilization or Hyperinflation Avoidance? The Case of the Austral Plan in Argentina, 1985–87", in Bruno, Michael *et al.* (eds) *Inflation Stabilization: The Experience of Israel, Argentina, Brazil, Bolivia and Mexico*, Cambridge, Mass.: MIT Press, pp. 153–90 [ch. 9].

CHACEL, Julian, SIMONSEN, Mário H., and WALD, Arnaldo (1970) *Correçao monetária* Rio de Janeiro: APEC [ch. 8].

CONJUNTURA ECONOMICA (1974) *Correção monetária—tema de interesse internacional*, May, pp. 110–14 [ch. 8].

CONJUNTURA ECONOMICA (1975) *Correção monetária—função e custos*, May, pp. 107–9 [ch. 8].

CONJUNTURA ECONOMICA (1976) *Correção monetária e realimentação inflacionária*, June, pp. 88–94 [ch. 8].

CONTADOR, Claudio (1976) *"Correção monetária, expectativa de inflação e a demanda por ativos financeiros"*, Revista brasileira de mercado de capitais, January–April, pp. 5–23 [ch. 8].

CONTADOR, Claudio (1983) *"Indexação: a experiência de duas décadas"*, Conjuntura Ecónomica, June, pp. 93–100 [ch. 8].

COTRIM, José (1984) "Accounting for Inflation in Latin America", *Price Waterhouse International Tax Review*, November–December, pp. 1–6 [ch. 8].

CUKIERMAN, Alex (1983) "Relative Price Variability and Inflation: A Survey and Further Results", *Carnegie-Rochester Series on Public Policy*, no. 19, Autumn 1983, pp. 1–47 [ch. 2].

CUKIERMAN, Alex and LEIDERMAN, Leonardo (1984) "Price Controls and the Variability of Relative Prices", *Journal of Money, Credit and Banking*, August, XVI, (3), pp. 271–84 [ch. 2].

CUKIERMAN, Alex and WACHTEL, Paul (1979) "Differential Inflationary Expectations and the Variability of the Rate of Inflation: Theory and Evidence", *American Economic Review*, September, pp. 595–609 [ch. 2].

CUKIERMAN, Alex and WACHTEL, Paul (1982) "Inflationary Expectations: Reply and Further Thoughts on Inflation Uncertainty", *American Economic Review*, June, 72, pp. 508–12 [ch. 2].

CUKIERMAN, Alex and WACHTEL, Paul (1982) "Relative Price Variability and Nonuniform Inflationary Expectations", *Journal of Political Economy*, February, pp. 146–57 [ch. 2].

DAVIDSON, Paul (1978) *Money and the Real World*, London: Macmillan, 2nd edn [ch. 5].

DORNBUSCH, Rudiger (1980) *Open Economy Macroeconomics*, New York: Basic Books [ch. 7].

DORNBUSCH, Rudiger (1982) "PPP Exchange Rate Rules and Macroeconomic Stability", *Journal of Political Economy*, February, 90, pp. 158–65 [ch. 7].

DORNBUSCH, Rudiger (1987) "Stopping Hyperinflation: Lessons from the German Experience in the Twenties", in Dornbusch, Rudiger *et al.* (eds) *Essays in Honor of Franco Modigliani* (Cambridge, Mass.: MIT Press [ch. 2].

DORNBUSCH, Rudiger and SIMONSEN, Mário Henrique (1987) "Inflation Stabilization with Incomes Policy Support," New York: Group of Thirty [chs 3, 6, 9].

THE ECONOMIST (1974) "How Brazil showed the way", April 27, pp. 82–3 [ch. 8].

THE ECONOMIST (1984) "Business Brief: Accountants SSAPed by Inflation", February 25, pp. 80–1 [ch. 8].

THE ECONOMIST (1985) "Son of Phillips?", September 21, p. 67 [ch. 3].

EDER, George Jackson (1968) *Inflation and Development in Latin America: A Case History of Inflation and Stabilization in Bolivia*, Ann Arbor: University of Michigan, Michigan International Business Studies no. 8 [ch. 6].

EISNER, Robert, and PIEPER, P. J. (1980) "A New View of the Federal Debt and Budget Deficits", *American Economic Review*, September, pp. 636–50 [ch. 6].

FEIGE, E. and PARKIN, M. (1971) "The Optimal Quantity of Money, Bonds, Commodity Inventories, and Capital", *American Economic Review*, June [ch. 5].

FELDSTEIN, Martin and SUMMERS, Lawrence (1978) "Inflation, Tax Rules, and Long-Term Interest Rates", *Brookings Papers on Economic Activity*, 1, pp. 61–100 [ch. 8].

FELIX, David (1961) "An Alternative View of the 'Monetarist-Structuralist' Controversy", in Hirschman, Albert (ed.) *Latin American Issues*, pp. 81–93 [ch. 3].

FIGLEWSKI, Stephen and WACHTEL, Paul (1981) "The Formation of Inflationary Expectations", *Review of Economics and Statistics*, February, 63, pp. 1–10 [ch. 2].

FISHER, Irving (1911) *The Purchasing Power of Money*, New York, 1911; repr. by Macmillan, 1971 [chs 2, 5].

FISHER, Irving (1930) *The Theory of Interest*, New York: Macmillan [ch. 5].

214 *Bibliography*

FISCHER, Stanley (1975) "The Demand for Index Bonds", *Journal of Political Economy*, June, pp. 509–34 [chs 2, 8].

FISCHER, Stanley (1977) "Long-term Contracts, Rational Expectations, and the Optimal Money Supply Rule", *Journal of Political Economy*, February, 85, pp. 191–205 [ch. 3].

FISCHER, Stanley (1979) "Corporate Supply of Index Bonds", *National Bureau of Economic Research* Working Paper no. 331, March [ch. 8].

FISCHER, Stanley (1983) "Welfare Aspects of Government Issue of Indexed Bonds", in Dornbusch, Rudiger and Mário Henrique Simonsen (eds) *Inflation, Debt and Indexation*, Cambridge, Mass.: MIT Press: ch. 9 [ch. 8].

FISCHER, Stanley (1985) "Israeli Inflation and Indexation,", in Williamson, John *Inflation and Indexation: Argentina, Brazil and Israel*, Washington, DC: Institute for International Economics [chs 8, 9].

FISCHER, Stanley (1986a) "Wage Indexation and Macroeconomic Stability", in Fischer, Stanley *Indexing, Inflation and Economic Policy*, Cambridge, Mass.: MIT Press, ch. 5 [ch. 8].

FISCHER, Stanley (1986b) "Indexing and Inflation", in Fischer, Stanley *Indexing, Inflation and Economic Policy*, Cambridge, Mass.: MIT Press ch. 6 [ch. 8].

FISCHER, Stanley (1986c) "On the Nonexistence of Privately Issued Index Bonds in the U.S. Capital Market", in Fischer, Stanley *Indexing, Inflation and Economic Policy*, Cambridge, Mass.: MIT Press, ch. 10 [ch. 8].

FISCHER, Stanley (1986d) "Toward an Understanding of the Costs of Inflation: II", in Fischer, Stanley, *Indexing, Inflation and Economic Policy*, Cambridge, Mass.: MIT Press, ch. 2 [ch. 2].

FISCHER, Stanley (1986e) "Relative Shocks, Relative Price Variability, and Inflation", in Fischer, Stanley *Indexing, Inflation and Economic Policy*, Cambridge, Mass.: MIT Press, ch. 3 [ch. 2].

FISCHER, Stanley and Franco MODIGLIANI (1986) "Toward an Understanding of the Real Effects and Costs of Inflation", in Fischer, Stanley *Indexing, Inflation and Economic Policy*, Cambridge, Mass.: MIT Press, ch. 1 [ch. 2].

FISCHER, Stanley (1987) "The Israeli Stabilization Program 1985–86", *American Economic Review*, May, 77, pp. 275–278 [ch. 9].

FISHLOW, Albert (1974) "Indexing Brazilian-Style: Inflation without Tears?", *Brookings Papers on Economic Activity*, no. 1, pp. 261–82 [ch. 8].

FOSTER, Edward (1978) "The Variability of Inflation", *Review of Economics and Statistics*, August, pp. 346–50 [ch. 2].

FRIEDMAN, Milton (1956) "The Quantity Theory of Money: A Restatement", in Friedman, Milton (ed.) *Studies in the Quantity Theory of Money*, Chicago, Ill.: University of Chicago [ch. 5].

FRIEDMAN, Milton (1971a) "Purchasing Power Bonds", *Newsweek*, April 12, p. 86 [ch. 8].

FRIEDMAN, Milton (1971b) "Government Revenue from Inflation", *Journal of Political Economy*, July–August, pp. 846–56 [ch. 8].

FRIEDMAN, Milton (1973) "More on Living with Inflation", *Newsweek*, October 29, p. 96 [ch. 8].

FRIEDMAN, Milton (1974) "Monetary Correction", in Giersch, Herbert (ed.) *Essays on Inflation and Indexation*, Washington, DC: American Enterprise Institute for Policy Research, pp. 25–61 [ch. 8].

FRIEDMAN, Milton (1977) "Nobel Lecture: Inflation and Unemployment", *Journal of Political Economy*, June, 85 [chs 2, 6].

FRIEDMAN, Thomas L. (1987) "The Lessons in Israel's Economic Recovery", *New York Times*, Section 3, p. 1, August 9 [chs 6, 9].

FRISCH, Helmut (1983) *Theories of Inflation* Cambridge: Cambridge University Press [ch. 3].

FRY, Maxwell (1988) *Money, Interest and Banking in Economic Development* Baltimore, Md: Johns Hopkins University Press [ch. 5].

GALBRAITH, John Kenneth (1975) *Money: Whence It Came, Where It Went*, Boston: Houghton-Mifflin [ch. 1].

GIORGIO, Luís Alberto (1989) *Crisis financieras, Reestructuración bancaria e hiperinflación en la Argentina*, working paper, December [ch. 9].

GLEJSER, H. (1965) "Inflation, Productivity and Relative Prices: A Statistical Study", *Review of Economics and Statistics*, February, 47 [ch. 2].

GOLDSMITH, Raymond (1986) *Brasil 1850–1984: Desenvolvimento financeiro sob um seculo de inflação*, São Paulo, Brazil: Harper and Row do Brasil [ch. 8].

GRAY, Jo Anna (1976) "Wage Indexation: A Macroeconomic Approach", *Journal of Monetary Economics*, April, 2, pp. 221–35 [ch. 8].

GRAY, Jo Anna (1978) "On Indexation and Contract Length", *Journal of Political Economy*, February, pp. 1–18 [ch. 2].

GRAY, Jo Anna (1983) "Wage Indexation, Incomplete Information, and the Aggregate Supply Curve", in Dornbusch, Rudiger and Mário Henrique Simonsen (eds) *Inflation, Debt and Indexation*, Cambridge, Mass.: MIT Press, ch. 2 [ch. 8].

GREIDER, William (1987) *Secrets of the Temple: How the Federal Reserve Runs the Country*, New York: Simon and Schuster [ch. 6].

GRUNWALD, Joseph (1961) "The 'Structuralist' School on Price Stability and Development: The Chilean Case", in Hirschman, Albert (ed.) *Latin American Issues*, pp. 95–124 [ch. 3].

GUÍTIAN, Manuel (1981) *Fund Conditionality, Evolution of Principles and Practices*, IMF Pamphlet Series no. 38 Washington, DC [ch. 7].

HALL, Robert E. (ed.) (1982) *Inflation: Causes and Effects*, Chicago Ill.: University of Chicago Press [ch. 3].

HAMMOND, Bray (1956) *Banks and Politics in America from the Revolution to the Civil War*, Princeton University Press [ch. 3].

HEILBRONER, Robert (1984) "Does Capitalism have a Future?", *New York Times* Magazine, August 15 [ch. 5].

HENDRICKS, Wallace E. and KAHN, Lawrence M. (1983) "Cost-of-Living Clauses in Union Contracts: Determinants and Effects", *Industrial and Labor Relations Review*, April, 36, pp. 447–60 [ch. 8].

HERCOWITZ, Zvi (1981) "Money and Dispersion of Relative Prices", *Journal of Political Economy*, April, 89, pp. 328–56 [ch. 2].

HEYMANN, Daniel (1989) "From Sharp Disinflation to Hyper and Back: The Argentine Experience, 1985–1989." Working Paper, United Nations Economic Commission for Latin America [ch. 9].

HIRSCH, Fred and GOLDTHORPE, John H. (1978) *The Political Economy of Inflation*, Cambridge Mass.: Harvard University Press [ch. 10].

HIRSCHMAN, Albert (1961) "Ideologies of Economic Development in Latin America", in Hirschman, Albert (ed.) *Latin American Issues*, pp. 3–42 [ch. 3].

HIRSCHMAN, Albert. (ed.) (1961) *Latin American Issues: Essays and Comments*, New York: The Twentieth Century Fund [ch. 3].

HIRSCHMAN, Albert (1981) "The Social and Political Matrix of Inflation: Elaborations on the Latin American Experience", in Hirschman, Albert, *Essays in Trespassing: Economics to Politics and Beyond*, Cambridge: Cambridge University Press, pp. 177–207 [chs 1, 4].

HOLLAND, A. Steven (1984) "Does Higher Inflation Lead to More Uncertain Inflation?", *Federal Reserve Bank of St. Louis Review*, February, 66 (2), pp. 15–26 [ch. 2].

HUME, David (1969) "Of the Balance of Trade, " *Essays Moral, Political, Literary*, excerpted in Cooper, Richard (ed.) *International Finance*, Harmondsworth: Penguin [chs 3, 7].

INTERNATIONAL MONETARY FUND (1987) "Israel Curbs Inflation, Improves Budget Balance", *IMF Survey*, September 14, pp. 260–64 [ch. 10].

JAFFEE, Dwight and KLEIMAN, Ephraim (1977) "The Welfare Implications of Uneven Inflation", in Lundberg, Erik (ed.) *Inflation Theory and Anti-Inflation Policy*, London: International Economic Association, pp. 285–307 [ch. 2].

JUD, Gustav Donald (1978) *Inflation and the Use of Indexing in Developing Countries*, New York: Praeger [ch. 8].

KAFKA, Alexandre (1974) "Indexing for Inflation in Brazil", in Giersch, Herbert (ed.) *Essays on Inflation and Indexation*, Washington: American Enterprise Institute for Public Policy Research, pp. 87–98 [ch. 8].

KAMPEL, Luiz Cezar and MIRANDA DO VALLE, Maria Tereza (1974) *Sistema Financeiro de Habitação* (Rio de Janeiro, 1974) [ch. 8].

KATONA, George and STRUMPEL, Burkhardt, *A New Economic Era*, New York: Elsevier [ch. 2].

KEYNES, John Maynard (1936) *The General Theory of Employment, Interest, and Money*, New York: Harcourt [chs 1, 5].

KIGUEL, Miguel (1988) "Ups and Downs in Inflation: Argentina Since the Austral Plan". Working Paper, World Bank [ch. 9].

KIGUEL, Miguel and LIVIATAN, Nissan (1989) "The Inflation-Stabilization Cycles in Argentina and Brazil." Working Paper, World Bank [ch. 9].

KIGUEL, Miguel and NEUMEYER, Pablo Andrés (1989) "Seignorage, Inflation Tax and the Demand for Money: The Case of Argentina," Working Paper, World Bank, 1989 [ch. 9].

KIGUEL, Miguel (1990) "Success and Failure of a Heterodox Shock: The Austral Plan", in Falk, Pamela (ed.) *Inflation: Are We Next: Hyperinflation and Solutions in Argentina, Brazil and Israel*, Boulder, Colorado: Lynn Rienner Publishers [ch. 9].

KLEIMAN, Ephraim (1977) "Monetary Correction and Indexation—the Brazilian and Israeli Experience", *Explorations in Economic Research* (NBER), Winter, 4 (1) [ch. 8].

KRUGMAN, Paul and TAYLOR, Lance (1978) "Contractionary Effects of Devaluation", *Journal of International Economics*, August, 8 [ch. 7].

LAIDLER, David E. W. (1975) *Essays on Money and Inflation*, Chicago Ill.: University of Chicago Press [ch. 3].

LEIDERMAN, Leonardo and LIVIATAN, Nissan, "Macroeconomic Performance before and after Disinflation in Israel", *World Bank Policy, Planning and Research Working Paper Series* no. 311, November [ch. 9].

LEVI, Maurice D. and John H. MAKIN (1978) "Anticipated Inflation and Interest Rates", *American Economic Review*, December, 68, pp. 801–12 [ch. 5].

LEVI, Maurice D. and John N.MAKIN (1980) "Inflation Uncertainty and the Phillips Curve: Some Empirical Evidence", *American Economic Review*, December, 70, pp. 1022–27 [ch. 3].

LIVIATAN, Nissan (1983) "On the Interaction between Wage and Asset Indexation", iDornbusch, Rudiger and Mário Henrique Simonsen (eds) *Inflation, Debt and Indexation*, Cambridge, Mass.: MIT Press, ch. 11 [ch. 8].

LIVIATAN, Nissan and LEVHARI, David (1977) "Risk and the Theory of Indexed Bonds", *American Economic Review*, June, pp. 366–75 [ch. 8].

LOGUE, D. and WILLETT, T. D. (1976) "A Note on the Relation between the Rate and Variability of Inflation", *Economica*, May [ch. 5].

LOPES, Francisco (1986) *O Choque heterodoxo: Combate a inflação e reforma monetária*, Rio de Janeiro: Editora Campus [chs 1, 6].

LUCAS, Robert E., Jr. (1973) "Some International Evidence on Output-Inflation Tradeoffs", *American Economic Review*, June, 63, pp. 326–34 [ch. 3].

LUCAS, Robert E., Jr. and SARGENT, Thomas (eds) (1981) *Rational Expectations and Econometric Practice*, Minneapolis: University of Minnesota Press [ch. 2].

LUCAS, Robert E., Jr. (1981) *Studies in Business-Cycle Theory*, Cambridge, Mass.: MIT Press [ch. 2].

MACEDO, Roberto (1983) "Wage Indexation and Inflation: The Recent Brazilian Experience", in Dornbusch, Rudiger and Mário Henrique Simonsen (eds) *Inflation, Debt and Indexation*, Cambridge, Mass.: MIT Press, ch. 6 [ch. 8].

MACHINEA, José Luis and FANELLI, José María (1988) "Stopping Hyperinflation: The Case of the Austral Plan in Argentina, 1985–87", in Bruno, Michael *et al.* (eds) *Inflation Stabilization: The Experience of Israel, Argentina, Brazil, Bolivia and Mexico*, Cambridge, Mass.: MIT Press, pp. 111–52 [ch. 9].

McKINNON, Ronald (1973) *Money and Capital in Economic Development*, Washington, D.C.: Brookings [ch. 5].

MEISELMAN, David (ed.) (1970) *Varieties of Monetary Experience*, Chicago, Ill.: University of Chicago Press: [ch. 3].

METZLER, Lloyd (1951) "Wealth, Savings and the Rate of Interest", *Journal of Political Economy*, April, pp. 93–116 [ch. 8].

MINSKY, Hyman (1982) *Can "It" Happen Again?: Essays in Instability and Finance*, Armonk, New York: M.E. Sharpe [ch. 4].

MODIGLIANI, Franco and MILLER, Merton (1958) "The Cost of Capital, Corporate Finance, and the Theory of Investment", *American Economic Review*, June, 48, (3) [ch. 8].

MULLINEAUX, Donald J. (1980) "Unemployment, Industrial Production, and Inflation Uncertainty in the United States", *Review of Economics and Statistics*, May, pp. 163–9 [ch. 2].

MUNDELL, Robert (1971) *Monetary Theory: Inflation, Interest and Growth in the World Economy*, Pacific Palisades, California: Goodyear Publishing Co. [ch. 3].

MUNDELL, Robert (1963) "Inflation and Real Interest", *Journal of Political Economy*, June [chs 2, 5].

NESS, Walter (1974) "Financial Markets Innovation as a Development Strategy: the Brazilian Experience", *Economic Development and Cultural Change*, April, pp. 453–72 [ch. 8].

NESS, Walter (1977) *A Influencia da correção monetária no sistema financeiro*, Rio de Janeiro: Instituto Brasileiro de Mercado de Capitais [ch. 8].

OKUN, Arthur (1971) "The Mirage of Steady Inflation", *Brookings Papers on Economic Activity*, 2, pp. 485–98 [ch. 2].

OLIVERA, Julio (1967) "Money, Prices and Fiscal Lags: A Note on the Dynamics of Inflation", *Banca Nazionale del Lavoro Quarterly Review*, no. 26 [ch. 3].

PARKS, Richard W. (1978) "Inflation and Relative Price Variability", *Journal of Political Economy*, February, 86, pp. 79–96 [chs 2, 5].

PATINKIN, Don (1965) *Money, Interest and Prices*, New York: Harper and Row, 2nd edn [chs 2, 3].

PIÉKARZ, Julio A. (1987) "El deficit cuasi fiscal del Banco Central", paper presented in the Seminar on Central Bank Quasi-Fiscal Operations, Brasília, Center for Latin American Monetary Studies, August [ch. 9].

PRÉBISCH, Raul (1981) *Capitalismo periférico: Crisis y transformación*, Mexico: Fondo de Cultura Económica [ch. 3].

RAGAZZI, Giorgio (1973) "Index-linking and General Welfare: A Comment", *Journal of Money, Credit and Banking*, May, pp. 261–3 [ch. 8].

RANGEL, Ignacio (1963) *A Inflação brasileira*, Rio de Janeiro: Tempo Brasileiro [ch. 1].

RATTI, Ronald A. (1985) "The Effects of Inflation Surprises and Uncertainty on Real Wages", *Review of Economics and Statistics*, May, 67, pp. 309–14 [ch. 8].

RODRÍGUEZ, Carlos A. and ALMANSI, Aquiles (1989) "Reforma monetaria y financiera en hiperinflación" Center for Macroeconomic Studies of Argentina (CEMA), *Série Documentos de Trabajo* no. 67, August [ch. 9].

SACHS, Jeffrey (1986) *The Bolivian Hyperinflation and Stabilization*, National Bureau of Economic Research Working Paper no. 2073 [chs 6, 9].

SAMUELSON, Paul and SOLOW, Robert (1960) "The Problem of Achieving and Maintaining a Stable Price Level: Analytical Aspects of Anti-Inflation Policy", *American Economic Review*, May, 50, pp. 177–94 [ch. 3].

SANTOMERO, Anthony and SEATER, John (1978) "The Inflation-Unemployment Trade-off: A Critique of the Literature", *Journal of Economic Literature*, June, pp. 499–544 [ch. 3].

SARGENT, Thomas and WALLACE, Neil (1981) "Some Unpleasant Monetarist Arithmetic", *Federal Reserve Bank of Minneapolis Quarterly Review*, Fall, pp. 1–18 [chs 6, 9].

SARGENT, Thomas (1982) "The Ends of Four Big Inflations", in Robert Hall (ed.) *Inflation*, Chicago, Ill.: University of Chicago Press, pp. 41–96 [ch. 2].

SARNAT, Marshall (1973) "Purchasing Power Risk, Portfolio Analysis, and the Case for Index-Linked Bonds: A Comment", *Journal of Money, Credit and Banking*, August, pp. 836–45 [ch. 8].

SCHEETZ, Thomas (1986) *Peru and the International Monetary Fund*, Pittsburgh, Pa.: University of Pittsburgh Press [ch. 7].

SCHYDLOWSKY, Daniel and WICHT, Juan (1979) *Anatomia de un fracaso económico: Perú, 1968–1979*, Lima, Peru: Universidad del Pacifico [ch. 10].

SELLEKAERTS, Willy and SELLEKAERTS, Brigitte (1984) "Both Anticipated and Unanticipated Inflation Determine Relative Price Variability", *Journal of Post Keynesian Economics*, VI (4) Summer, pp. 500–8 [ch. 2].

SHARON, Emanuel (1990) "Israel and the Success of the Shekel: The Key Years, 1984–1987", in Falk, Pamela (ed.) *Inflation: Are We Next: Hyperinflation and Solutions in Argentina, Brazil and Israel*, Boulder, Colorado: Lynn Rienner Publishers [ch. 9].

SHAW, Edward (1973) *Financial Deepening in Economic Development*, New York: Oxford University Press, [ch. 5].

SHESHINSKI, Eytan and WEISS, Yoram (1977) "Inflation and Costs of Price Adjustment, "*Review of Economic Studies*, June, pp. 267–303 [ch. 2].

SHLEIFER, Andrei and SUMMERS, Lawrence (1988) "Breach of Trust in Hostile Takeovers", in Auerbach, Alan (ed.) *Corporate Takeovers: Causes and Consequences*, Chicago, Ill.: University of Chicago [ch. 10].

SIEGEL, Jeremy (1974) "Indexed versus Nominal Contracting: A Theoretical Examination", unpublished paper, University of Chicago [ch. 8].

SILVA, Adroaldo Moura da (1977) "*A Conjuntura económica brasileira, 1974/ 1976*", Tibiriçá, January-March [ch. 8].

SILVA, Adroaldo Moura da and KADOTA, Décio, (1902) "Inflação e preços relativos: O caso brasileiro, 1970/1979", *IPE-USP Estudos Económicos*, April, 12 (1), pp. 5–30 [ch. 2].

SIMONSEN, Mário Henrique (1970) *Inflação: Gradualismo x tratamento de choque*, Rio de Janeiro: APEC Editora S. A. [chs 1, 4, 8].

SIMONSEN, Mário H. (1975) "*Correção monetária—a experiência brasileira*", *Conjuntura Economica*, July, pp. 65–9 [ch. 8].

SIMONSEN, Mário Henrique (1983) "Indexation: Current Theory and the Brazilian Experience", in Dornbusch, Rudiger and Mário Henrique Simonsen (eds) *Inflation, Debt and Indexation*, Cambridge, Mass.: MIT Press, ch. 5 [ch. 8].

SLAWSON, W. David (1981) *The New Inflation: The Collapse of Free Markets*, Princeton, N.J.: Princeton University Press [ch. 1].

TANZI, Vito (1977) "Inflation, Lags in Collection and the Real Value of Tax Revenue", *IMF Staff Papers*, 1 [ch. 3].

TANZI, Vito (1980) *Inflation and the Personal Income Tax*, Cambridge: Cambridge University Press [ch. 8].

TANZI, Vito (ed.) (1984) *Taxation, Inflation, and Interest Rates*, Washington, D.C.: IMF [ch. 2].

TAYLOR, John B. (1979) "Staggered Wage Setting in a Macro Model", *American Economic Review*, March, 69, pp. 108–13 [ch. 4].

TAYLOR, John B. (1981) "On the Relation between the Variability of Inflation and the Average Inflation Rate", in Brunner, Karl and Allan Meltzer (eds) *The Costs and Consequences of Inflation*, Carnegie-Rochester Conference Series on Public Policy, Autumn, pp. 57–85 [ch. 2].

TAYLOR, Lance (1979) *Structuralist Macroeconomics: Applicable Models for the Third World*, New York: Basic Books [ch. 1].

THORP, Rosemary and WHITEHEAD, Laurence (eds) *Inflation and Stabilisation in Latin America*, London: Macmillan [ch. 7].

TOBIN, James (1961) "Money, Capital and Other Stores of Value", *American Economic Review*, May [ch. 5].

TOBIN, James (1963) "An Essay on the Principles of Debt Management", in Commission on Money and Credit, *Fiscal and Debt Management Policies*, pp. 143–218 [ch. 8].

VINING, Daniel R. and ELWERTOWSKI, Thomas C. (1976) "The Relationship between Relative Prices and the General Price Level", *American Economic Review*, September, 66, pp. 699–708 [ch. 2].

WALLACE, Neil (1981) "A Modigliani-Miller Theorem for Open Market Operations", *American Economic Review*, June, pp. 267–74 [ch. 8].

WEISSKOPF, Richard (1990) "The Political Economy of the Israeli Inflation", in Falk, Pamela (ed.) *Inflation: Are We Next: Hyperinflation and Solutions in Argentina, Brazil and Israel*, Boulder, Colorado: Lynn Rienner Publishers [ch. 9].

WICKSELL, Knut (1936) *Interest and Prices* (1898), translated by R. F. Kahn, London: Macmillan [ch. 5].

WILLIAMSON, John (1981) *Exchange Rate Rules: The Theory, Performance and Prospects of the Crawling Peg*, London: Macmillan [ch. 7].

WILLIAMSON, John (ed.) (1983) *IMF Conditionality*, Cambridge, Mass.: MIT Press [ch. 7].

Index